Advance Praise for *How the Best Did It*

"A discerning examination of what all of us can learn from some of our most effective leaders who have held—and wielded—ultimate power at the highest level."

—Jon Meacham

"In *How the Best Did It,* Talmage Boston demonstrates rare gifts in sifting gold nuggets from the endless gravel beds of known facts about eight leading presidents, then delivering them concisely and persuasively. In his insightful study of George Washington, he finds the core of America's first great leader without exaggerating his talents, and makes him someone from whom we can learn and cherish."

—David O. Stewart, author of *George Washington: The Political Rise of America's Founding Father,* on the George Washington chapter

"Thomas Jefferson was one the most effective American leaders of his time, creating a political party that dominated American politics for more than a quarter of a century. With great insight and clear writing, Talmage Boston brings Jefferson to life as the talented leader who shaped the course of early American society."

—Annette Gordon-Reed, Pulitzer Prize–winning historian and coauthor of *Most Blessed of the Patriarchs: Thomas Jefferson and the Empire of the Imagination,* on the Thomas Jefferson chapter

"Talmage Boston offers a wise and wide-ranging understanding of Lincoln's leadership qualities. What makes Boston's chapter distinct is the personal questions that challenge the reader to apply Lincoln's values to their lives today."

—Ronald C. White Jr., author of *A. Lincoln* and three other notable books on Lincoln, on the Abraham Lincoln chapter

"Talmage Boston has entered the field of leadership studies with a head full of steam and a barrel full of fresh ideas. His investigation into Theodore Roosevelt's distinguished record as US president is deeply illuminating and highly recommended!"

—Douglas Brinkley, author of *The Wilderness Warrior: Theodore Roosevelt and the Crusade for America,* on the Theodore Roosevelt chapter

"No president has been more successful than FDR in moving public sentiment forward one step at a time. And no one has been more successful in analyzing the secret of that success than Talmage Boston. His terrific chapter on FDR provides a riveting account of the critical role Roosevelt's rhetorical skill played in saving our democracy."

—Doris Kearns Goodwin, Pulitzer Prize–winning author of *No Ordinary Time: Franklin and Eleanor Roosevelt: The Home Front in World War II,* on the FDR chapter

"Talmage Boston has provided business leaders—really, any kind of leader—with a fascinating roadmap of the qualities, both subtle and larger than life, that made Dwight Eisenhower a great president. You will wonder, why don't we have more leaders like Ike? And, if you pay attention, you may learn how to become one."

—Evan Thomas, author of *Ike's Bluff: President Eisenhower's Secret Battle to Save the World,* on the Dwight Eisenhower chapter

"Talmage Boston uses his discerning lawyer's mind to lay out a compelling case for why John F. Kennedy deserves his lofty historical standing as one of America's finest presidents. While acknowledging his dark side and outsize flaws, Boston provides keen insight into JFK's enduring greatness: his propensity to learn on the job, prowess as a crisis manager, and power as an orator."

—Mark Updegrove, author of *Incomparable Grace: JFK in the Presidency,* on the JFK chapter

"While most people agree that Reagan was a consequential president, Talmage Boston shows just how and why he was. Combining extensive research and trenchant insights with compelling prose, Boston distills the essence of Reagan's leadership qualities. The happy result is a unique blend of expert history and leadership lessons for the twenty-first century."

—Will Inboden, author of Reagan-Prize winner *The Peacemaker: Ronald Reagan, the Cold War, and the World on the Brink,* on the Ronald Reagan chapter

Also by Talmage Boston

1939: Baseball's Tipping Point
Baseball and the Baby Boomer: A History, Commentary, and Memoir
Raising the Bar: The Crucial Role of the Lawyer in Society
Cross-Examining History: A Lawyer Gets Answers From the Experts About Our Presidents

How the BEST DID IT

Leadership Lessons From Our Top Presidents

Talmage Boston

Foreword by John Avlon

Post Hill Press

A POST HILL PRESS BOOK
ISBN: 978-1-63758-697-6
ISBN (eBook): 978-1-63758-698-3

How the Best Did It:
Leadership Lessons from Our Top Presidents

Cover design by Cody Corcoran

Post Hill Press
New York • Nashville
posthillpress.com

Published in the United States of America
1 2 3 4 5 6 7 8 9 10

To David O. Stewart

Great Lawyer and Eminent Historian

Mentor and Friend

The Man Who Inspired This Book

"The one quality that can be developed by studious reflection and practice is the leadership of men."

- Dwight D. Eisenhower -

"The powerful, painful, grinding process by which an ideal emerges out of history draws us to the glory of the human effort to win meaning from the complex and confused motives of men and the blind ruck of events.

Looking back, we see how individual men,
despite their failings, blindness, and vice,
may affirm for us the dignity of life.

And in our contemplation of history, some of the grandeur of these men, in the midst of the confused issues, shadowy chances, and brutal ambivalences of our life and historical moment, may rub off on us.

And that may be what we yearn for after all."

- Robert Penn Warren -

TABLE OF CONTENTS

FOREWORD

The study of history is much more than a succession of names and dates. What makes history come alive is the *stories*—the heroes and villains, the struggles and successes that have an enduring impact on our world today. Just below this storytelling level, there is a different drama: the search for useful wisdom that we can apply to our own lives.

That is the essence of applied history. It is mining true stories for inspiration and actionable insight. Seen from this vantage point, history is not relegated to the past because it can inform decisions in real time. It offers perspective on our problems, which is the thing we have least of in current events. Applied history can also take extraordinary individuals from any era and turn them into friendly acquaintances whom we can indirectly ask for advice. Their stories not only illuminate our path into the murky future; they mean that we are never truly alone.

The book you are about to read—*How the Best Did It: Leadership Lessons from Our Top Presidents* by Talmage Boston—is decidedly a work of applied history. It distills the leadership lessons of eight great American presidents into a book that is brisk, enjoyable, and above all, useful.

Talmage correctly identifies that one of the chief challenges of our time is the fact that too many people have short attention span, brought on by constant digital distractions. As a corrective, he condenses these presidents' stories, drawing on dozens of biographies as research. You can read this book straight through or dip into different presidencies as the spirit moves you and find that the lessons apply to many arenas in your life and career. Accuracy is ensured by the fact that each chapter has been reviewed by at least two major biographers of the president in question; from Doris Kearns Goodwin and Doug

Brinkley on the Roosevelts to Evan Thomas and Mark Updegrove on Ike and JFK, respectively.

The result is a survey of the American presidency, but it is not a remedial history. In detailing the twenty-four distinct leadership traits that were demonstrated by these presidents, Talmage does not rely on overly familiar anecdotes but instead offers real analytic insights amid often surprising quotations by contemporaries. In the process, we get a more granular sense of how some of our most effective leaders rose to the pinnacle of power and implemented their executive strategies inside the White House, from the people who knew them best.

Each of these eight presidents lived in different eras, faced distinct challenges, and left unique legacies. But each achieved the larger goal of not only restoring America's faith, in itself, but also, in the words of Reagan biographer Will Inboden, in "restoring the world's belief in America—not as a perfect nation, but as a strong and good nation."

These leaders had starkly different personalities, combining great strengths with personal weaknesses. They were, in a word, human. Talmage does not flinch while discussing their shortcomings alongside their nation-shaping successes. Taking historical figures off the pedestal makes their wisdom more accessible. As a result, we gain insights into the contradictions and complexities of these men at work. For example, we learn that Jefferson was shy and avoided the public eye but was a master of persuasion in private meetings with congressmen. Theodore Roosevelt's boundless energy might be diagnosed as manic depression today, but he was far more self-disciplined than his aggressive posture would suggest, making him an excellent diplomat. Franklin Roosevelt learned to compartmentalize private despair over his disability to project a jaunty confidence that could move popular opinion in his desired direction. Eisenhower was a decisive executive with a collaborative leadership style committed to forging a "middle way" in American politics but he could be ruthless when any figure—domestic or foreign—tested his boundaries or betrayed his word.

Given their varied personalities, perhaps the thing these Oval Office occupants have most in common is a reliance on the example of past presidents to provide courage and comfort in what is sometimes described as the loneliest job in the world. Lincoln took inspiration from Washington and Jefferson. Theodore Roosevelt viewed Lincoln as a personal and political model. In turn, FDR consciously modeled much of his career on his famous distant cousin. Eisenhower admired his fellow soldier-turned-statesman George Washington while often invoking Lincoln. And Ronald Reagan, surprisingly, often quoted his youthful idol but ideological opposite, FDR, as part of his successful effort to sway the voters who became known as "Reagan Democrats." These relationships across the centuries are in some ways the most powerful evidence of the success that comes from applied history in action.

These profiles in presidential leadership remind us that character is the essential quality in a president, while the importance of partisan affiliation fades over time. It is also a reminder of how much we Americans need a shared civic history, especially in times of rapid change. As the only nation founded on an idea rather than a tribal identity, the United States depends on unifying stories to create a cohesive sense of national purpose. We have got to make the old stories new again for each generation.

Applied history is a powerful way to engage people: by learning leadership lessons from America's greatest presidents and applying them to our own lives. That is what *How the Best Did It* does. As you pour through these pages, you will appreciate the labor of love that created this accessible and insightful look into how our greatest presidents boldly rose to power and wisely led the nation. Thanks to Talmage Boston's great new book, you can learn from the best and then carry those lessons forward to create your own American life.

John Avlon
Sag Harbor, New York
February 1, 2024

INTRODUCTION

Most people with ambition aspire to lead. Success requires not only doing what it takes to rise to the top, but also staying there for a good long run. The seed for this book is the thought that those with the horsepower necessary to attain and then sustain themselves in high organizational positions in their little corners of the world can up their leadership games by knowing enough history to emulate the four men whose faces are carved on a mountain in South Dakota, and their four successors who arrived at the White House after Gutzon Borglum began chiseling the granite there in 1927.

Much is known about the men who look out from Mount Rushmore, thanks to the many biographers who have pored over the evidence of their subjects' lives, wrestled with the tough questions about how those presidents did what they did, and drawn sound conclusions. Their books allow us to know those big faces not as immovable rock, but as flesh and blood human beings who led the country with distinction during their eras, and thereby earned a high place in history.

The carving in South Dakota stopped when its government funding ran out. Four subsequent presidents then picked up the torch that had previously passed from Washington to Jefferson to Lincoln to Theodore Roosevelt. The Rushmore-deserving titans who led the nation to new heights in the last hundred years are Franklin D. Roosevelt, Dwight Eisenhower, John F. Kennedy, and Ronald Reagan. The well-known history chronicled in the many biographies of these eight great presidents is more than sufficient to teach us what needs to be known about them from a leadership standpoint.

The goal of the book in your hands is to provide takeaways for current and future leaders in all walks of life, about these eight great presidents' most important leadership traits. Grasping exactly what caused this octet to make their marks in the annals of history, and then incorporating that information into their command repertoire, should expedite progress toward achievement in one's chosen field. An organizational leader now struggling with a knotty issue can find clear guidance from the pages that follow about what George Washington did, what Abraham Lincoln said, or what Dwight Eisenhower thought, and then have the newfound knowledge of history move the needle of prudent decision-making to a more informed place.

To get some buy-in to this premise, here are examples of potential presidential history applications to likely challenges at hand in a modern enterprise, that are explored fully in the chapters that follow:

- For someone who wants to move up in his group's pecking order without appearing to be a shameless self-promoter, see what George Washington did to continue his upward surge throughout his military and political careers.
- For someone whose organization is now dysfunctional because of conflicts between factions that produce gridlock and ill will, read how Thomas Jefferson built positive relationships with his Federalist foes in the aftermath of the Sedition Act, which allowed him to make progress as president by proactive consensus building.
- For someone confronting hostility on many fronts, examine how Abraham Lincoln treated his adversaries and always took the high road when he dealt with them.
- For someone confronting entrenched, seemingly insurmountable opposition that blocks an important objective, see what Theodore Roosevelt did to achieve his goal of busting the nation's largest trusts when the odds were stacked against him.
- For someone confronted by an unforeseen obstacle that appears to block all hope for a brighter future, be inspired by Franklin D. Roosevelt's approach to dealing with the paralysis of polio after the virus hit him at age thirty-nine in the middle of his political career.

- For someone having to deal with misbehaving colleagues who think they can get away with shenanigans, learn how Dwight Eisenhower played hardball with the miscreants in the 1956 Suez Crisis who willfully but unsuccessfully sought to disrupt world stability by seizing the canal in violation of Ike's instructions.
- For someone whose organization is in an all-or-nothing fight for survival, and has his support team panicking as they look at possible calamity on the horizon, observe how John F. Kennedy maintained calmness amid his high-strung subordinates, which led to his sound decisions that ended the Cuban Missile Crisis.
- For someone with wise, well-articulated beliefs and a long-term vision for exactly what his group needs to do to advance, and despite it, manages to attract mass quantities of critics, absorb how Ronald Reagan maintained a strong steady eloquent approach to bringing down the Soviet totalitarian regime, and thereby brought an end to the Cold War without firing a shot.

Having now put some meat on the bones regarding this book's value to actual and potential leaders, I will add that writing it was based on the assumption that most people in the twenty-first century are too consumed with work and other activities to find time to do what I do for fun in my free time: pick up thick presidential biographies, peruse their pages, and then synthesize the leadership lessons that subtly emanate from each historian's carefully researched work on his subject's life story.

One of my favorite things about presidential history is the way each generation of the brilliant people who write about it stand on the shoulders of those who covered the same ground in the past. The protagonists' letters, diaries, speeches, and public documents, as well as the earlier biographies of them, get read, digested, evaluated, and synthesized by a new wave of historians with each passing decade.

Through every round of analysis, the picture of what actually happened in the past usually gets clearer, and the conclusions drawn more reliable. Because of the way knowledge and insights evolve over time, no biographer who has written about the eight leaders featured in this book had to start from scratch, and most have built their work off others' past scholarship and then done their part to advance our understanding of their subjects.

Alas, it is one thing to learn a lesson from the life of a great person; it is something else to apply it in real time. Recognizing that fact, may this book open minds more readily to trying these time-tested approaches for achieving success in leading a group. May it also instill a deeper passion for appreciating the blessings all of us have because at key moments in the past, our most dynamic, astute, and emotionally intelligent presidents did what it took to preserve the American Dream. And yes, taking on that responsibility made them carry the weight of our country on their ready, willing, and able shoulders.

Talmage Boston
Dallas, Texas
February 1, 2024

CHAPTER ONE

HOW TO MOVE UP THE LADDER—LIKE GEORGE WASHINGTON

Imagine being a long-term participant in a large speculative venture, and during the early years, it faces four dissimilar turning points in succession on which the future of the enterprise depends. To confront these challenges, assume that the leaders who will have full responsibility for the upcoming tests, and are yet to be chosen, must have different skillsets to do what it will take to keep things moving through each trial. With high expectancy, the people await learning the outcome of who will be chosen to lead the group when the next crossroads event is about to begin.

With that scenario in mind, now picture a series of four messengers who arrive on the scene at the headquarters of the enterprise right before the start of each venture-changing effort. When it is his turn, the courier steps up and delivers the day's breaking news, announcing that after considering the qualifications of all possible candidates, the selection committee has made its decision, and picked the same individual to take charge of the next big job as was chosen to lead in the last big job. Each messenger then ends his report on an upbeat note, saying to the crowd that the folks who made the most recent leadership choice reached their decision...UNANIMOUSLY!

This scenario may be hard to believe, but it is *exactly* what happened in our country from 1775 to 1792.

First task: Lead an untrained army against an enemy's veteran troops in a war that has already begun, knowing that unless the novice soldiers achieve a miraculous victory, the new nation will not gain its independence from England. In June 1775, two months after Lexington and Concord's "shot heard round the world," the members of the Second Continental Congress had to select as commander-in-chief of the Continental Army the leader most likely to win the war despite the unfavorable odds. Every one of them chose George Washington.

Second task: After the Revolutionary War ended, it became clear that because the Articles of Confederation didn't provide for a strong federal government, the future of the new nation was—in a word—bleak. A new Constitution to fix what was broken in the Articles would have to be drafted, debated, negotiated, and finalized in short order. The process would be accomplished at a convention of strong-willed political leaders from all over the country who would arrive in Philadelphia with conflicting priorities. For the first order of business, those in attendance would have to elect a chairman of the proceedings with the political muscle necessary to pull the group together and agree on a final product. In 1787, the delegates unanimously chose George Washington.

Third task: After the Constitution had been signed and ratified, then, per its terms, the electors from each state—some chosen by their state legislators, some by the outcome of a popular election in their state—had to vote for a chief executive to lead the new country as its first president. During that four-year term, he would have to establish precedents for how the new position should be performed in the many areas not expressly addressed in the Constitution. In December 1788 to January 1789, every voting elector chose George Washington.

Final task: At the end of the first four-year term, during which time the two political parties were formed and became increasingly consumed with going at each other's throats, a new group of electors had to choose the nation's chief executive for the next four years. They knew that rapidly aging, increasingly hard-of-hearing, and weary-to-the-bone George Washington was eager to leave the presidency and return home to Mount Vernon to enjoy the rest of his life as a simple planter. He especially wanted to remove himself from future government leadership because he knew that the second time around, the president's main job would be to act as a peacemaker between the government's warring factions and prevent Congress and the Cabinet from self-destructing. After bitter enemies Thomas Jefferson and Alexander Hamilton (who could agree on only one thing—President Washington for a second term!) succeeded in talking Washington out of retirement on the ground that *only he* could keep the parties from annihilating each other, in November to December 1792, electors again unanimously chose George Washington, hoping he had enough energy left in reserve for him to keep the wheels of government turning for four more years.

These decidedly different tasks—military commander, Constitutional Convention chairman, first-term president setting up a new government struggling to gain traction on the slippery slope of making this new republic thing work, and second-term president mediating order out of partisan dysfunction—all fell on the shoulders of George Washington, chosen for these four fundamentally different jobs by differing sets of his compatriots over the course of seventeen years. *Not one* dissenter stepped forward out of all those responsible for selecting the right person to take on each position, and, amazingly, the fellow they picked *never said one word* to enhance his chances of being chosen.

My recognition of this unique achievement came in February 2021, with the publication of historian David O. Stewart's biography of George Washington[1] that focused on his subject's political rise. With tongue planted in cheek, here is how Stewart initially described his seemingly-reluctant and definitely-reticent subject's unique rise during the last twenty-four years of his life: "It was magic."[2] Yes, on the surface, the unanimous results that kept going Washington's way seemed magical, though Stewart then proceeded to explain how "nothing about his success was easy,"[3] and why Big George kept getting chosen to lead without opposition because of his ironclad self-discipline, unrelenting perseverance, and plain ol' hard work in building a spotless reputation and achieving steady success in almost everything he did. No, it wasn't magic, but sustained excellence in the performance of all challenges accepted that made it impossible for the four groups who chose Washington to seriously consider anyone else for the new nation's top positions.

The balance of this chapter reveals the leadership traits that led Light-Horse Harry Lee to provide his immortal tribute to George Washington shortly after his death: Our greatest Founding Father was "first in war, first in peace, and first in the hearts of his countrymen."[4] May understanding the particulars of Washington's well-executed strategy for attaining top leadership positions accelerate you toward a higher level of success.

Leadership Trait #1: Learning from Mistakes

George Washington went through life making fewer mistakes than most people. A relentless self-critic from the time he was young, he made sure his occasional blunders became learning experiences never to be repeated.

Washington made most of his worst mistakes in his early twenties during the French and Indian War, which was the conflict where colonial militiamen joined forces with the British army and certain Indian tribes to fight the French and other native tribes on the issue of who would control the western lands that adjoined the thirteen colonies.

Although the Brits, colonists, and their Indian allies ultimately won the war (which lasted several years), it wasn't before they suffered setbacks in which young Washington played a significant role. He started off well, named a full colonel at age twenty-two by Robert Dinwiddie, the British governor of Virginia, after Washington led a successful scouting expedition and then successfully attacked thirty-five French Canadians led by Joseph de Jumonville in Fayette County, Pennsylvania. Things soon went downhill from there.

A little more than a month after the Jumonville Affair, Washington and his men built Fort Necessity in southwestern Pennsylvania at a location on low ground that they soon learned was susceptible to flooding. Shortly after the small fort was finished, Jumonville's brother, seeking revenge, led a French-Canadian regiment joined by tribal warriors who attacked the colonial and British troops as they worked on deepening trenches outside the new fort. While the French and the Indians fired their guns from behind trees within musket range of the fort, Washington's men first attempted to defend themselves in their trenches. When a torrential rainstorm made their sitting (and drowning) duck position untenable, they retreated to positions inside their small fort. There, seeing that his men's outnumbered position was hopeless, Washington realized he had no viable option but to surrender (for the only time in his military career). The surrender document Washington signed (which he didn't understand because it was written in French), contained a confession that he had "assassinated" Jumonville. The embarrassing defeat combined with the mistaken admission of murder, and Dinwiddie's decision to reorganize the levels of rank in his army, soon resulted in Washington's being demoted from colonel to captain. This so angered him that he resigned from the war effort—albeit temporarily.

After Washington cooled off and rejoined the military, he hoped to have more success serving under newly arrived British Major General Edward Braddock than he had had with Dinwiddie. A year after the

Fort Necessity fiasco, as Braddock pursued the initiative of attempting to take Fort Duquesne from the French, Washington participated in another disastrous loss. As he and others under Braddock slowly built a road over the Allegheny Mountains through thickly wooded terrain amidst dense brush ten miles from their destination, French soldiers and Indians attacked them from all sides, in what became known as the Battle of Monongahela. His fellow soldiers panicked and mistakenly started shooting each other in friendly fire until they fled in retreat. Throughout the battle, Washington fought gallantly while bullets whizzed all around him, and his surviving the attack was so incredible that it seemed providential, causing many to conclude that he was a "Child of Destiny."[5] When the fighting stopped, rather than remain stoically silent about the devastating outcome in which Braddock had been killed, Washington displayed arrogant insensitivity and bad judgment by demanding a pay raise and criticizing the British soldiers' cowardice.

Soon after that, knowing he would need a better effort from the colonial militiamen in the future, Governor Dinwiddie named Washington "Commander in Chief of the Virginia Regiment." The title sounded good, but in the next two years, Washington fought no battles with the French, had to deal with a series of murderous Indian raids, and spent most of his time training hack soldiers prone to desertion. In that role, Washington attempted to instill order among his underperforming men through a series of severe beatings.

While biding his time training the inept troops, and looking for something to raise his spirits, Washington decided his pain would be dulled if he received a royal commission from his British superiors. He left his post and traveled to Boston where he made his request to William Shirley, the acting British commander-in-chief after Braddock's death. Shirley refused it. Undeterred, Washington came up with a new plan for obtaining the coveted prize. A year after Shirley's rejection, he went over Governor Dinwiddie's head and took his case to the leading British official in the colonies at the time, Lord Loudoun, who chose to ignore Washington's pitch for the elusive commission. Angry over the double rejections, Washington got on his horse and rode away from the war effort a second time.

After clearing his head at Mount Vernon for four months, and knowing how important achieving some level of military success would be to elevating his stature later in life, ever ambitious George Washington rejoined the British and colonial army in March 1758. He soon became part of a new effort to move a regiment toward Fort Duquesne in hopes of taking it from the French. In that endeavor, he again got crosswise with a British superior, this time, General John Forbes. Their conflict arose over the best route for the soldiers to take in getting to the fort, with Washington insisting that his way through Virginia (instead of Forbes' preference for going through Pennsylvania) was best. Though he lost the argument with Forbes, the trek ultimately resulted in their taking over a surprisingly undefended Fort Duquesne. With that box checked, Washington was ready to end his service in this war, return to Mount Vernon, and focus on his new political career while attempting to amass serious wealth.

In reviewing Washington's record in the French and Indian War, Stewart summarized the downside:

> He could claim no battlefield triumph, only the sad memory of the "friendly fire" encounter.... Washington had largely alienated those to whom he had reported.... His lack of connection with common soldiers showed in his enthusiasm for harsh discipline. He was often too disgusted by the militia to use them well. He acquired little actual combat experience and never commanded a large unit. Perhaps most troubling, he proved he could be impatient, self-promoting, and ready to leapfrog the chain of command.[6]

Despite these failings, because of the courage he had repeatedly shown in combat, as proven by the horses shot under him and the bullet holes in his hats and uniforms, Stewart said Washington had "emerged as Virginia's premier military man,"[7] which would certainly be a feather in his cap from that day forward.

Eminent historian Ron Chernow (author of the Alexander Hamilton biography that inspired the hit musical) wrote a Pulitzer-winning biography of Washington that came out in 2010. Here is what he concluded about his subject's French and Indian War experience, acknowledging the setbacks but also looking at the upside of the tough times and lessons learned:

> The war had humbled him with cruel ironies and unexpected setbacks, leaving him more philosophic and reflective.... He had proved his toughness and courage in the face of massacres and defeats. He had learned to train and drill regiments and developed a rudimentary sense of military strategy. He had shown a real capacity to lead and take responsibility for fulfilling the most arduous missions.... Forced to deal with destructive competition among the colonies, dilatory legislative committees, and squabbling, shortsighted politicians, he had passed through an excellent dress rehearsal for the prolonged ordeal of the American Revolution.[8]

Educated at a young age in a variety of ways through these searing experiences, and moving forward with his life after the war, Washington never again did anything to provide ammunition for criticism that he was an obnoxious self-promoter, confrontational with superiors and equals, inclined to resign over disappointments, or careless in evaluating risks. Chernow hit the nail on the head when he said the French and Indian War proved to be like a "dress rehearsal" for Washington's later experience in the Revolutionary War. Mistakes made in a dress rehearsal don't matter as long as they are recognized, corrected, and not repeated during the run of the show. In Washington's case, the run of the show that opened when his French and Indian War service ended was almost flawless.

Leadership Trait #2:
The Power of Nonverbal Communication, "Less is More" Public Remarks, and the Gift of Silence

At a young age, George Washington had a respiratory illness that presumably contributed to his speaking with a soft breathy voice from then on.[9] In the eighteenth century, long before the microphone's invention, weak pipes ordinarily crippled ambitious people. Later in life, his speech was also hampered by dwindling teeth and primitive dentures. Somehow these problems with his speech didn't impact his effectiveness.

He dealt with the hindrance by being more of a doer than a speaker as he went about his business, letting his actions speak for themselves. He noted, "With me, it has always been a maxim to let my designs appear *from my works* rather than my expressions."[10] When Washington found himself in a political conversation or forum, he listened more than he spoke, more engaged in sizing up his peers than attempting to impress them with efforts at passionate or eloquent rhetoric emanating from a breathy voice.

Washington knew there were ways for a man to make a strong impression without saying much. Among his silent tactics, he made it a habit to look at others with a full straight-on face highlighted by penetrating eyes that so dazzled portrait artist Gilbert Stuart he drew this conclusion: "Had Washington been in the forest, he would have been the fiercest among the savage tribes."[11] His tall trim stature (6'3", 180 pounds) also allowed him to stand out in a crowd, so physically impressive that Stuart's wife Charlotte said Washington was "the most superb looking person I have ever seen."[12]

As for the other nonverbal means that enhanced the power of his presence, Washington moved with the grace of a natural athlete; was always well-groomed; maintained erect posture at all times; dressed immaculately with quiet elegance; expertly rode a gleaming white horse; out-danced every other man at parties; was an accomplished fox hunter; moved on his own timetable such that he never seemed in a hurry; habitually showed respectful deference to others (after learning his lesson in the French and Indian War); avoided speaking outside his areas of expertise; and *never* philandered, smoked, got drunk, or swore (except when he occasionally lost his temper).

In short, rigid self-discipline and attention to detail allowed Washington to present himself to everyone he met, and in every circumstance (even when no one was looking), with as perfect an image of command presence as he could visualize, appearing to be right out of central casting for looking and acting the way strong leaders should project themselves to everyone they encounter.

In addition to inspiring respect in ways that didn't require much speaking, Washington also elevated his standing in groups by being a steady pleasant networker. When the day's work ended, he had no desire to be alone. Instead, he made sure to join gatherings of his colleagues at dinners where he could build rapport and draw conclusions about them based on how they conversed, reacted, and relaxed.

Because of all these nonverbal traits and strategies, supplemented by his well-known track record of having displayed heroic battlefield courage in the French and Indian War and successful leadership as well as bravery in the Revolutionary War, when the stars aligned and the occasion ripened for Washington to speak, those in his presence were all ears. Long before the advent of self-help books, he grasped the communication precept that unfortunately is not followed by many leaders in the modern era: less is more. And to bring additional force to his infrequent public statements, historians David and Jeanne Heidler in their fine biography of Washington noted that, "He paused and hesitated when he spoke, but that made him seem thoughtfully averse to hair-triggered opinions."[13]

Historian Mark Updegrove in his book *Baptism by Fire* noted how important Washington's verbal reserve was in holding the new nation together as factional discord ratcheted up with conflicting viewpoints that diverged mainly on the issue of how strong the new federal government should be. "Conscious that political passions threatened to split the country, he largely kept his voice still so as not to add to them...keeping his opinions in check until policy decisions were required so as not to add to the divisions."[14]

On occasion, Washington even tactfully took his "less is more" communication approach to an extreme, being emotionally intelligent enough to know that in some circumstances, the best approach for sending a clear message is by saying nothing at all. John Adams referred to this as his predecessor's "gift of silence."[15] Chernow described Washington as "the maestro of eloquent silences."[16]

Here are two examples of his using timely silences effectively. First, Virginia's Speaker of the House and Treasurer from 1738 to 1766 was a man named John Robinson. During Robinson's final years in office, he illegally distributed large sums of the state's money to his cronies. This scheme of illicit handouts became public knowledge shortly after Robinson's death, and it caused quite a stir and brought deserved condemnation upon his legacy. Washington, a member of the Virginia House of Burgesses at the time, had regarded Robinson as something of a friend, and said nothing about it. Why? Stewart's answer:

> Washington's reticence seems to reflect the calculation that he had little to gain by attacking a dead man with many friends. Moreover, Robinson had supported Washington, an obligation that he would not repay by disparaging Robinson after his death. Washington's silence also previewed the caution he was learning, which would characterize his future conduct. He occupied a tricky middle ground in the Robinson scandal: He was part of the emerging generation of Virginia leaders and was uninterested in Robinson-style self-dealing, yet had been an intimate of Robinson's. In negotiating such treacherous terrain, silence can be the wisest course.[17]

A second example of Washington's using his gift of silence to produce the desired effect occurred during John Adams' presidency, when the new nation appeared to be a potential target for an invasion by the French. To prepare for such an attack, Adams had to move quickly to put together a new American navy and army (after they had disbanded following the Revolutionary War), so he asked Washington to lead the army. Despite being happily retired at Mount Vernon and completely worn out by his past public service, Washington couldn't decline the call of duty and accepted Adams' invitation. Soon, however, they got into a disagreement over who would serve immediately below him in the new army. Washington wanted Alexander Hamilton as his major general, whom Adams despised, and, therefore, he rejected Washington's request. Washington then made his future leadership of the new army conditioned upon having Hamilton by his side. In that pickle, the president had no choice but to accept the ultimatum. Recognizing he had boxed Adams into an embarrassing predicament and prevailed in their epistolary confrontation, in Washington's next letter to Adams, Chernow described how "with consummate tact, he made no mention of the controversy over the major generals and simply inquired about Abigail's failing health."[18]

Yes, not only can nonverbal communication create a strong impression, and fewer words are usually more potent than too many words, George Washington demonstrated repeatedly that sometimes the most effective way to make a statement when conflict or controversy rears its ugly head is by total silence.

Leadership Trait #3: Humility That Embraces Collaborative Decision-Making

An occupational hazard for many a leader is to believe and project to his peers that he is the smartest guy in the room, regardless of which room he enters and who else is in it. George Washington knew enough about his strengths *and weaknesses* to know that he was *not* high IQ brilliant, but could still function ably amidst great minds by taking advantage of the bright people's smarts in his inner circle.

An example of Washington's awareness of his limitations, and how he used it to achieve a good result, took place in 1787, before the start of the Constitutional Convention. It was acknowledged among Washington's circle of friends that someone should write a solid first draft of the document that could provide a springboard for more focused discussion once the gavel came down in Philadelphia. Washington knew that his close confidante (at the time), James Madison, had studied world political history more thoroughly than anyone else and had the steel-trap mind necessary to pick out the best practices from around the globe that could be used in setting up the new government's structure. So, with Washington's blessing, before the convention began, Madison authored the draft that he called the Virginia Plan, which provided for a strong federal government with checks and balances within three branches.[19] The Plan ably served its purpose in that the final version of the Constitution aligned with most of its key provisions.

As another example of Washington's willingly deferring to the superior horsepower of another, during his presidency, as the federal and state governments attempted to deal with nation-threatening post-war insolvency, he knew that coming up with practical solutions to address the desperate economic conditions the country faced was outside his wheelhouse. Rather than pretend that he could come up with a sensible plan for addressing the issue, Washington turned the problem over to his Treasury Secretary Alexander Hamilton, believing correctly that if anyone could get the country out of the ditch, it was the financial genius.[20] Hamilton succeeded at his assigned task just as Madison had with his. Washington also relied on Madison's word power in writing his First Inaugural Address[21] and Hamilton's in crafting his Farewell Address.[22]

For a final example of having the humility and self-awareness to recognize the need to use others' intelligence, as the problems during his presidency became more complex, Washington increasingly depended on his entire Cabinet to provide counsel on a variety of issues. In gleaning their advice, Washington followed the same practice with his department heads that he had used successfully with his top military advisors during the Revolutionary War—that is, whenever a challenging situation arose that had no readily apparent solution, Washington asked each of them to submit a written memorandum that argued their position on the issue at hand. He knew that as president, *he*, of course, would have to make the final decision on what to do, but he didn't want to make it until *after* he had considered the best input from his brain trust. As an intuitive master of leadership skills, he knew that not only did he need their sage advice to supplement his own thoughts, but he presumably recognized that nothing elevates the spirits of a support team like knowing the boss values his subordinates' opinions.[23]

Chernow noted that Washington's approach in making tough decisions only after gaining as much input as he could from those on all sides of an issue meant that although he didn't reach his conclusions quickly, his process paid dividends by the quality of the results: "Washington's inestimable strength, whether as a general, a planter, or a politician, was prolonged deliberation and slow, mature decisions."[24]

Consistent with Chernow's conclusion, here was Thomas Jefferson's assessment of Washington's collaborative leadership process: "The strongest feature in his character is prudence, never acting until every circumstance, every consideration, was maturely weighed; refraining if he saw a doubt but, when once decided, going through with his purpose whatever obstacles opposed.... No judgment was ever sounder."[25]

Leadership Trait #4:
Acting as Conscience-in-Chief

The Heidlers zeroed in on the most important component of their subject's greatness as a leader. In his every venture—be it leading the Continental Army in the Revolutionary War, presiding over the Constitutional Convention, or serving as President of the United States—all could see that he would always act as the group's "conscience-in-chief" and be guided accordingly. The husband-and-wife biographers provided the following explanation of the impact of his conscience on his constituencies (which synchronizes nicely with his Leadership Trait #3 regarding his gift for collaborative leadership):

> People trusted Washington to do what was right rather than what was smart. It mattered not at all that he was not brilliant, for the world was full of brilliant but bad people. Americans preferred his wisdom born of experience, *the certainty of self that feared no other man's greater intelligence,* and *the moral compass that always pointed the way to promises kept.*[26]

Along the same lines, Stewart repeatedly marveled in his book at Washington's unique "ability to inspire trust."[27] How did he do it? The biographer concluded that it was because his subject never did anything to make people think of him as a "political operator" or to suspect that he ever made a decision based on self-dealing.[28]

Additional facts that confirm Washington's straight-arrow integrity and how it heightened his stature in the public eye, as president, he made all his appointments based on merit, and *never* due to family or friendship relations.[29] He once explained why this was important to him: "My political conduct in nominations, even if I were uninfluenced by principle, must be exceedingly circumspect and proof against just criticism, for the eyes of Argus are upon me, [i.e., he knew there was strict scrutiny on his every move], and no step will pass unnoticed that can be improved into a supposed partiality for friends or relatives."[30]

On another important front where his conscience inspired him to make a good decision during his presidency, many partisan newspapers defamed him during his second term. In response to the unjust criticism, Washington did nothing to restrict their First Amendment rights, unlike his thin-skinned successor John Adams. Here's how Washington explained his confidence in the reward for following his conscience, regardless of having to deal with the libelous comments made in the press: "I have a consolation within that no earthly efforts can deprive me of, and that is, that neither ambitious nor interested motives have influenced my conduct. The arrows of malevolence, therefore, however barbed and well pointed, never can reach the most vulnerable part of me."[31]

Why was Washington totally consumed with maintaining his integrity? Because he knew that for a person in leadership to minimize its importance in any situation will likely result in conduct that permanently tarnishes his reputation. Washington obsessed as much over keeping his reputation spotless as he did over Mount Vernon's being run as an earthly paradise.[32] Again Thomas Jefferson sealed the point: "Washington's integrity was most pure. His justice was the most inflexible I have ever known, no motives of interest or consanguinity, or friendship or hatred, being able to bias his decision.... He errs as other men do, but he errs with integrity."[33]

As a final example of Washington's putting his conscience on display as a non-negotiable force for making sound decisions, one of the most controversial issues of his presidency came during his second term when he sent his Supreme Court Chief Justice John Jay abroad to negotiate a treaty with the British over issues that had arisen after the Revolutionary War. Items on the table included import-export imbalance, the Brits' occupation of certain forts in America's western territories, and their seizure of American sailors and supplies on the open seas. Though the deal Jay ultimately struck did little to advance the new nation's position, it at least helped avoid a second war with the British.

Under the Constitution, in order to become effective, all treaties must be ratified by a two-thirds majority of the Senate and then approved by the president. In the face of an outpouring of public protest over Jay's Treaty once its disappointing terms became known, Federalists led by Hamilton argued and editorialized in support of it, but final acceptance came largely from a letter President Washington wrote that circulated throughout the country. Here was Stewart's perspective on Washington's message that calmed the masses:

> He wrote that he had always sought the happiness of all Americans. He pledged to consider every argument about the treaty while respecting the Constitution, which was "the guide I never can abandon." He stressed that the Senate and he, as president, have the

> power to make treaties because we can judge "without passion, and with the best means of information, those facts and principles upon which the success of our foreign relations will always depend." He would ultimately decide [whether to support the treaty], "by obeying the dictates of my conscience."[34]

The public's trust in Washington's conscience-led decisions allowed him to gain the needed support for Jay's Treaty. In his book *Presidential Courage,* eminent historian Michael Beschloss explained why Washington's leadership in getting Jay's Treaty approved had major historical significance: "The precedent Washington set with his leadership on Jay's Treaty was that a president should not merely preside. He must use his unique standing—even if it made him unpopular or cost an election—to convince Congress and the American people to accept unpopular notions that may be in their long-term interest."[35]

Abiding by the dictates of his conscience allowed George Washington to have complete credibility with every group he touched throughout his era. Those who knew him and those who knew of him always took comfort from the fact that no matter what happened, he would never compromise on his commitment to *do the right thing,* as he saw it. More than any other of his virtues, the well-recognized mandate that Washington's conscience provided him drove the public's trust in his judgment.

Leadership Trait #5: Advancing Unity

One of the most important traits for an effective leader is to be seen as an effective force for bringing a group together and keeping it unified. Per Jesus Christ's words in Matthew 12:25 of the New Testament, as used famously by Abraham Lincoln, "A house divided against itself cannot stand."[36] Thus, a great leader must prioritize keeping his house from imploding due to internal conflict. Washington's uniquely successful track record in being a unanimous pick for top leadership positions chosen by different constituencies is certainly proof that across the board, he was perceived by all as being more likely than anyone else to keep American citizens on the same page and functioning as a productive unit.

Just as he had made it a practice to ride through his military camps daily to make sure his soldiers knew he was fully engaged with them throughout the Revolutionary War, shortly after the inauguration for his first term as president, Washington decided to showcase his commitment to fostering unity among the American people by making a tour of all thirteen colonies, which he did on intermittent trips over the four years. Each trip was marked by major receptions in his honor given in every town he entered. Historian Nathaniel Philbrick in his book *Travels with George* explained what drove his subject's decision to see the entire country: "From the first, Washington hoped to use the power of his immense popularity to foster a sense of unity and national pride that had not previously existed."[37] In furtherance of his effort to bond with all parts of the new American society, Philbrick noted that on the trips, Washington spent every night in a public tavern.[38]

In addition to prioritizing face-to-face contact with his subordinates, another ingredient in Washington's recipe for building unity among his constituents was by developing a well-known track record for sound decision-making. The Heidlers cited Jefferson's awareness of it shortly after Washington's death: "His almost supernatural ability to pluck the best solution from an abundance of advice made him 'in every sense of the words, a wise, a good, and a great man.'"[39]

Yes, people are more likely to become unified as a group behind a leader perceived to consistently have the right answers to tough questions. As a corollary to that precept, sometimes there is no readily apparent good solution to a thorny problem and the difference of opinion over what should be done about it can cause polarization. When that circumstance arose, Washington still knew what to do to unify a group, as demonstrated when he served as a delegate to the First Continental Congress in 1774. Stewart noted that,

> Through the tedium and the excitement, Washington listened and watched. As he had done before [in the Virginia House of Burgesses], he evaluated the arguments and the delegates, stating his views in conversation but avoiding floor debate. He was affable and polite. He described his role in that first Congress as that of "an attentive observer and witness." Months later, when Congress convened for its second session, it would become clear that Washington had exercised his gift of winning the trust of others.[40]

Washington's talent for unifying was also tied to the sense of optimism he managed to project to those he led, even on dark days. Chernow gave a good summary of how this trait was crucial to victory in the Revolutionary War:

> He was a different kind of general fighting a different kind of war, and his military prowess cannot be judged by the usual scorecard of battles won and lost. His fortitude in keeping the impoverished Continental Army intact was a major historic accomplishment. It always stood on the brink of dissolution, and Washington was the one figure who kept it together, the spiritual and managerial genius of the whole enterprise: he had been resilient in the face of every setback, courageous in the face of every danger.... His stewardship of the army had been a masterly exercise in nation building. In defining the culture of the Continental Army, he had helped to mold the very character of the country, preventing the Revolution from taking a bloodthirsty or despotic turn.[41]

A vivid post-war example of Washington's using his talents to unify in the context of quieting conflicting voices on the political front came during his first presidential term, as he watched the two brightest stars in his Cabinet, Hamilton and Jefferson, become more estranged with each passing day. This disturbed the president for the reasons Philbrick explained:

> What bothered him were not the philosophical differences between his two warring Cabinet members but their unwillingness to work cooperatively. "Differences in political opinions are as unavoidable as, to a certain point, they may perhaps be necessary," he wrote to Hamilton. What both Hamilton and Jefferson needed, Washington seemed to be saying, was a little more humility and self-doubt. Because no one—not even the two most brilliant men of their age—had all the answers. Unlike Hamilton and Jefferson, Washington didn't need to be right all the time. He just wanted to make things work. He understood that feasible change is not attained by righteous indignation; it's understanding *that the road ahead is full of compromises if life is actually going to get better.*[42]

In the midst of the widening division between Hamilton and the Federalists, on the one hand, and Jefferson and the Republicans, on the other, in 1790, the two biggest issues that confronted them—whether the federal government should assume the states' debts and where the nation's capital should be permanently located—resulted in the trade that the feds *would* assume the states' debts to make Hamilton happy and the capital city *would* be located on the Potomac near Virginia to make Jefferson happy.

This vitally important deal had to have been engineered behind the scenes by President Washington,[i,43] and Stewart gave this expla-

---

i Thomas Jefferson later wrote that the deal was struck during a private dinner at his home attended by him, Madison, and Hamilton. Neither of the other attendees ever corroborated Jefferson's account of the alleged dinner. Never being reluctant to claim an elevated place in history, and sometimes opportunistic in his willingness to use poetic license to enhance his stature as a leader, the credibility of Jefferson's version of what induced the Compromise of 1790 is left to you, the reader. See: Nathaniel Philbrick, *Travels with George: In Search of Washington and His Legacy* (Viking 2021), 340–341.

nation for that inferential conclusion: "The president won *everything* he wanted. Assumption was a linchpin of his program to retrieve public credit and strengthen the government. A Potomac residence [for the nation's government] fulfilled his years of effort to promote his home region."[44]

Yes, for the two key issues in the Compromise of 1790, Hamilton and Jefferson each won one and lost one, while Washington, the mediator-unifier, won them both. Only a leader like George Washington could resolve extreme conflict between bona fide enemies, and at the same time come out of it triumphant in achieving all his objectives.

As another example of Washington's commitment to doing all he could to enhance a spirit of unity during his presidency, Stewart explained how the first president subtly projected a tone of optimism in his address to Congress in December 1790. Mindful of the ongoing need to foster unity, Washington chose to focus his speech on the *good things* happening in America, and gave short shrift to what caused heartburn:

> The address slighted important questions. Washington mentioned Indian unrest near the Wabash River, but not reports that an expedition had met a bloody defeat there. Neither did he refer to the proposal for a national bank that Congress soon would address. The omissions reflected his understanding of the power of information, which he released to suit his purposes, and also his instinct to skirt controversial matters in order to tamp down forces of disunion.[45]

In at least one critical area, Washington's commitment to unity appears to have prevailed over his commitment to act as the nation's conscience-in-chief. As will be discussed later in this chapter, one of Washington's few moral blind spots was on the issue of slavery. During the Revolutionary War, he witnessed many African American slaves who fought courageously with the Continental Army. Thereafter, *privately,* he wrestled with his conscience over what should be done to end it, and he never came up with an answer that inspired him to change his ways. As for the *public* arena, until his death, Washington *never* said *anything* about slavery. Stewart offered this explanation for his subject's unfortunate silence:

> The slave system posed the greatest test of Washington's political skills. For virtually all his life, he failed it. He made no public statement nor took any public action that questioned the legitimacy of slavery, *fearing that it would upend the republic for which he sacrificed so much*. On the most pressing moral question facing the nation, its greatest leader did not lead.[46]

In summary, to be a successful unifier, the most important traits Washington exhibited were that he made sure those he led saw him face-to-face and could verify his engagement with them; he developed a well-known reputation for making good decisions using a process that required his consideration of all pertinent information and advice available to him; he knew the importance of steadily building rapport with people on all sides of the political spectrum; he was largely silent on the issues of his time that defied a clear answer until enough evidence was provided that allowed him to make a final decision; he refused to debate controversial issues because it would make him appear divisive; when necessary, he could cram down a compromise to bring closure to a conflict; and he remained steadily optimistic and focused on doing what it took to achieve his goals regardless of any setbacks, which inspired others to hang in there with him and not give up on his cause.

Leadership Trait #6:
Avoiding the Image of Self-Promoter

Mere mortals make no effort to conceal their lust for powerful positions. They believe that by letting their ambitious intentions be known, others will take action to help them rise to the top, and a failure to deliver a direct message about their desired advancement runs the risk of being passed over because selectors will overlook them.

As covered earlier in this chapter, in his early twenties, during the French and Indian War, George Washington acted as a mere mortal and left no stone unturned in communicating to his British superiors his expectations for being chosen to go up the army's rank and recognition ladder. Since his overt self-promotional efforts didn't work for him in that war (presumably, it dawned on him that "nobody likes a diva"), as a relentless critic of himself, he surely took note of the fact that such efforts failed to achieve his desired results. From that time forward, he used a new subtle approach to move himself up the ladder that inspired *others* to shine their lights on his basket so he wouldn't have to do it himself.

Between his time of service in the French and Indian War and the Revolutionary War, the sixteen years from 1759 to 1775, Washington served continuously in the Virginia House of Burgesses. Slowly but surely, he elevated his political stature in each session by paying his dues as a tactful diligent legislator. Here was how Stewart described Washington's political education in those years that paid huge dividends later in life: "He saw at close hand how political interests clash, how alliances are formed and opinions shaped, and how legislators can be persuaded. He worked at reading men's intentions, a talent he would master."[47]

As confirmation of Stewart's assessments about this crucial but uncelebrated time in his life that became instrumental to his subsequent move up the career ladder, Washington once explained to his stepson the unglamorous but effective priorities he followed while serving in the House of Burgesses: "to be punctual in attendance, hear dispassionately, and determine coolly all great questions."[48] Notice that none of his rules for being an effective legislator involved speaking.

During those sixteen years in the Virginia House, Washington built strong, steady, mutually respectful relationships with his colleagues by knowing their strengths and weaknesses, and never boring them with longwinded verbosity nor offending them with arrogance. He learned how to retaliate effectively but with civility when others caused problems, and quietly took advantage of opportunities for advancement when they came along. He also had enough awareness of what was coming down the track to avoid situations that could potentially tarnish his reputation or create ill will with others.[49] Doing all these things, together with his commanding physical presence, strategic use of nonverbal, "less is more," and sometimes silent communication (described earlier), and his fame from the valor he had shown during the French and Indian War, Washington not only won the trust of his peers in the Virginia House of Burgesses, he also became viewed as its backbone.

As problems with the Brits grew in the early 1770s, the colonies' leading political figures quickly realized they would have to band into a united effort if they were to have any hope of disconnecting themselves from British rule. Thus, they assembled in Philadelphia as the First Continental Congress in September to October 1774 and the Second Continental Congress beginning in May 1775 (one month after Lexington and Concord). Washington was a delegate at both.

The Congresses recognized that a new Continental Army would *have to be formed* and organized immediately for the cause of independence to have any chance of success. Therefore, a commander-in-chief to lead the army *had to be chosen*. Under those circumstances, Washington went to the Second Congress knowing that he *was*, and *was viewed* by others, as the most qualified person to take charge of the colonies' embryonic military enterprise. Despite having a huge competitive advantage as the candidate most likely to be chosen to lead the new army, presumably remembering how his obvious self-promotional efforts during the French and Indian War had backfired, this time around, *he said nothing* that would cause any delegate to think he was seeking the job.

How to be offered the command leadership post without specifically asking for it? Here Washington flashed genius in the art of nonverbal communication. Wherever he went during the meetings of the Second Congress, he *always* wore his pristine, well-tailored Virginia militiamen uniform, which conveyed the clear but unstated message: "I'm here, if you want me."[50] When the time came for the delegates to make their choice, Washington's striking attire, enhanced by how he wore it on his impressive frame, supplemented by his steady smooth networking at the Congress, and his well-known past courageous military service, all combined to speak louder than any self-promotional words he could have spoken.

The war effort then continued for the next eight years. Washington proved himself to be the best possible commander-in-chief, given the Continental Army's many disadvantages and setbacks, by holding his troops together often without pay through the bitter winters; making progress in defeating the larger and better-equipped Brits by implementing an effective strategy that often used sneak attacks; tactfully keeping his troops away from predictable losing battle situations that were likely to occur whenever his army was outnumbered; and persevering through the many tough times to outlast the enemy. Here was how Philbrick weighed in on Washington's nontraditional but successful military leadership during the Revolutionary War:

> Washington did not win the war so much as endure an eight-year ordeal that would have destroyed just about anyone else. In the early years of the conflict, he'd been repeatedly second-guessed by the Continental Congress, even though that legislative body proved powerless to provide the food and supplies his army desperately needed. After the entry of France into the war, Washington spent three frustrating years pleading with his obstinate ally to provide the naval support that ultimately made possible the victory at Yorktown. And then, in the months before the evacuation of the British from New York City, Washington was forced to confront a group of his own officers who threatened to march on Philadelphia and demand their pay at gunpoint. By persuading his officers to remain at their encampment on the Hudson River, Washington prevented the military coup that would have destroyed the Republic at its birth.[51]

Just as Washington had enhanced his standing with his peers in the Virginia House of Burgesses and Continental Congresses, he did the same thing in wartime—maintaining close contact with his troops, staying deferential to Congress (regardless of how many times they failed to get him what the war effort needed), brainstorming strategy and tactics with those ranking directly below him, staying calm and persevering in the toughest times, never letting fame or power go to his head, and consistently making good decisions.

The ultimate *pièce de résistance* in Washington's winning the adoration of Americans from all walks of life in an act that involved few words, but elevated his stature the next time a leader needed to be chosen for a top position, came when the Revolutionary War ended in triumph. Rather than stay on at the helm as commander-in-chief or insist on continuing to hold power in the now fully-independent government, he voluntarily relinquished his position to return home to Mount Vernon and resume life in the private sector. When England's King George II learned of his walk away from supreme power, he called Washington "the greatest man in the world."[52]

Put all these traits and accomplishments together, carry through with them year after year, and achieve the ultimate goal of military victory and national independence; then step down gracefully in a historically unprecedented relinquishment of power. By the time the United States needed to find a leader to help it take the next step forward, a still ambitious George Washington didn't need to wear a uniform, beat on his chest, remind people of his past achievements, or send messages to insiders to communicate his desire to be chosen for the next vaulted position. A person having the stature of being a man among boys *does not need to say or do anything* to promote himself for future leadership positions.

Post-war, the Constitutional Convention was scheduled to convene in late May 1787. Knowing how important the convention would be to the new nation's future, and knowing as well that he was the best person to lead it, but presumably playing coy, Washington acted like he didn't want to go to Philadelphia. James Madison had to beg him to attend, finally persuading him on the basis that the convention couldn't possibly fulfill its mission without him there, and if the new nation didn't have a new "Supreme Law of the Land" in place that worked, everything Washington had fought for in the war would have likely been for naught.[53]

For the reasons stated previously, at the Constitutional Convention, when it came time to pick a chairman, though Washington knew he would be the best person for the job, he said and did nothing to suggest his having an interest in it because he *knew* there was no choice to be made. Upon being chosen unanimously as the chair, Washington knew how essential it was for the country to throw away the Articles of Confederation and have a new strong Constitution. He also knew that the final document shouldn't vary much from Madison's Virginia Plan, regardless of how heated the discussions got. He also knew most of the delegates well. Those he didn't know certainly knew who he was and recognized him as an American hero. He also knew not to interject himself into debates (and thereby become a divider rather than a unifier) other than to keep the proceedings moving and show no favoritism to anyone. When the Constitution was finally approved, in hopes of aiding the upcoming ratification effort, Washington signed his name at the top, making it clear to all that the country's most revered figure had endorsed it. Without his giving such a clear stamp of approval, he presumably knew that there would have been little chance of its being ratified by the states.

Upon its ratification, the Constitution provided for three branches of government, including the executive branch to be led by a president. The same foregone conclusion that led the decision-makers to make a unanimous choice of Washington to lead the Continental Army in 1775 and the Constitutional Convention in 1787 kicked in again for choosing the first president in 1789. He again said or did nothing to indicate his desire to be chosen for the country's highest office. Chernow explained why:

> He regarded any open interest in power as unbecoming to a gentleman. As a result, he preferred to be drawn reluctantly from private life by the irresistible

> summons of public service. He eschewed the word *president*, as if merely saying it might connote an unsavory desire on his part. The only way he could proceed, it seemed, was to show extreme reluctance to become president, then be swept along by others.[54]

Alexander Hamilton used the same tactic to get the seemingly reluctant Washington to accept the presidency as Madison had used on him to attend the Constitutional Convention: Telling him in no uncertain terms that if he refused to take the job, the new independent American nation would surely disintegrate, and all his past heroic efforts would have been in vain. Big (and coy) Washington finally said "Yes," and the rest is history.[55]

George Washington's Flaws

When I embarked on writing this book, my friend Mark Updegrove, the author of many fine books on presidential history, made this suggestion: "Talmage, I'm sure you'll do this along the way, but I'd strongly suggest that in examining what made these leaders great at key times, you should also show their warts. Those flaws will be important in making the eight presidents relatable—not distant and daunting Mount Rushmore and Mount Rushmore-like icons but flesh and blood leaders who walked on feet of clay, ultimately finding the best in themselves to rise to the challenges that defined their presidencies."

Though I accepted that good advice from Mark, it hasn't been easy to execute in this chapter because after George Washington learned his lessons in the French and Indian War about what *not* to do, from that point on, he had only a few notable flaws in what he *did*. He had a hot temper that was so extreme Thomas Jefferson described it as "*naturally irritable and high-toned,* but reflection and resolution had obtained a firm and natural ascendancy over it. If, however, he broke its bonds, *he was most tremendous in his wrath*."[56] Yes, Washington's temper was a thorn in his side that never left him, but as Jefferson noted in his comment, Washington's self-awareness and self-discipline caused him to minimize its frequency.

As mentioned previously in the discussion of Leadership Trait #5 on unity, Washington's largely unbothered view of slavery was a serious blind spot on his otherwise clear conscience. He was born, grew up, and lived almost his entire life in a Virginia world where virtually everyone he knew and respected owned slaves, and none of them made any known statements of feeling guilt or having remorse about it. Washington at least began to *wrestle* with his conscience about slavery during the Revolutionary War as African American slaves fought and died with valor on the American side, yet he failed to *say or do* anything to right the wrong of slavery being permitted across America. In his private life, he owned slaves at Mount Vernon until he revised his will during his final health decline, emancipating his slaves upon his death. In his *political life*, with his *never doing* anything about slavery publicly, Stewart said it best: "On the most pressing moral question facing the nation, its greatest leader did not lead."[57]

Washington also received criticism for his treatment of Native Americans during the Revolutionary War by refusing to let them prevent the colonies' westward expansion that he deemed necessary for the war effort. When he offered to purchase their lands at what he considered a fair price, and they rejected his terms, Washington seized their lands and had them removed.

For this author at least, it's problematical to evaluate Washington's eighteenth-century attitudes and conduct toward African Americans in slavery and Indians by using twenty-first century racial sensibilities. Having said that, you can draw your own conclusions of how much aspersion to cast on Washington for what he thought and did or did not say or do about the rough treatment of minorities during his era, which took place long before the abolitionist movement in America had gained any traction, in the context of how his conduct and mindset compared to his peers.

Having now identified Washington's few major flaws, when added together, do they qualify him to be viewed as a man with "feet of clay"? After learning life lessons from the French and Indian War, obviously he was still *not* a flawless person. Nonetheless, in comparison to other mortals, especially those who lived in the American colonies and then the newly independent United States of America prior to 1799 (the year he died), George Washington surely ranks at the top of his class from a moral excellence and emotional intelligence standpoint.

Personal Application

For those now considering how to apply George Washington's traits into their personal repertoires in a quest for achieving greater success in being chosen for higher leadership positions, providing honest answers to the questions below should help with that process. I recommend that this self-awareness exercise take place in a quiet room with the door closed, perhaps joined by one's closest and most candid friend.

You now know how George Washington would have answered the following questions. How do *you* answer them?

- How frequently do you inventory and attempt to avoid repeating the mistakes you have made?
- Do you evaluate how much you *do* on the same plane as how much you *say*?
- How much do you *listen* compared to how much you *talk*?
- Do you consistently dress and groom yourself in a manner most likely to make a strong favorable impression on those you encounter?
- Do you maintain erect posture when you stand, walk, and sit?
- In conversation, do you make sure you maintain eye contact?
- Are you respectful to *all* regardless of their social stature?
- Do you consistently appear to be unhurried (and, thus, adept at time management)?
- How often do you speak on a subject outside your knowledge?

- Do you have any bad habits that you know are offensive to at least some people?
- Do you stay proactive in enhancing the *quality* and *quantity* of your relationships?
- Do you make it a point to go deep in evaluating what makes someone else tick who is important to your current situation?
- Are your peers likely to say that either you talk too much or without precision in your choice of words?
- Do you connect with people whom you believe to be strong in the areas where you know you are weak, and then use them as a resource?
- Before making an important decision, do you solicit and review the opinions of others you respect?
- Do you make major decisions quickly or deliberately?
- Are you guided by your conscience in *all* your decisions and situations?
- Do you consider yourself more of a unifier or a divider?
- Do you prioritize having face-to-face encounters with your subordinates?
- Do you have a well-established track record for making sound decisions?
- Do you typically listen and show respect to a person having a point of view that's materially different from your own?
- When you speak on a subject in which you're heavily invested, do you project a sense of optimism?
- When two sides disagree on an important issue in which you're involved, do you typically choose a side or do you attempt to mediate their areas of disagreement?
- When you become aware of a higher position that you deem desirable to advance your career, are you aggressively

pushy with your self-promotional efforts or do you find subtle (often unstated) ways to motivate those involved in the selection process and quietly rely on others' awareness of your worthiness when the time comes for the leadership choice to be made?

May the lessons and leadership traits of George Washington's life guide you as you reflect on these questions. Digging deep with full transparency in this question-and-answer exercise should move the needle not only toward enhanced self-improvement, but also improving your chances of moving up the career ladder at a faster pace.

CHAPTER TWO

HOW TO MAXIMIZE HARMONY, IMAGINATION, LONG-TERM VISION, AND POWER— LIKE THOMAS JEFFERSON

Writing about Thomas Jefferson is a tough assignment in the twenty-first century because those who do it must deal with "the Jefferson Conundrum," articulated by Walter Isaacson in his book *The Code Breaker*: "To what extent can you respect a person for great achievements ("We hold these truths") when they are accompanied by reprehensible failings ("are created equal")?"[58]

The Conundrum crystallized for me during my interview of Jon Meacham in February 2013 as we discussed his book *Thomas Jefferson: The Art of Power* that had just been released. I asked him this hypothetical question:

> Assume it is 2013, but the Jefferson Memorial has never been built. Assume also that a Congressperson submits a bill *today* that seeks several million dollars in federal funding for the construction of such a memorial in our nation's capital.
>
> Knowing what we *now* know about Thomas Jefferson, and what was going on with him and the slaves at Monticello throughout his adult life, does the current Congress pass that bill?

When I finished, Meacham paused, then smiled, and then answered in a quiet voice, "No, that bill wouldn't pass today." After the program, he inscribed in my copy of his Jefferson biography, "To Talmage, who asked me the best question of 2012–2013" during his national book tour. Seven years later, in his foreword to the book *In the Hands of the People,* Meacham wrote, "Jefferson represents the *best* of us and the *worst* of us."[59]

In accordance with this book's purpose, the pages that follow in this chapter will be devoted mainly to Jefferson's "best" leadership traits that are worthy of emulation. His "worst" flaws will also be addressed, though in much less detail, to let the "warts and all" span of his life be available for your final evaluation of the man and the conundrum he presents to the ages.

Having opened this chapter acknowledging the moral deficiencies that have altered the assessments of Jefferson in recent years, the facts remain that his face still appears on the nickel, the two-dollar bill, and Mount Rushmore; the Jefferson Memorial still stands on the shore of the Potomac River and attracts over 3 million visitors annually; and an average of 440,000 people travel to Charlottesville each year to see Monticello and its slave quarters. Furthermore, in the most recent C-SPAN presidential ranking polls (in which the 150 voters are recognized historians), despite his slavery issues, Jefferson has maintained his stature in the top ten, ranked seventh in both 2017 and 2021.

Acknowledging the good and bad in this mixed-bag scenario, it is undeniable that only an exceptional person could have authored the American Creed found in the opening of the Declaration of Independence; championed the rise of democracy and human freedom in the new republic of the United States; built and fueled (without ever taking credit for it) the political party engine that controlled the presidency for thirty-six of the nineteenth century's first forty years; and doubled the country's size by consummating the Louisiana Purchase.

These achievements were effected by a dazzling compartmentalized man whose internal inconsistencies led one of his leading biographers, Merrill Peterson, to conclude (after studying his subject for thirty years) that Jefferson's "personality remains elusive" since he was "the least self-revealing of his contemporaries," and that is what makes him "an *impenetrable* man."[60] Another biographer, Peter Onuf, who has also spent most of his adult life studying and writing about Jefferson, says that "the search for a single, definitive, 'real' Jefferson is a fool's errand."[61] Maybe Jefferson was "impenetrable"; clearly, he cannot be seen in only one certain way, and thus, to assess him given the vast complexity of his personality is certainly quite a challenge for a historian.

The author of this chapter has *not* studied Jefferson continuously for decades and, therefore, will not attempt to penetrate the impenetrable and is hopefully not on a fool's errand. Regardless of Jefferson's complexity and personal baggage, he was certainly one of our country's greatest leaders, and Peterson explained why: "No other founder had a longer or larger influence on the life and the hopes of the New World prodigy than Thomas Jefferson. He embodied the nation's aspirations for freedom and enlightenment."[62] With that introduction, let's see what the man and his stellar accomplishments can teach us about best practices in leadership.

Leadership Trait #1: To Maintain Progress in the Midst of Conflict, Be Proactive in Building Harmony Among Friends and Foes

Hard to believe, but true: The political friction that escalated during the presidencies of George Washington and John Adams was every bit as intense as it has been throughout the White House years of Donald Trump and Joe Biden. Things got so out of control in our country's first decade that the Federalists (who then held the majority of seats in Congress) passed the Sedition Act in 1798, which imposed criminal penalties, including incarceration, for anyone who criticized President Adams or Federalist policies. Thomas Jefferson called the years when the Act was in effect "the reign of witches," because, as he wrote to his daughter, "Politics and party hatreds destroy the happiness of every being here. They seem like salamanders, to consider fire as their element."[63] Thankfully, the Act expired at the end of Adams' single term.

Pulitzer Award–winning historian Annette Gordon-Reed and Onuf co-authored the book *"Most Blessed of the Patriarchs": Thomas Jefferson and the Empire of the Imagination.* In it, they set the stage as to how, prior to Jefferson's election in 1800, at that time of hatred and fire, "Republicans characterized Federalists as the 'English party' while Federalists claimed that Republicans were intent on revolutionizing America into yet another French puppet state…. In this era of intense partisan rancor, Jefferson's Franco-American persona grew so polarizing that the conflict-averse gentleman from Virginia became a *lightning rod* for political conflict"[64] since the new direction of the nation's foreign policy was incredibly important to the American people at the time.

Into that hornet's nest stepped Jefferson, leader of the opposition "faction" to the Federalists, despite having served as John Adams's vice president.[i] Jefferson narrowly defeated Adams (the electoral vote

---

i To clarify as to exactly what was meant by political "parties" in the eighteenth century, Chernow stated in his biography of George Washington that during the new nation's first decade, the opposing groups were "not political parties in the modern sense so much as clashing coteries of intellectual elites, who operated through letters and conversations instead of meetings, platforms, and conventions."

split was 73–65, with Jefferson carrying nine of the sixteen states) in the election he called "the people's triumph," though the newly elected president quickly decided his days as a political "lightning rod" needed to end.

Outgoing President Adams was so upset at failing to get reelected and having to turn the country over to his then-archenemy Jefferson (they reconciled decades later) that he headed home to Massachusetts before his successor was sworn in, displaying a level of embittered bad form repeated only by three other departing presidents: Adams' son John Quincy (after he was beaten decisively by Andrew Jackson in the 1828 election), Andrew Johnson (after he narrowly dodged an impeachment conviction bullet), and Donald Trump (who avoided impeachment convictions twice).

Foreshadowing Abraham Lincoln's Second Inaugural Address (in which the Great Emancipator urged the divided country to look at each other after four years of death and devastation in the Civil War, "with malice toward *none*; with charity for *all*..."), in March 1801, upon taking the oath of office, Jefferson addressed the gathering at his inauguration with carefully chosen (but softly spoken) words aimed at calming the partisan storm that threatened to become a nation-destroying cataclysm. He knew that for the new nation to get back on track, Americans needed to return to the same sense of "Spirit of '76" unity that had spurred them to victory a quarter century before in the Revolutionary War.

His conciliatory message on that pivotal occasion, which his biographer Joseph Ellis said he "worked on with the same diligence he had once given to the Declaration of Independence," created a turning point that reduced the nation's feverish political temperature from its surge during Adams' presidency:

> ...Let us, then, fellow-citizens, unite with one heart and one mind. Let us restore to social intercourse that harmony and affection without which liberty and even life itself are but dreary things.... Every difference of opinion is not a difference of principle. We

> have called by different names brethren of the same principle. *We are all republicans,*[ii], [65] *we are all federalists*.... Let us, then, with courage and confidence pursue our own federal and republican principles, our attachment to union and representative government.[66]

Though Jefferson's First Inaugural Address is regarded as a rhetorical masterpiece, it proved to be the *only* impactful speech of his life. From the outset of his political career, he had accepted the inconvenient truth that he was a poor public speaker, although he had once been an effective lawyer in the courtroom. His awareness of this usually fatal weakness for politicians made Jefferson avoid talking to large groups whenever possible. During his years in the Virginia House of Burgesses and the Continental Congress, he almost never spoke during legislative sessions, and in the eight years of his presidency, his two inaugural addresses were the only speeches he made.

Despite his prudent unwillingness to pontificate to the masses, Jefferson knew he had a unique gift for communicating in small gatherings. There he could charm and disarm anyone within earshot regardless of their political affiliation, and in time, turn them into friends or at least admirers. Even John Quincy Adams, who opposed essentially all of Jefferson's political positions, had to admit that a person "never can be an hour in his company without [experiencing] something of the marvelous."[67]

Since using his lackluster oratorical skills was not a viable option, President Jefferson decided that to bring down partisan strife during

---

ii In Ellis's book, *American Sphinx: The Character of Thomas Jefferson*, which won the National Book Award, he noted that "in the version of the address printed in the *National Intelligencer* and then released to the newspapers, "the 'R' in 'Republicans' and the 'F' in 'Federalists' were capitalized." Ellis explained that "by capitalizing the operative terms, the printed version had Jefferson making a gracious statement about the overlapping goals of the two political parties. But in the handwritten version of the speech that Jefferson delivered, the key words were *not* capitalized. Jefferson was, therefore, referring not to the common ground shared by the two parties but to the common belief, shared by all American citizens, that a republican form of government and a federal bond among the states were most preferable." See: Joseph Ellis, *American Sphinx: The Character of Thomas Jefferson* (Knopf 1997), 182.

his administration, he'd need to pursue a plan by which he would assemble small group gatherings where he could turn on his extraordinary engagement powers and build rapport with hostile Federalists and also deepen his bond with fellow Republicans.

In formulating his socialization plan, Jefferson had seen enough heated debates and arguments over the years to know that such confrontations *never* resulted in anyone changing his position. He reached the same conclusion Dale Carnegie later addressed in rhyme in *How to Win Friends and Influence People* on the folly of participating in verbal quarrels: "A man convinced against his will is of the same opinion still." Jefferson also embraced the idea that inspired Abraham Lincoln's approach to moving the needle on public sentiment: "You can't change someone's mind until you first change his heart."

Throughout diplomatic history, a well-known strategy for building fellowship among wary acquaintances has been to do it while sharing food, adult beverages, and comfortable talk around a table. Recognizing the potential of hospitality to enhance his political influence, Jefferson decided on a plan in which he implemented a social stamina-testing string of frequent (three times a week) small (eight to twenty people) dinners that he carried on throughout his presidency, where he displayed impeccable manners as he hosted and schmoozed with other government leaders. Jefferson gave this explanation for why he chose dinner diplomacy:

> I cultivate personal intercourse with the members of the legislature that we may know one another and have opportunity of little explanations of circumstances, which, not understood might produce jealousies and suspicions injurious to the public interest; and are best promoted by harmony and mutual confidence among its functionaries. I depend much on the members for the local information necessary on local matters, as well as for the means of getting at public sentiment.[68]

Meacham shed additional light on the plan's inspiration:

> Jefferson appreciated how to handle lawmakers *for he had been one*. Even then a president's attention meant the world to politicians. For all his low-key republican symbolism, he understood that access to the president himself could make all the difference in statecraft—hence his dinners with lawmakers.[69]

To Jefferson, warm-hearted conversations among government colleagues at dinner epitomized how people in the new republic's public arena were *supposed* to operate. In his book *The Mind of Thomas Jefferson,* Onuf confirmed that, for Jefferson, "political life could be seen as a conversation among friends, recognizing diverse perspectives and interests while seeking common ground and a common good."[70]

As he sought to maximize the mileage from the dinners, Jefferson imposed three rules that he always followed: (1) never invite Republicans and Federalists to the same dinner; (2) never discuss controversial political business at a dinner; and (3) never impose seating arrangements. Meacham explained the third rule's rationale: "To Jefferson, each guest who came into his orbit was significant and…he had no patience with the trappings of rank."[71]

Among Jefferson's key insights in heightening the impact of the dinners was his awareness that (1) his first two rules were necessary because any significant conflict between two or more at the table would almost certainly poison an evening (Gordon-Reed and Onuf said the rules worked because his "aversion to conflict [at the dinners] enabled men of feeling to forge enduring bonds with each other")[72]; and (2) guests typically enjoyed their time at the table more if their host orchestrated the flow of conversation so that *they* did most of the talking and *he* did most of the listening. The historian co-authors gave this account of how Jefferson went about his business of confrontation avoidance and relationship building through talking less and listening more at meal time:

> "In conversation," Daniel Webster reported, "Mr. Jefferson is easy and natural, and apparently not ambitious." He was "not loud" and did not seek to command the "general attention," instead usually addressing "the person next to him" on topics suited to "the character and feelings of the auditor." Thomas Jefferson Randolph recalled that his grandfather "never indulged in controversial conversation." He was, rather, a good "listener": the closer a visitor came, the more Jefferson would seek to draw him or her out, deflecting conversation away from himself, and "if anyone expressed a decided opinion differing from his own, he made no reply, but changed the subject."[73]

When, after waiting his turn, President Jefferson finally weighed in with his thoughts on the topic at hand, his relationship-building genius kicked into overdrive. Again, Gordon-Reed and Onuf wrote: "Conversation in private, intimate settings was his distinctive métier. He proved adept at drawing colleagues and acquaintances into his personal realm and thus making 'friends' who shared his fundamental values and commitments."[74]

Meacham quoted a Jefferson dinner guest so impressed by the fellowship dinner experience that he rhapsodized about it in a letter to his wife:

> The food was excellent, cooked rather in the French style.... Wine in great variety, from sherry to champagne, and a few decanters of rare Spanish wine.... [For the conversation around the table] Literature, wit, and a little business with a great deal of miscellaneous remarks on agriculture and building filled every minute. There is a degree of ease in Mr. Jefferson's company that everyone seems to feel and enjoy.[75]

Just as Stewart encapsulated (with tongue in cheek) George Washington's seemingly effortless political rise in one word, that same word might well describe a conclusion made in jest about the power of Jefferson's smooth charisma at his dinners: It was "magic." Like Washington's rise, Jefferson's gracious hospitality and flair for promoting scintillating conversation was definitely *not* magic but rather the result of his serious attention to analyzing best practices in socializing. Meacham described how Jefferson went about developing kinship with Federalists during their evenings together:

> The *subtext* [of each word Jefferson said,] as he discussed the violin and books: "We may be political opponents, but we are men of culture who share a love of common things..." Jefferson believed in the politics of the personal relationship.... He governed personally...and believed in constant conversation with lawmakers.[76]

A frequent President's House[iii] dinner guest was the Federalist Senator William Plumer from New Hampshire, who recognized that his initial partisan hostility toward Jefferson came down *incrementally* with each passing meal they shared: "The more critically and impartially I examine the character and conduct of Mr. Jefferson, the more favorably I think of his integrity.... I have a curiosity which is gratified by seeing and conversing with him. I gain a more thorough knowledge of his character, and of his views, and those of his party—for he is naturally communicative."[77]

Jefferson's focus on building rapport with Federalists was not limited to his dinners. Supreme Court Justice William Paterson, a Federalist appointed to the court by Adams, gave this account of the before-and-after effect of the Jefferson Schmooze Treatment, after the two men had traveled together on business: "No man can know Mr. Jefferson and be his *personal* enemy. Few, if any, are more opposed

iii The residence of the President of the United States was not called the "White House" until Theodore Roosevelt formalized the name's dedication in 1901.

to him as a politician than I am, and until recently, I utterly disliked him as a man as well as a politician." After spending time with the president, Paterson concluded, "I was highly pleased with his remarks, for though we differed on many points, he displayed an impartiality, a freedom from prejudice."[78]

Just as every structure that gets constructed goes up board by board, brick by brick, Jefferson knew that for the new nation's government to function with less friction during his presidency, he would have to engage in the slow, steady process of building positive relationships with people on both sides of the aisle, man by man, interaction by interaction. He realized that establishing a solid measure of harmony with someone holding a conflicting position rarely happened in one encounter or conversation. Chemistry and mutual respect flowered and bloomed *over time* as the essence of both people in the new fellowship dynamic became more clearly established to each other.

Obviously, no one can be a successful leader without having the capacity to attract large numbers of followers. Loyal support toward a leader usually comes to fruition based on trust, personal fondness, and earned esteem. Although Jefferson's commitment to civility and relationship-building throughout his presidency clearly did *not* bring an end to partisan hostility, it at least made a dent in it. With his constant, congenial, one-on-one, and small-group approach, he served as a role model for best practices in promoting civil discourse and good will inside the federal government for others to follow. As Meacham concluded, "the tension between social harmony and the demands of politics was not one that Jefferson—or anyone else—could ever be resolved. It could only be managed."[79]

But Jefferson "managed" it. As time passed, most Federalists and Republicans began to accept President Jefferson's belief that they would *have* to do a better job at peacefully coexisting and compromising when necessary if the new nation's government had any chance of fulfilling its potential.

In summary, Thomas Jefferson displayed exemplary leadership by committing himself, in Meacham's words, to "a constant campaign to win the affection of whomever was in front of him,"[80] taking every opportunity to make sincere, positive, up-close-and-personal impressions on those who crossed his path during his presidency. Using that approach, he often succeeded in turning foes into friends. His proactive spirit in building fellowship through almost non-stop, well-orchestrated gatherings turned the new nation's political tide toward having a more stable two-party equilibrium, which allowed it to function with greater productivity for the third president than it had for his two predecessors.

Leadership Trait #2:
Use the One-Two-Three Sequence of Knowledge Base, Imagination, and Peer Feedback to Formulate Long-Term Vision

Among the most important traits for any successful leader to have is long-term vision for how things should operate in the future. Working backwards, what ultimately becomes a clear vision for how best to approach the road that lies ahead typically starts with a spark from one's imagination that falls within the realm of reason and ignites off a base of knowledge. Such a chain of idea development usually starts when the person destined to have the epiphany has blocked out all distractions and positioned himself in a place of solitude.

Thomas Jefferson understood and applied this sequence. He knew his mind had the capacity to fire on all cylinders *only* when no one was around and silence filled his space. Then and only then could he read, write, and above all *think* at his highest level. Presumably, this was what inspired President John F. Kennedy to say to a White House ballroom filled with Nobel laureates in April 1962 that it was "the most extraordinary collection of talents that had been gathered together at the White House with the possible exception of when Thomas Jefferson dined *alone*."

No one ever accused Jefferson of being lazy. His carefully scheduled times in solitude were not spent playing solitaire; instead, he consumed his hours by himself either reading great books (he famously said in a letter to John Adams, "I *cannot live* without books") or writing his most important thoughts in letters, which kept him in a mode of thoughtful engagement with his network of smart friends and provided him with an avenue for exploring ideas. Gordon-Reed and Onuf determined that "letter writing was the principal means by which he imagined and structured his life."[81] To give you an idea of Jefferson's prodigious correspondence output, Ellis counted 677 letters his subject wrote during his first year as president.

Gordon-Reed and Onuf's previously mentioned biography was subtitled *Thomas Jefferson and the Empire of the Imagination* (its title: "*Most Blessed of the Patriarchs*"), and they gave this tight summary of what activated his creativity:

> The empire of his imagination was a place created out of the books he read, the music he played [on the violin], the songs he sang [he was well-known for singing frequently to himself], the people he loved and admired, his observations of the natural world, his experiences as a revolutionary, his foreign travels, his place at the head of society and government, his religion, and his role as one who enslaved other men and women.[82]

In short, Jefferson's active mind had plenty of material to work with whenever he sat down to think and write about what should come next in making the future better than the present. On most days, his brainstorming agenda consumed him, and the authors verified that his "writing life required great discipline and *as much solitude as possible* for contemplation and composition."[83]

Throughout Jefferson's presidency, Ellis explained how, except for the time spent at the evening dinners described earlier, Jefferson operated largely in solitude and *never* made public appearances:

> The chief business of the executive branch under Jefferson was done almost entirely in writing.... A historically accurate picture of him as president would have him seated at his writing table about ten hours

> a day.... The real work of the job played right into his remarkable hand, which could craft words more deftly than any public figure of his time, and into Jefferson's preference for *splendid isolation*, where improvisational skills were unnecessary, control over ideas was nearly total and making public policy was essentially a textual problem.... The art of making decisions was synonymous with the art of drafting and revising texts. Policy debates within the Cabinet took the form of editorial exchanges about word choice and syntax.[84]

In addition to solitude, for a writer's imagination to have maximum productivity while remaining anchored to reality, it must have mass quantities of readily accessible reliable information that can be synthesized and used in new ways that advance one's position. Per Meacham's assessment, with decades of book learning wired into his retentive brain, Jefferson had the knowledge and the imagination to couch his arguments using "philosophy and history to create emotional appeals to shape broad public sentiment. Leadership...meant *knowing how to distill complexity into a comprehensible message to reach hearts as well as the minds.*" With this knowledge-based creative approach, he could "use his pen and his intellect to shape the debate.... Information was power."[85]

Thus, Jefferson's approach to formulating his long-term visions had a sequential one-two-three punch: (1) educate the mind through a steady diet of reading great books to have maximum information available when the time comes to pursue new ideas; (2) generate and refine new ideas in solitude largely by letting one's imagination (tempered by the limits of reason) stream into the pen as new (and sometimes unexpected) words pour onto the page every day; and (3) share one's best thoughts from the private brainstorming sessions with a ready-made sounding board of colleagues while socializing in the evening. Using this process, his long-term visions were developed, tested, and refined at an expedited pace.

To keep his heightened levels of fast-paced thinking in check, Jefferson also used his best friend James Madison as the clearinghouse for his ultimate conclusions. In his book *Madison's Gift: Five Partnerships that Built America,* Stewart described the Jefferson-Madison collaborative friendship as "the most influential political partnership in the nation's history."[86] Ellis described Madison as "Jefferson's lifetime lieutenant and protégé, a fellow member of the Virginia dynasty, a battle tested veteran of the political wars of 1790, and the shrewdest student of the Jefferson psyche ever placed on earth."[87]

Peterson determined that his subject knew "as a rule, Madison was a man of cooler judgment than Jefferson. Madison recognized that there was a habit in Mr. Jefferson as in others of great genius of expressing in strong and round terms, impressions of the moment."[88]

Meacham pinpointed why Madison's counsel was so important to Jefferson: He was "an affectionate, respectful, discreet check on Jefferson's episodic flights of philosophy. Madison would always be there for Jefferson, reminding him—deftly—of his own core convictions about the limits of politics, the imperfections of government, and the realities of human nature."[89]

The collaboration lasted from 1786 until Jefferson's death in 1826. During those forty years, Jefferson ran most of his major ideas by Madison before taking a public position on them. When Madison said "no" (as he did in 1799 when Vice President Jefferson wanted to advocate a state's right to nullify what it believed to be the unconstitutional Alien and Sedition Acts), Jefferson followed his friend's advice and "receded readily" from taking such an extreme position in the public arena.

For those who decide to use Jefferson's systematic sequential approach to vision formulation, the potential rewards are great. Perhaps it will inspire the same type of blockbuster final product that Jefferson generated. His most prominent visions included the following that Ellis called "the central themes of the emerging American republic," and their power made him "electromagnetic":[90]

- Per the Declaration of Independence he wrote, his visions included:

  In the new nation, the people (the bottom-up), rather than a king (the top-down), would have sovereignty and, thus, power; causing the will of the majority to become society's natural law and the basis for deciding how the rights of all men would be protected.

  Therefore, *equality* among people would become one of American society's most important values, and would serve to guarantee individual liberty.

- Per his Bill for Religious Freedom, which he got through the Virginia House of Burgesses in 1786, that disestablished the Anglican Church from Virginia, his vision was:

  The church and the state must be separate.

- Per his sending Meriwether Lewis and William Clark on their expedition to the West, and his consummating the Louisiana Purchase, the vision was:

  Expanding the new nation as far west as it could go would be critical to its survival.

Nick Saban, the most successful coach in college football history, drills into his teams "the process." If his players abide by his process every day in practice—which includes weight training, conditioning, film-watching, maintaining good eating and sleeping habits, as well as perfecting their techniques in all aspects of playing their position in the game—then their commitment and discipline will almost always produce the desired outcome on gameday and the final score will take care of itself.

Similarly, Jefferson's *process for envisioning* what needs to be achieved in the future is also worthy of emulation: educate oneself enough to have an expansive knowledge base; commit to scheduling blocks of solitude to maximize output from the imagination; assemble a sounding board network of smart people able to provide quick and constructive feedback; and have a trusted, joined-at-the-hip friend available to assert veto power when necessary. By committing to this process, one's long-term vision will take care of itself.

Leadership Trait #3: Once the Vision Is Set for Moving a Group Forward, Turn It into Reality Through Principled Pragmatism

The term "principled pragmatism" first entered my lexicon as a result of studying the career of former Secretary of State James A. Baker III, recognized as "the man who ran Washington" from 1981–1993 during the Ronald Reagan and George H. W. Bush presidencies. Baker earned the moniker because of his unique ability to "get things done" and "make government work" amid partisan strife that made others dysfunctional inside the political hurley-burley of party, country, and world.[91]

A principled pragmatist has two essential dimensions, both of which, when taken to extreme, prevent progress. A person who is totally consumed with "principles" stands on them rigidly, refuses to compromise, and typically falls on his sword without achieving his goal. A person totally consumed with "pragmatism" is willing to compromise his principles all the way down to abandoning them, doing whatever it takes to make a deal, regardless of whether the final agreement bears any relationship to the inspiration that initiated it.

Implementing the best slant on the two perspectives, a principled pragmatist knows how to strike a balance between the ideal and the real and consummate a transaction that accomplishes most of his objectives, bringing to fruition a "happy medium" result that is good but not perfect, and definitely causes things to be better than they were before.

Meacham described Thomas Jefferson as a principled pragmatist who could "bend the world to his will."[92] This final leadership tool in the Jeffersonian toolkit that is worthy of study and aspiration was his having the means to affect his desired objectives by pulling the right levers with the right interpersonal lubrication to move the American enterprise forward.

A. Jefferson's Main Principles as President

During the first term of his presidency,[iv] three principles that flowed from his long-term visions became the most prominent. Joyce Appleby (in her biography of Jefferson in Arthur Schlesinger Jr.'s *The American Presidents* series) identified the first two: "his radical commitment to limiting government *and* his eradication of elite practices in the federal government"...where he used "his discretionary powers to promote new, democratic manners for the United States."[93]

The third dominant principle was his commitment to westward expansion, epitomized by his consummating the Louisiana Purchase. Ellis explained why it was so important to Jefferson:

> The West was America's future. Securing a huge swath of it for posterity meant prolonging for several generations the systematic release of national energy that accompanied the explosive movement of settlements across the unsettled spaces.... It was a self-renewing engine that drove the American republic forward... [and it would be] America's fountain of youth.[94]

After recognizing that Jefferson had these key principles fixed in place to guide him during his presidency; the next question becomes: Exactly *how strong* was his allegiance to them? Short answer: very strong, unless they got displaced by something stronger. Ellis determined that Jefferson's principles rose to the level of "moral impera-

iv Historians agree that Jefferson's first term was a spectacular success, but his second term was not. The effectiveness of his leadership traits definitely peaked from 1801–1805; thus, that time period will be what this segment of the chapter will focus upon. He used the same traits with less success in his second term—most notably in his support of the Embargo Act's economic sanctions against Great Britain and France, which will be discussed in the "flaws" section of this chapter.

tives," because only with that level of psychological intensity "could he fully mobilize his political energies."[95] Historian Henry Adams (John Adams's descendant who from 1889–1891 wrote nine volumes on the Jefferson and Madison presidencies) concluded that "through difficulties, trials, and temptations of every kind, Jefferson *held fast to his ideas*...pliant and yielding in manner, but *steady as the magnet itself in aim*."[96] Thus, Jefferson's bond with his principles was airtight, although as will be discussed later in this chapter, changing circumstances sometimes caused the prioritization of his principles to shift, which resulted in the lessening of his commitment to one because of heightened passion for another.

For his first moral imperative, he started his presidency seeking to limit the size and power of the federal government. To that end, he directed his efforts toward reducing the national debt and lowering federal spending and taxes. Appleby's research revealed that he achieved success on all three fronts. During his administration, the debt decreased from $83 million to $77 million, spending went down by 30 percent, the size of the civil service staff materially shrunk, and he abolished federal taxes.[97]

He gave this explanation for why he wanted less government in the nation's capital: "The states are independent as to everything within themselves, and united as to everything respecting foreign nations."[98] Obviously, in time, commencing with Franklin D. Roosevelt's New Deal, Jefferson's states-rights based rationale for the need to have a more limited federal government evaporated into the dust of ancient history, but it certainly held its ground for well over a century.

For his second principle, removing all traces of (British-type) elitism from the federal government and implementing a more democratic approach to how people in his administration were chosen and went about their business, Jefferson also achieved success. When he was sworn in as president on March 4, 1801, it marked the first transfer of power from one party to another in the new nation's history—moving from the back-to-back Federalist policy-driven administrations of Washington and Adams to the adamant anti-Federalist Jefferson, who always claimed he was not a member of any political party, even though the Republican Party came into being because of its organizers' total commitment to all things Jefferson. Thankfully, as a pleasant surprise to many, the United States withstood the potentially explosive changing of the guard without incident, though that did *not* cause the country's discordant political passions to subside.

Recognizing the fragile emotional state of affairs in the nation's capital upon the commencement of his presidency, to effectuate his second principle, Jefferson tactfully managed to remove Federalists from their patronage positions without producing major heartburn and replaced them with Republicans. Unlike his predecessors, all his choices to fill the jobs were based on merit, not family lineage. He also maintained an anti-regal low profile as president, devoid of pomp and circumstance, and never making a public appearance to satisfy a craving for adulation and applause. Emphasizing his idea that the president was definitely *not* like a king, whenever he met with his Cabinet to consider issues, he told them his vote would count no more than theirs.

In furtherance of the idea that the nation's *people,* operating in the *present* (not the past), were in charge of the government, he surprisingly attempted to minimize the importance of the Constitution as a "be-all and end-all" sacred document. Onuf determined that Jefferson never fully embraced the concept of the Constitution's being the Supreme Law of the Land because he believed it "jeopardized the union [of the states] by putting too much power in the federal government."[99] On top of that, Jefferson believed (as he said in a 1789 letter to Madison shortly after the Constitution was ratified):

> The earth belongs in usufruct *to the living,* that the dead have neither powers nor rights over it.... No society can make a perpetual constitution, or even a perpetual law.... Persons and property make the sum of the objects of government. The constitution and the laws of their predecessors extinguished them in the natural course of those who gave them being.[100]

Fortunately, such thoughts which were intended to justify Jefferson's limited respect for the long-term staying power of the Constitution never gained traction. Gordon-Reed and Onuf noted that Madison, the "Father of the Constitution," "threw as much cold water as he could on his friend's potentially incendiary doctrine,"[101] attempting to talk Jefferson off the cliff with his principle of generational sovereignty. Despite the outrageousness of this perspective (which, thankfully, Jefferson never advocated to the multitudes), it nonetheless demonstrated his commitment to maximizing the influence of the people, in the present, to hold more sway during their lives than was held by any past controlling authority.

Finally, to ice the cake on his second key principle, Jefferson did his best to project himself to all people he encountered as Every Man. A diplomat of his era observed that Jefferson was "careful in every particular of his personal conduct to inculcate upon the people his attachment to a republican simplicity of manners and his unwillingness to admit the smallest distinction, that may separate him from the mass of his fellow citizens."[102]

Addressing Jefferson's third dominant principle of his presidency—the need for the new nation to have westward expansion—is complicated. Yes, he was as committed to it (in fact more so, as discussed below) as he was to the first two principles. Yes, he again achieved his objective by his consummation of the Louisiana Purchase. And yet... And yet...his bringing it to fruition violated his first two principles. By doing what it took to double the size of the country, Jefferson maximized (not minimized) the power of the federal government; and by quickly pushing it through Congress to obtain the massive property before Napoleon changed his mind and walked away from the deal, rather than obtain a constitutional amendment (which he had acknowledged on the front end was a necessary legal prerequisite before the transaction could be closed), he took power *away* from the people and let the federal government take charge of getting the deal done.

Operating in a mode of contradiction never bothered Jefferson. He saw it as merely making choices between competing priorities. To lose the Louisiana property and thereby lose the greatest real estate deal in American history (the purchase price was $15 million for 827,000 square miles, which came to about three cents an acre) for the sake of holding on to lesser principles would have transformed Jefferson's place in history from genius statesman to bonanza-losing buffoon. Furthermore, had Jefferson not acquired Louisiana, the new nation would have probably had to engage in extensive turf battles over the land mass with Native Americans and Europeans who likely would have tried to exert power in the region. Thus, making the purchase was a matter of national preservation for the United States.

Shortly before completing the deal, Jefferson's thirst for westward expansion was still not quenched, as proven by his sending Lewis and Clark on an expedition to the territories west of the Louisiana landmass. His instructions: go as far as they could until they reached the Pacific Ocean, in hopes he could stake an American claim on the Far West that would eventually be added to the country by a future president.

B. Jefferson's Pragmatic Approach to Implementing His Principles

As stated previously, to lay the foundation for his efforts to operate effectively and find mutually agreeable solutions amid conflicting perspectives, Thomas Jefferson *hated* interpersonal conflict and did everything he could to avoid it by schmoozing with his adversaries until he removed at least some of the friction. He knew that the less noise his opponents made about his future initiatives, the more likely his positions were to be heard, read, and ultimately approved by the people. Jefferson had such confidence in the ultimate wisdom of his views that he believed once he shared them in an effective way (through conversations, letters, and the public documents he authored), then his stated goals would quickly gain traction and ultimately become reality.

Given the vast historical record of what Jefferson said and did during his years in politics, it is clear that to make his points resonate across a wide variety of opinions, he was *not* above being purposefully vague or saying different things to different people to shape their thinking to where he wanted them to go. If non-disclosure and semi-duplicity were part of what it took to unify people behind the great things he wanted to accomplish for the country, then, in his mind at least, the end justified the means.

Part of what it took to build bridges with those who opposed him was to minimize his apparent connection with his allies. That is why even though he was regarded as the "standard bearer" of the Republican Party since the time of its emergence (which ultimately evolved into today's Democratic Party), he *never* identified himself as a member of the party during his presidency because doing so would have necessarily diminished his potential to move the needle toward achieving his goals with Federalists.

Presenting himself as being unaligned with a party positioned him *above* the partisan fray and, thus, made him more appealing as a leader who operated in a mode of high pragmatism to consummate acceptable deals, which had sufficient appeal for both sides. In furtherance of that objective, with few exceptions, Jefferson engaged in his interactions with allies in a mode of being friendly but distant. His friend Margaret Bayard Smith said he had an "affability that precluded familiarity," which "produced a degree of restraint in those who conversed with him."[103]

His push-pull back strategy for socializing was epitomized by the way he habitually greeted others, regardless of their political persuasion—with a graceful bow followed by a conversation in which, for the duration, he kept his arms *folded across his chest*—in essence, saying, "I'm honored to know you, but we are *not* going to be as close as you might like." Ellis said this semi-distant approach to social engagement gave Jefferson an "accessible mysteriousness,"[104] which surely enhanced his persona as he went about pursuing his goals between conflicting sides.

Along these lines of Jefferson's strategic interactions as he went about his business of getting things done, Meacham classified him as "more of a chess player than a traditional warrior, thinking out his moves and executing them subtly rather than reacting to events viscerally and showily."[105] Chess provides a grandmaster with the opportunity to use any and every tactic that advances his position. Thus, Meacham said Jefferson recognized that "diplomacy, grace, and mercy had their place. So did steel, vengeance, and strength. Jefferson was quite capable of deploying whatever weapon he thought best."[106]

To Ellis, Jefferson's moving through conflict with a chess player's mentality meant *avoiding* "behind-the-scenes arm twisting and cajoling;" and to the extent any direct confrontations needed to occur, Jefferson "preferred to work through *surrogates,* [being] skillful at covering his tracks."[107] His favorite surrogate was Madison, and Ellis painted this vivid picture of how the two men worked together with their complementary strategies to achieve their objectives in dealing with partisan friction:

> It seems fair to concur with those Federalists who considered Madison the "General" and Jefferson the "Generalissimo" of the emergent Republican opposition. Jefferson was the psychological superior and senior member of the team. He *orchestrated* the strategy and Madison *implemented* the tactics. Jefferson could afford to emphasize the broadest contours of a political problem because Madison was silently handling the messier specifics. (If God was in the details, so the story went, Madison was usually there to greet Him upon arrival.) The advantages of this arrangement were obvious: It placed an extremely talented spokesman at the point of attack while allowing Jefferson to remain behind the scenes and above the fray.[108]

When Jefferson's desired outcome was in doubt, what helped put him over the top to get what he wanted was his ever-present optimism. Onuf attributed his subject's "perennial" optimism (which made him the "Apostle of Hope") to "his belief in the liberating power of words, and his faith in man's natural sociability and capacity for self-government."[109] Gordon-Reed and Onuf concluded that Jefferson's optimism was so strong that he "*never* revealed any self-doubt or inner conflict."[110] Ellis agreed with them that Jefferson had "utopian expectations,"[111] while Meacham said Jefferson "offered the example of a president who can operate at two levels, *cultivating the hope of a brighter future,* while preserving the political flexibility and skill to bring the ideal as close as possible to reality."[112]

These interpersonal strategies—avoiding conflict, shaping his word choice and/or tweaking his position to have maximum appeal to whomever was on the receiving end of his messages, being more of a chess player than a warrior, appearing to stand on neutral ground by never coming on too strong to foe or friend, using surrogates to do the head butting when confrontation was necessary, and maintaining unbridled optimism—and emotionally intelligent tactics combined with Jefferson's unmatched persuasive word power to undergird his pragmatic approach to bringing his objectives to fruition and allow him to achieve most of what he sought to do, and he was fine with that.

In a letter to Congressman John Randolph during his presidency's first term, Jefferson offered this thought on why *compromise* was an essential part to effectuating his political goals because it produced progress (and thereby unlocked gridlock) in a democracy:

> I see too many proofs of the imperfection of human reason to entertain wonder or intolerance at any difference of opinion on any subject; and acquiesce in that difference as easily as on a difference of feature or form: experience having taught me the reasonableness of mutual sacrifices of opinion among those who are to act together, for any common object, and the expediency of doing what good we can, when we cannot do all we wish.[113]

The most famous compromise of his political career took place in 1790 when he served as Secretary of State in Washington's Cabinet alongside Treasury Secretary Alexander Hamilton, the one enemy he could not avoid. At the time, two major issues were hopelessly stuck in the federal government: where the nation's capital should be permanently located *and* whether the federal government should assume the states' massive post-war debts. Jefferson ultimately struck a deal with Hamilton whereby they agreed they would each win the issue that was more important to one of them and lose the one that was less important. Since he never had any talent for dealing with financial matters (as demonstrated by the fact that he was insolvent at the time of his death), Jefferson prioritized locating the capitol in the southern part of the country near his home state of Virginia, while the financial genius Hamilton cared more about the federal government's taking control over how the states' debts would be addressed. In his biography of Hamilton, Chernow stated that the federal assumption of the states' debts was "the linchpin of his economic program."[114]

At the hidden hand urging of President Washington, the two adversaries struck their deal in Jefferson's dining room. Though Jefferson later regretted the trade, Chernow stated that had the deal not been made, the conflict over the two issues was "so venomous that it seemed the Union might dissolve in acrimony."[115] Thus, Jefferson's having the pragmatism necessary to do the good but not perfect deal may well have saved the country from fracturing, and (knowing that Jefferson *always* had presidential aspirations), it sure made his commute from Monticello (outside Charlottesville, Virginia) to the President's House much easier during his presidency from 1801–1809 by having the capital in Washington, DC as opposed to the Eastern cities (New York and Philadelphia) as favored by Hamilton.

For his third and final major initiative, Jefferson's orchestration of the Louisiana Purchase provides the ultimate example of principled pragmatism. Ellis encapsulated it: "His nearly mystical sense of the American West made him more flexible in the implementation of his political principles [with the Purchase] than at any other time in his public life. To seize an empire, it turned out, required an imperial [so, *not* a republican] president."[116]

What led to the acquisition started in 1800 when Spain relinquished whatever rights it had in much of North America (though the relinquishment did not include their property interests in Florida, Texas, and Mexico) to France (i.e., Napoleon). Whereas Spain's presence had never been perceived as threatening to the security of the United States, such was *not* the case with Napoleon's gaining control of the territories west of the new nation. Although Jefferson had originally favored France as an ally over England for well over a decade since the end of the Revolutionary War, once the French took control of New Orleans and the lands west of the Mississippi River, his position flipped, believing: "From that moment, we must marry ourselves to the British fleet and nation."[117]

As a first stop in dealing with the threatening situation, Jefferson decided that an immediate diplomatic initiative to Napoleon might well avoid future warfare, so he sent his friend James Monroe to Paris as a special envoy to work with US Minister to France Robert R. Livingston in hopes that he could solve the potential problem by *buying* the land rather than fighting over it. Monroe and Livingston, as willing buyers, found Napoleon to be a willing seller since France was engaged in fighting a war with Britain in 1802 and his war chest was running low on funds. Furthermore, Napoleon's thirst for having his troops gain control over lands in the western hemisphere dried up when his 25,000-man expeditionary force traveled to the Caribbean colony of Saint-Dominique in hopes of putting down a slave insurrection. In a shocking result, the slaves annihilated the French troops, and the setback made Napoleon abandon his dreams of future North American conquests.

The land deal between Monroe/Livingston and Napoleon was formalized in a treaty signed April 30, 1803. Jefferson initially believed that for the federal government to acquire land from a foreign country required a constitutional amendment, a cumbersome and problematic task likely to take at least three years to effectuate. By the time the purchase treaty was presented to Congress for ratification in October 1803, however, Jefferson, the pragmatist, feared that a delay in ratification would kill the deal.[v,118] Therefore, he changed his mind about a constitutional amendment's being required, and for the first time in the nation's history, Jefferson invoked the doctrine of necessity (later used by Abraham Lincoln to revoke the right of habeas corpus during the Civil War, as described in Chapter Three) to justify his decision to disregard what he believed was required procedurally by the Constitution. Jefferson provided this explanation for how he got comfortable with the way things played out: "It is the case of a guardian, investing the money of his ward in purchasing an important adjacent territory; and saying to him when of age, 'I did this for your own good.'"[119]

Always wanting to cover his tracks, Jefferson put out the word among his key players in the nation's capital, "the less that is said about my constitutional difficulty, the better; and it will be better for Congress to do what is necessary *in silence*,"[120] claiming that in time, when the fruits of his efforts became appreciated by the people, they would surely come to understand why he had done what he did: "The good sense of our people will correct the *evil* of [broad] construction when it shall produce ill effects."[121]

Once Congress ratified the treaty with France, the next issue for the Louisiana property became what type of government should preside over the territory. Again, acting in conflict with one of his prior top principles, Jefferson decided that the territories' new government should *not* be republican where the people had voting power, but rather it should operate under the authority of a governor and a senate-type body *selected by the president*. Ellis pointed out that by implementing this decision, Jefferson, "the old enemy of George III now wielded more arbitrary power over the residents of Louisiana than any British king had wielded over the American colonists."[122] How could he live with himself in the context of how the governance of

v In a letter he wrote to then Secretary of the Treasury Albert Gallatin, Jefferson said, "You will find that the French government, dissatisfied with their late bargain with us, will be glad of a pretext to avoid it. It will be necessary, therefore, that we execute it with punctuality and without delay." See: Jefferson's letter to Albert Gallatin, August 23, 1803.

Louisiana was implemented—with an *enlargement* of federal government power and a purposeful *rejection* of democracy in the huge new territory? Ellis believed it was all about prioritizing his principles.[123] To Jefferson, advancing the cause of expanding the new nation westward and making sure the new lands would *not* be led by someone capable of jumping the train off Jefferson's track, simply *eclipsed* the importance of all other causes.

Meacham neatly summarized history's assessment of the Louisiana Purchase and Jefferson's complicated leadership throughout the acquisition:

> The story of the Louisiana Purchase is one of strength, of Jefferson's adaptability, and, most important, his determination to secure the territory from France, doubling the size of the country and transforming the United States into a continental power. A slower or less courageous politician might have bungled the acquisition; an overly idealistic one might have lost it by insisting on strict constitutional scruples. Jefferson, however, was neither slow nor weak nor overly idealistic.[124]

Bottom line, for all three of Jefferson's top principles during the most productive years of his presidency, he fully embraced them on his own timetable; fulfilled his plan to achieve them while he was focused on each of them; and when they conflicted, dealt with the situation based on how he prioritized them. Though criticized for sometimes abandoning his republican principles during the run of his two terms, as the third president leading the country during the second decade of its existence, he recognized that changing circumstances necessitated invoking new approaches for dealing with uniquely fabulous opportunities that could greatly enhance his ultimate political achievements. Being frozen in his tracks by holding on to conflicting principles would have stopped all progress. Given these circumstances, Jefferson accepted the criticism associated with his changed positions because achieving his highest goals for the country was a "moral imperative" that demanded every strategic thought and tactic he could use on the chessboard.

To close this thought, Onuf said Jefferson never lost sight of being "responsive to the historical moment."[125] He certainly maintained that perspective amidst the multitudes of changes that arose during his presidency's many moments.

Thomas Jefferson's Flaws

In the twenty-first century, the fact that Jefferson owned an average of two hundred slaves throughout his adult life (from the 1770s through the 1820s) to aid in the running of Monticello, is disturbing, though not surprising given the legalities of that time and the economic conditions in the agrarian South that existed throughout his adult life. Slavery is properly regarded today—as it has been in most parts of the country since the end of the Civil War in 1865—as an evil and immoral institution. During Jefferson's era, however, slavery was permissible under the Constitution and the laws of most states, and became entrenched because of the absence of an available alternative labor force in the South. Thus, most plantation owners totally depended on enslaved people to perform the necessary work on their property.

Sadly, the man who in 1776 wrote into the Declaration of Independence that "all men are created equal," did not regard enslaved African American men as men. Although he devoted a chapter in the only book he ever wrote, *Notes on Virginia* (published in the early 1780s), to American slavery's many disturbing issues, in it he said that the only specific way he could think of to end it was with colonization (a.k.a. transporting America's enslaved people to foreign lands). Although it was clearly impractical, the idea of colonization for enslaved Americans was nonetheless advocated by many other statesmen well into the nineteenth century (even for a while by Abraham Lincoln). After putting his thoughts into print in his only book, for the last four decades of his life, Jefferson *did nothing* to change any aspect of slavery in the United States, and he certainly did nothing to free any of his own slaves except for the few he fathered with Sally Hemings, whom he emancipated in his final years.

Some reading this chapter may believe that Jefferson's "owning" hundreds of enslaved people until his death in 1826 made him an evil and immoral person unworthy of receiving honor for the many things he did to advance the country during its formative years. Others (including this author) choose to evaluate Jefferson's sense of morality in the context of the legal rights and societal norms as they existed during his era, and have problems with the idea of imposing the ever-evolving social consciousness of subsequent generations as the means for judging a man who lived two centuries ago.

Having said that, Jefferson's moral flaw that has become accepted as fact in recent years, which is inexcusable and unforgivable in any context, arises from his sexual relationship (beginning in France where the newly widowed Jefferson was serving as an American diplomat, and then at Monticello for the rest of his life) with an enslaved girl named Sally Hemings, who was the half-sister of Jefferson's wife Martha. Virginia planter John Wayles was the father of both Sally and Martha. The forty-year Jefferson-Hemings relationship started when she was fourteen and he was in his early forties. During that time, she gave birth to seven of his children (two of whom died in infancy), and the four who survived into adulthood he treated as slaves until the last few years of his life.

As Gordon-Reed has pointed out, assessing the Jefferson-Hemings relationship is "tricky."[126] He kept the promises he made to Hemings early on about how she and their children would be treated. Though Jefferson kept her and their children enslaved until he finally emancipated them, for the most part, they had a better quality of life with more privileges than the other slaves, and he prepared the children for life after slavery. He ultimately freed the children, thereby giving them a forty-year head start on emancipation.

How best to process the long-term existence of such an (presumably non-consensual) arrangement and the treatment of her and their children is definitely a great challenge for anyone. It is surely what led Meacham to say: "Jefferson represents the best of us *and the worst of us*."

Outside of his slavery black box, Jefferson's two other major flaws pale in comparison. Ellis summarized them. First, while Jefferson played all conceivable angles to move people to go where he wanted them to go (as described previously in the section of this chapter on "Principled Pragmatism"), in many instances, he could accurately be described as "a devious manipulator who played cowardly games with the truth."[127] Ellis pointed out that the man recognized as Jefferson's most well-known biographer, Pulitzer-winner Dumas Malone, author of the multi-volume biography *Jefferson and His Time*, acknowledged that there were times when his subject "crossed the dim line between courtesy and deception."[128]

Secondly, Ellis recognized that Jefferson's "second term was as disastrous as his first term was glorious."[129] The worst decision he made during his last four years was pushing through Congress the Embargo Act in 1807, which was intended to prevent America from going to war by taking our ships and seamen out of harm's way in the Atlantic, where they were likely to be captured either by British or French ships (who at the time were at war with each other).

The Embargo Act *stopped* American trade with foreign nations and it also weakened the American navy. Pushing it through Congress meant Jefferson became the nation's leading advocate for using the power of a strong federal government, meaning he once again completely *reversed his course* from where he started his presidency. Though the Act succeeded in keeping the United States out of war, it created a major divide among the American people, totally decimated the economy, and caused America to have a lesser navy, which likely impacted our perceived vulnerability in the years leading up to the War of 1812. Jefferson left office in such a serious state of decline and disapproval that Ellis gives it as the explanation for why he wanted no mention of the fact that he had served as president of the United States on his tombstone.[130]

In his assessment of this major flip flop on an issue, Meacham provided this explanation for why Jefferson was not bothered by advocating the need for less federal government *and* more federal government *simultaneously*: "He believed in limited government except when it needed to be expansive."[131]

Unlike Washington, Jefferson's flaws, especially in the context of his relationship with Sally Hemings, give him glaringly unappealing feet of clay. Because of that, it's difficult to think of him as a man of moral excellence.

Fortunately, this book is *not* about judging the moral compass of our greatest presidents. It *is* about learning exactly what they did that made them successful leaders. Based on that premise, the thrust of this chapter has attempted to convey Jefferson's specific approaches to sound leadership that can be readily applied today for those inspired to implement them.

Personal Application

You now know how Thomas Jefferson would have answered the following questions. How do *you* answer them?

- Does your current business or enterprise of some sort (that you're either currently leading or aspiring to lead) operate in a mode of ongoing conflict and discord?
- If so, what are you *doing* to *reduce* the conflict/discord and *increase* the harmony?
- Are you being proactive about building rapport with those on the other side of the conflict?
- Have you shared a meal (or a drink) with him or her in the recent past?
- Have you attempted to have purely social conversations with him/her where business issues were not discussed?

  - If so, did you do more listening than talking during those conversations?
  - If not, are you willing to actively engage in setting up such conversations?

- What is your current approach for formulating long-term vision for your business or enterprise?
- Can you quickly identify long-term visionary thoughts you have had in the last five years that you turned into action items and then executed on them? If so, what were they?
  - If not, why not?
- Do you deliberately schedule times to think in solitude?
- Do you write down most of your important thoughts?
- Do you have a small group or at least one person in your network whose judgment you trust and who is readily available to act as a sounding board when you need to bounce ideas off others before going public with them?
- Do you abide by certain principles that shape your work life and/or efforts at leadership?
  - Can you list them?
  - Do you *always* follow them or do you maintain flexibility because of changing circumstances that suggest the need for reconsideration of them in the context of your having conflicting principles?
- Have you ever held principles that came into direct conflict with one another?
  - Did you resolve the conflict by choosing the higher principle?

- When conflict arises that initially prevents your goal from being achieved, are you willing to compromise?
- When in the middle of friction and/or conflict, how careful are you about your choice of words, tone, and body language?
- When dealing with friction/conflict, are you more of a chess player or a warrior?
- Which of those two problem-solving approaches appeals most to you?
    - Which do you think is more effective?
- Would you rather be in the middle of the fray or above the fray? If the latter, what steps are you taking to stay above the fray?
- Do you know how to use surrogates in a way that keeps *you* above of the fray?
- Do you project yourself to your business/enterprise as an optimist?
- When problems arise, do you avoid showing any signs of self-doubt or inner conflict?

May the leadership traits of Jefferson's life guide you through the answering of these questions. Digging deep with intellectual honesty in this personal application exercise should also improve your chances of handling conflict, maximizing harmony, imagining prudent long-term vision, and exercising power—just like Thomas Jefferson did.

CHAPTER THREE

HOW TO BE THE MOST SUCCESSFUL AND ESTEEMED LEADER IMAGINABLE—LIKE ABRAHAM LINCOLN

To write about Abraham Lincoln and attempt to say something new or different is a daunting task. Only Jesus Christ has had more biographical coverage. As a role model for successful leadership, historians view him in a class by himself. In all four C-SPAN presidential ranking polls in the twenty-first century (which are taken upon a new president's being inaugurated), Lincoln has finished first among his peers.

Those who have not previously studied Lincoln's life in depth may wonder at the outset of this chapter why most historians believe he stands at the top of the mountain in presidential leadership. The answer: Unlike anyone else who has ever been the nation's chief executive, Lincoln was a multi-dimensional *genius* in the fields of politics,[i] word power,[ii] warfare,[iii] law,[iv] and, by the end of his life, theology.[v,132] Furthermore, his inestimable brainpower equaled his emotional intelligence and moral compass. Do not take *my* word for it. Here are evaluations of Lincoln by two of history's greatest thinkers over the last two centuries. First, international political scientist Hans Morgenthau wrote:

> Lincoln's political philosophy was not the result of theoretical reflection and study nor even of experience, but of innate qualities of character and mind. The qualities of his mind were as extraordinary as the quality of his character. His sheer brainpower must have exceeded that of all other presidents, Jefferson included. The manifestations are the more astounding, as Lincoln's mind was virtually untrained, his spo-

i Only a political genius could go from being a one-term congressman from 1847–1849 to being elected president of the United States in 1860.

ii No other American president comes close to his potent eloquence.

iii He could see what needed to be done to win the Civil War, which none of his early generals could see—that victory would only come from an aggressive, non-stop hard war.

iv As a lawyer, whether talking to a judge, jury, or appellate court, he pursued legal positions that were almost always successful because of his ability to discern an argument's most important angle and present it with maximum persuasion using the best possible word choice and tone for his audience.

v Eminent theologian Reinhold Niebuhr concluded, "Lincoln's religious convictions were superior in depth and priority to those held by the religious leaders of his day.... He puts the relation of our moral commitments in history to our religious reservations about the partiality of our judgments more precisely than any statesman or theologian has ever put them." See: Reinhold Niebuhr, "The Religion of Abraham Lincoln," in *Lincoln and the Gettysburg Address*, ed. Allan Nevins (Urbana: University of Illinois Press, 1964), 72–73.

> radic formal elementary schooling having amounted altogether to about one year. That extraordinary intelligence revealed itself in a philosophic understanding of public issues, in a judicious concern with politically relevant detail, in a mastery of political manipulation, and in military judgment.[133]

Second, and more laudatory than Morgenthau, was the assessment of Leo Tolstoy, author of *War and Peace,* arguably the greatest novel ever written that's filled with history and philosophy. Tolstoy said of Lincoln in 1908, forty-three years after the latter's assassination:

> Of all the great national heroes and statesmen of history, he is the only real giant. Alexander, Frederick the Great, Caesar, Napoleon, Gladstone, and even Washington stand in greatness of character, in depth of feeling, and in a certain moral power far behind Lincoln. He was a man of whom a nation has a right to be proud; he was a Christ in miniature, a saint of humanity, whose name will live thousands of years in the legends of future generations. We are still too near to his greatness, and so can hardly appreciate his divine power; but after a few centuries more, our posterity will find him considerably bigger than we do. His genius is still too strong and too powerful for the common understanding, just as the sun is too hot when its light beams directly on us.[134]

Given these admiring conclusions drawn by profoundly wise men, synthesizing Lincoln's leadership traits into a single chapter definitely requires a plan. One of this book's goals is to avoid repetition of its conclusions. This requires identifying the best leadership traits of the eight leaders covered in these pages *without* praising more than one president for a particular trait. Surely a reader would get bored in reading about the trait of integrity as exemplified by five different presidents.

Thus, in Chapter One, this book covered George Washington's leadership virtues of learning from his mistakes; communicating in a mode of "less is more"; demonstrating the humility that enhanced his collaboration; acting with such an elevated level of integrity that he became the nation's Conscience-in-Chief; doing everything he could to advance unity among the people; and avoiding shameless self-promotion. Abraham Lincoln had all these traits, but explaining how he used them will *not* be covered in this chapter because it would constitute making the same point twice about the desirability of a leader's having these virtues.

Similarly, in Chapter Two, the book covered Thomas Jefferson's talents for consensus-building, long-term vision, and principled pragmatism. Lincoln also had these traits, and again, there is no need for double coverage.

It is my hope that through the accounts in this chapter of Abraham Lincoln's magnanimity coupled with equanimity, and his steadfast resolve in keeping promises, the specifics of how he demonstrated those two traits will shine the light on the fact that by possessing them, he thereby embodied all of Washington's and Jefferson's best leadership traits.

Leadership Trait #1: Magnanimity Coupled with Equanimity

Throughout his presidency, Abraham Lincoln wrestled daily with the uphill tasks of winning a major war, reuniting a divided nation, and abolishing the institution of slavery on which the Southern economy depended. Dealing with such high-pressure responsibilities, he necessarily had to interact with legions of people amid a crisis and made decisions that impacted him, them, and the nation. A well-known insomniac, given how little he slept during his four years and one month in office, and burdened by having the fate of the nation heaped upon his shoulders (thereby becoming the "American Atlas" in the words of one of his secretaries, William Stoddard) every single day of his presidency, the tragic passing of his beloved eleven-year-old son Willie, the frequent disruptive conduct of his wife Mary, and knowing that so many deaths and permanent injuries (75 percent of wartime "surgeries" were amputations) had been caused by the war, it is a wonder Lincoln had any capacity at all for maintaining grace and calmness under pressure during his years as the nation's chief executive. Yet in displaying magnanimity coupled with equanimity, his cup runneth over.

Magnanimity and equanimity are words rarely used because they describe so few people. The word "magnanimity" comes from Latin, meaning "greatness of spirit." Someone who is magnanimous forgives others and doesn't show resentment. Its antonym is "vindictiveness." The word "equanimity" comes from Latin, meaning "even mind." A person with this trait stays level-headed under stress. Its antonym is "agitation."

Lincoln presumably became inspired to pursue magnanimity at a young age by absorbing the wisdom of one of his favorite writers, William Shakespeare, whose works he not only devoured but often memorized with his sponge-like memory. Shakespeare addressed the subject in "Sonnet 94":

> They that have *pow'r to hurt and will do none,*
> That do not do the thing they most do show,
> Who, moving others, are themselves as stone,
> Unmoved, cold, and to temptation slow,
> They rightly do inherit heaven's graces
> And husband nature's riches from expense;
> They are the lords and owners of their faces,
> Others but stewards of their excellence.

In his insightful book about Lincoln's early years, *Honor's Voice: The Transformation of Abraham Lincoln,* Douglas L. Wilson connected the dots between his subject's ferocious ambition, (which he stated at age twenty-three, "to be truly esteemed of my fellow-men, by rendering myself worthy of their esteem"), and how he became consistently magnanimous to help achieve that goal. Wilson: "Shakespeare here [in

"Sonnet 94"] calls attention to the self-evident superiority of those who have the power to hurt but choose to withhold it. In this perspective, [Lincoln knew that] to achieve the level of recognition and public admiration at which others become the stewards of one's own excellence, it is necessary not so much to use one's power to hurt as to master it."[135]

Here are several instances from Lincoln's presidency that demonstrate how he called into play his magnanimity, and managed to deliver it with equanimity:

A. Toward His Cabinet and Other Government Officials

Before the start of his first term in March 1861, Lincoln famously chose a "team of rivals" for his Cabinet, some of whom had opposed him at the Republican Convention in 1860. This unique assemblage of talent was immortalized by Doris Kearns Goodwin in her award-winning book with that title. Despite being initially disrespected by New York senator William Seward (whom he chose as his secretary of state), Ohio governor Salmon Chase (his secretary of the treasury), and former US Attorney General Edwin Stanton (his secretary of war), Lincoln refused to take their slights personally, and chose them to serve in his Cabinet, believing he would need their skills to lead the country during his presidency, which he knew from the start would be tempestuous. He explained his decision: "These were the strongest men…and I had no right to deprive the country of their services."[136]

It did not take Seward or Stanton long to see that their negative first impressions of Lincoln were off the mark. Soon after assuming their Cabinet positions, they recognized how extraordinary Lincoln was and became some of his greatest admirers. After serving under Lincoln only two months, Seward told his wife, "His magnanimity is almost superhuman. His confidence and sympathy increase every day."[137] A month later, he said to her, "Executive skill and vigor are rare qualities. The President is the best of us."[138] Stanton's being overwhelmed by Lincoln's greatness culminated in his tribute immediately after his boss's death. It stands out in history (and aligns with

Morgenthau's and Tolstoy's conclusions) as the ultimate assessment of Lincoln's never-fading legacy: "Now he belongs to the ages."[vi,139]

Chase, however, could never get past his insufferable ego to appreciate Lincoln. During the three years he led the Treasury Department, he made no secret of his belief that *he*, not Lincoln, should be in charge of the country, and for a time in early 1864, he sought to replace Lincoln on the ticket as the Republican nominee for president. When Lincoln accepted Chase's resignation from his Cabinet post in June 1864, the president not only forgave his unrelenting rival's interpersonal shortcomings, but six months later, he chose Chase to succeed Roger Taney as chief justice of the US Supreme Court.

Goodwin pointed out that when Lincoln told his colleagues of his intention to nominate his former Treasury secretary for the Court's top position, they reminded him of Chase's past "myriad intrigues against him." Lincoln's response: "Now, I know meaner things about Governor Chase than anyone can tell me, but we have stood together in time of trial, and I should despise *myself* if I allowed personal differences to affect any judgment of his fitness for the office."[140] Goodwin accentuated the point by referencing a subsequent quote by Lincoln to Republican Senator Zachariah Chandler, "I would rather have swallowed his buckhorn chair than to have nominated Chase [to the Supreme Court] but the decision was right for the country."[141]

As of December 1864, Lincoln knew that the Supreme Court would probably be reviewing the constitutionality of the Emancipation Proclamation soon, and he had confidence that Chase would support it. Goodwin wrote: "Lincoln trusted that Chase would help secure the rights of the black man, for which he had fought throughout his career,...and Chase quickly justified Lincoln's confidence in this

---

vi In his Pulitzer-winning Lincoln biography, David Herbert Donald gave this vivid description of Stanton before he said his immortal words, upon seeing that the president had just passed away on his deathbed: "Standing at the foot of the bed, his face covered with tears, Stanton paid tribute to his fallen chief: with a slow and measured movement, his right arm fully extended as if in salute. He [then] raised his hat and placed it for an instant on his head and then in the same deliberate manner removed it." See: David Herbert Donald, *Lincoln* (Simon & Schuster 1995), 599.

regard," by permitting a black lawyer to argue a case before the Supreme Court for the first time.[142]

Lincoln's magnanimous treatments of Seward, Stanton, and Chase were not isolated incidents among government leaders during his presidency. Upon hearing one of his Congressional supporters delight in the 1862 mid-term election defeat of an adversary, the president responded, "You have more of that feeling of personal resentment than I. A man has not time to spend half his life in quarrels. If any man ceases to attack me, I never remember the past against him."[143]

Lincoln's statement showing his willingness to forgive others aligned with his close friend Leonard Swett's conclusion: "He was certainly a very poor hater. He never judged men by his like or dislike for them. I do not believe he ever removed a man because he was his enemy or because he disliked him."[144] Swett's statement dovetailed with what Ralph Waldo Emerson said of Lincoln shortly after the president's death. "His heart was as great as the world but there was no room in it to hold the memory of a wrong."[145]

B. Toward His Generals

Prior to his appointment of Ulysses Grant as commanding general of the Union Army in March 1864, Lincoln had to suffer through the dismal military leadership of generals who demonstrated that despite their experience, they had no grasp of how to win the war. General George McClellan took over the Army of the Potomac early in the war and Lincoln later chose him to become general-in-chief of the Army. When the commander-in-chief asked McClellan whether he could handle both jobs, the cocky general replied, "I can do it all!"[146]

Despite the prestigious appointments and support he received from Lincoln, in a letter to his wife, McClellan told her that he viewed his commander-in-chief as a "well-meaning baboon."[147] When Lincoln, Seward, and John Hay (Lincoln's personal secretary) made an unexpected visit to McClellan's residence one night in November 1861 hoping to discuss strategy, they waited there an hour before the general finally came home from the theater. When McClellan entered his house, he went upstairs, kept his guests waiting downstairs for a half hour, and then had his servant tell Lincoln that he was not up to seeing him and his group that night. Seward and Hay were appalled by McClellan's insolence, but Lincoln responded without bitterness, telling Hay, "It is better at this time not to be making points of etiquette and personal dignity."[148]

Lincoln would continue to deflect McClellan's incivility until the general's continued refusal to obey the president's orders to advance the war effort (culminating in his failure to pursue Confederate general Robert E. Lee after the Battle of Antietam), caused the commander-in-chief to remove him from his command post on November 5, 1862. In his fine book, *President Lincoln: The Duty of a Statesman,* William Lee Miller gave this perspective on what drove his subject's magnanimity and equanimity in dealing with McClellan:

> The root of Lincoln's conduct was not solely his modesty and lack of ego; it was also—or rather primarily—his concentration on the immense national purpose of which he was the instrument. What Lincoln dealt with was too vast for mere personal pride. If McClellan will bring us victories, he might have said, then I will overlook repeated snubs and hold a dozen horses. Deference to me is not the point; victory is the point; a preserved and reborn United States of America is the point.[149]

In one of his letters, Lincoln reiterated this crucial message with a tight statement that should be the mantra of all leaders with major responsibilities: "I shall do nothing in malice. What I deal with is too vast for malicious dealings."[150] What did Lincoln mean by "malice"? One of his finest biographers, Ronald C. White, defined it this way: "Malice is not simply evil; it is *directed* evil, the intent to harm people."[151] Lincoln confirmed his alignment with White's definition in a statement he made in November 1864, after being reelected: "So long as I have been here, I have not willingly planted a thorn in any man's bosom."[152]

Another underwhelming general among Grant's predecessors was George Gordon Meade, who led the Union Army at the Battle of Gettysburg in early July 1863. Although Meade successfully drove Lee's army out of Pennsylvania, he then inexplicably failed to pursue the Confederates into Virginia where his troops likely would have routed the enemy and thereby shortened the war. Lincoln was privately incredulous that Meade let Lee get away.

Without the president's permission, chief of staff Henry Halleck notified Meade in a telegram of Lincoln's dismay. Pulitzer–winning historian James McPherson, in his Lincoln biography *Tried by War: Abraham Lincoln as Commander in Chief*, noted that upon getting Halleck's message, Meade sent back a telegram offering his resignation. When Lincoln received it, he composed a strong letter to the general that recited the pertinent facts that led to this devastating conclusion, "Your golden opportunity is gone and I am distressed immeasurably because of it." After completing the letter, however, Lincoln slept on his thoughts, and the next morning decided *not* to send it, believing it would totally demoralize his leading general at the time. McPherson wrote: "Within a couple of days, the president recovered his equanimity."[153]

C. Toward Union Soldiers

As the Civil War raged on during Lincoln's presidency, the Union Army became beset by the court-martials of young soldiers who either fell asleep on guard duty or ran out of battlefield courage and deserted their regiments. Inevitably, some of them sought pardons after being convicted. As commander-in-chief, Lincoln had the final say on who got pardoned. He devoted countless hours to performing the task, and usually erred on the side of forgiveness, believing that the exhausted and frightened young men whose fate he held in his hands were worthy of a second chance.

Attorney general Edward Bates's pardon clerk wrote of his boss that "his most important duty was to keep all but the most deserving cases from coming before the kind Mr. Lincoln at all; since there was nothing harder for the president to do than put aside a prisoner's application and he could not resist it when it was urged by a pleading wife and a weeping child."[154] Lincoln's personal secretary, John Hay, noted the "eagerness with which he caught at any fact that would justify him in saving the life of a condemned soldier."[155] Lincoln acknowledged that whenever he found "a good excuse for saving a man's life, I go to bed happy as I think how joyous the signing of my name will make him and his family and friends."[156] He was particularly forgiving when he thought the soldier's misconduct was the result of "sudden passion and not premeditation."[157]

D. Toward the Confederate States of America

In responding to the Kansas–Nebraska Act of 1854 with his first major speech, and asserting his opposition to slavery's being extended into new territories or states, Lincoln said, "I have no prejudice against the Southern people. They are just what we would be in their situation. If slavery did not now exist amongst them, they would not introduce it. If it did now exist amongst us, we should not instantly give it up."[158]

The fracturing of the country over slavery was ultimately inevitable. Between the time of his election in November 1860 and taking the oath of office on March 4, 1861, seven Southern states seceded and formed the Confederate States of America (CSA), an act the new president regarded as treasonous. Despite that opinion, in his First Inaugural Address, Lincoln's tone toward the seceders was *not* harsh, but rather conciliatory. Early in the speech, he assured Southerners, "I have no purpose directly or indirectly, to interfere with the institution of slavery in the states where it exists. I have no right to do so, and I have no inclination to do so."[159]

After explaining why it was his constitutional duty to restore the Union and reclaim the seceded states, he said he would pursue that goal as peacefully as possible: "Beyond what may be necessary for these objects, there will be no invasion, no using of force against or among the people anywhere." Whatever might happen in the future, "my best discretion will be exercised...with a view and hope of a peaceful solution of the national troubles and the restoration of fraternal sympathies and affections."[160]

After explaining his commitment to the Constitution and his belief that although there would always be majority and minority positions on critical issues, this did *not* give the minority the right to secede, he closed his First Inaugural Address with these famous words:

> In your hands, my dissatisfied fellow countrymen, and not in mine, is the momentous issue of civil war. The government will not assail you. You can have no conflict without being yourselves the aggressors. You have no oath registered in Heaven to destroy the government, which I shall have the most solemn one to "preserve, protect, and defend it."
>
> I am loath to close. We are not enemies, but friends. We must not be enemies. Though passion may have strained, it must not break our bonds of affection. The mystic chords of memory, stretching from every battle-field, and patriot grave, to every living heart and hearth-stone, all over this broad land, will yet swell the chorus of the Union, when again touched, as surely they will be, by the better angels of our nature.[161]

Despite the conciliatory eloquence of the address, five weeks into Lincoln's presidency on April 12, 1861, the Confederate Army fired on the federal troops stationed at Fort Sumter, South Carolina and the Civil War began. It lasted four years and caused over 750,000 people to die and millions more to suffer severe injuries. While it lasted, Miller pointed out President Lincoln "did not demean or demonize the enemy, as war leaders generally do. From that first post-Sumter Sunday afternoon in April 1861, when he dissented from the dismissive remarks others were making in his office about the South, through to the generosity of the Second Inaugural, he did not deal in disdain or contempt for the adversary. Much of his distinction on this point, in other words, would rest in what he did *not* say, which another in his place would have said."[162]

By the time Lincoln gave his Second Inaugural Address on March 4, 1865, the end of the War was in sight. Union general William Tecumseh Sherman had marched through Georgia and the Carolinas and Lee would surrender to Grant a month later on April 9. The issue for Lincoln and the country to face going forward was how best to bring the country back together and resume operating as a nation. Though the speech lasted only six minutes, it was a classic case of "less is more," and provided the overflow crowd with the president's ultimate reflection on the war and how best Americans should move forward in the future.

Ronald White, author of four great books on Lincoln, has called the Second Inaugural Address "Lincoln's Sermon on the Mount." He described the speech as "sermonic," in the context that during his first term, Lincoln's faith had grown exponentially as he attended church regularly and heard the sermons of Pastor Phineas Gurley at his New York Avenue Presbyterian Church in Washington, DC. Whenever someone interrupted Lincoln's rare moments of solitude during his presidency, they usually found him reading his Bible. White believed this is why Lincoln's Second Inaugural Address "mentions God 14 times, quotes the Bible four times, and invokes prayer three times."[163]

After reviewing the history of the war and intuiting its meaning and purpose to be God's punishment for the nation's allowing slavery to exist for so long, Lincoln closed his Second Inaugural with what White calls an "imperative ethic," and "a timeless message of reconciliation." They are the most magnanimous words ever spoken by an American president, and were aimed at the people of the North *and* South:[164]

> With malice toward none;
> with charity for all;
> with firmness in the right,
> as God gives us to see the right,
> let us strive on to finish the work we are in;
> to bind up the nation's wounds;
> to care for him who shall have borne the battle,
> and for his widow and for his orphan—
> to do all which may achieve and cherish
> a just, and a lasting peace,
> among ourselves, and with all nations.[165]

White said this about what Lincoln was attempting to drive home with the stirring ending: "In this final paragraph, he declared that the true test of the aims of war would be how we now treat those who have been defeated."[166]

After the speech, as the surrender of the Confederacy became imminent, Lincoln's magnanimity toward the enemy kicked into overdrive, as expressed by Ron Chernow in his terrific biography *Grant*:

> As they pondered postwar reconciliation, Lincoln preached leniency toward the South, saying he didn't want reprisals. Facetiously he added that he didn't want to *hang* Confederates so much as hang *on* to them. Though he couldn't say so publicly, he hinted he would be happy if Jefferson Davis fled the country, avoiding a treason trial that might inflame sectional tensions. "I want no one punished; treat them liberally all around," Lincoln advised. "We want those people to return to their allegiance to the Union and submit to the laws."[167]

When Lincoln visited Richmond on April 4, 1865, five days before Lee's surrender at Appomattox, the president gave his thoughts to Union General Godfrey Weitzel on how to treat those of the enemy who were now under his control, reflecting his ultimate strategy for achieving post-war reconciliation: "We must extinguish our resentments if we expect harmony and union. If I were in your place, I'd let 'em up easy, let 'em up easy."[168]

His statement to Weitzel in Richmond aligned with what Lincoln had told Grant, Sherman, and Admiral David Porter a week earlier at their Hampton Roads war counsel meeting aboard the *River Queen* on March 28:

> Let them all go, officers and all, let them have their horses to plow with, and, if you like, their guns to shoot crows with. Treat them liberally. We want these people to return to their allegiance and submit to the laws. Therefore, I say, give them the most liberal and honorable terms.[169]

Alas, all of Lincoln's magnanimous intentions were extinguished by John Wilkes Booth. In 2022, renowned journalist-historian John Avlon released his book *Lincoln and the Fight for Peace,* which paints a vivid picture of how his subject was ready, willing, and able to fully engage with a magnanimous approach to reconciliation once the Confederate states reentered the Union. Avlon properly concluded that "Lincoln understood that if you do not win the peace, you do not really win the war."[170]

Exactly how dramatically different and better the Reconstruction period would have gone for the nation under Lincoln's magnanimous leadership is something on which we can now only speculate, and then shake our heads in sorrow over the vast potential of "what might have been" if he had lived past April 15, 1865. Lincoln's close friend Noah Brooks, a journalist for the *Sacramento Daily Union,* was stationed in Washington, DC during the war and he later wrote an acclaimed biography of the fallen president. Brooks properly determined that Reconstruction "would demand the highest statesmanship, the greatest wisdom, and the firmest generosity."[171] With Lincoln in office, those traits were all in place. Upon his death, they went away and Reconstruction became a disaster.

E. Toward His Wife Mary

Although Lincoln was inspired at a young age by Shakespeare about the prudence of conducting himself with magnanimity, he became especially accomplished at *using* the trait because of having to invoke it on an almost daily basis in dealing with his wife Mary.

Why was he attracted to her in the first place? White determined that Lincoln became attracted to his future wife because they both "prized education...such that they were soul mates in intellectual curiosity and learning. They had a mutual enjoyment of ideas and politics."[172] In addition, at social functions in Springfield, she could turn on her personality, and be "the very creature of excitement"—to use local lawyer James Conkling's description of her.[173] Lincoln's law partner William Herndon, who later grew to despise Mary, had to acknowledge her strong first impression: she was "young, dashing, handsome—witty...cultured—graceful and dignified...and an excellent conversationalist."[174]

Beyond these reasons, it is an accepted fact among historians that Mary was every bit as ambitious as Lincoln was throughout their time together. Knowing that a woman was not going to get elected president in the nineteenth century, Mary decided (and commented to others) that the best she could hope to become was the wife of a president. Early in their courtship, Mary saw something in Lincoln that no one else did: he had all the tools necessary to lead the country one day.[175] Throughout their marriage, her ambition pushed his ambition, and this drove them up the political ladder together.

Having noted Mary's strengths that drew Lincoln to her initially, it did not take long for her favorable first impression to melt away and be replaced by an opposite extreme. Michael Burlingame is among the most esteemed of Lincoln's biographers, though he is also known for being Mary Todd Lincoln's most severe critic. In 2021, he released his book *An American Marriage: The Untold Story of Abraham Lincoln and Mary Todd*. It provides a detailed account of how Mary Lincoln spent much of her over twenty-two years of marriage doing seemingly everything she could to drive her husband toward anxiety and depression, and her efforts intensified during Lincoln's presidency.

Though Lincoln was *not* an easy spouse to live with (due to his melancholy personality, which often made him gloomy and uncommunicative), nonetheless, between their November 4, 1842 wedding day until he became president on March 4, 1861, Burlingame's research established with mass quantities of credible evidence that, among other things, Mary had an "ungovernable temper;" "seemed to take a special delight in contradicting her husband and humiliating him on every occasion;" "was a very nervous, hysterical woman who was incessantly alarming the neighborhood with her outcries...such that she became a laughingstock;" and "couldn't keep a hired girl because she was tyrannical."[176]

Amid all of Mary's exasperating conduct, Lincoln managed to maintain his equilibrium by spending six months a year away from her, riding horseback around the legal circuit, an area larger than Connecticut made up of the fourteen counties that surrounded Springfield. Unlike the other lawyers and judges who traveled the circuit, Lincoln did *not* return home to be with his wife on the weekends. David Herbert Donald wrote that, "traveling the circuit gave him relief from a domesticity that he sometimes found smothering."[177] During the half of each year Lincoln stayed in Springfield, he often left home in the evenings and on weekends to spend time alone in his law office rather than deal with Mary's temperamental explosions.

Throughout Lincoln's presidency, Mary accelerated the destructive tactics of her torturous personality toward her husband by having ongoing relations with shady characters, engaging in excessive spending habits that ran up debts in the tens of thousands of dollars, making deals (i.e., accepting bribes) that put money in her pocket in consideration for attempting to get the president to grant favors, developing conflicts with the wives of government and military leaders, holding seances in the White House in hopes of reconnecting with their son, Willie, who had died there in 1862, and repeatedly demonstrating hostility toward African Americans.

To further cement the fact that Mary was more of a burden than a blessing to Lincoln, Avlon described an event that took place on the morning of April 9, 1865, the day Lee would later surrender to Grant at Appomattox and only six days before Lincoln's death. On board the *River Queen* in Chesapeake Bay, Lincoln read aloud to those near him from his favorite play *Macbeth*. Avlon wrote: "It is a cautionary tale set amid civil war—the story of a striver with *a wife who simultaneously drives him upward toward power and downward toward despair*."[178] Yes, Mary Todd Lincoln drove her husband upward throughout his career and also downward as he struggled to abide her difficult temperament and hostile antics. Somehow, as the marriage went on, he endured the many bad days with her in a mode of consistent magnanimity and equanimity.

Despite his many criticisms of Mary, Burlingame concluded his book with a positive spin by saying that although the marriage was surely a "fountain of misery" for Lincoln, "from it flowed incalculable good for the nation. Lincoln may not have had such a successful presidency, during which he showed a preternatural ability to deal with difficult people, if he had not had so much practice at home."[179] Burlingame cited Lincoln's close friend Henry C. Whitney, an eyewitness to the marriage, who later became his biographer, for this conclusion:

> Lincoln possessed "an equanimity and patience, which captivated the masses, while it tired out petulant grumblers, like [Horace] Greeley, [Wendell] Phillips, etc.; which enabled him to force unwelcome policies on his Cabinet, on Congress, and on the nation; which allowed him to bear his 'faculties with meekness,' and finally to restore peace to his bleeding country, and give physical freedom to the blacks and political freedom to the whites." Whitney speculated that if Lincoln had not undergone the harsh "domestic discipline" he experienced at the hands of his difficult wife, he might well have failed as president. "The nation is largely indebted to Mary Todd Lincoln for its autonomy," Whitney concluded.[180]

In summary, after dealing with his imbalanced and often hostile wife Mary for more than eighteen years in a steady mode of magnanimity and equanimity before he became president, upon taking the oath of office, Abraham Lincoln's maintaining civility, generosity of spirit, and professionalism toward the likes of antagonists Salmon Chase, George McClellan, and Jefferson Davis may have seemed like a walk in the park.

LEADERSHIP TRAIT #2: Keeper of Promises

Mary Todd Lincoln was not only instrumental in her husband's demonstrations of superhuman magnanimity and equanimity, she also played a key role in the development of one of his other great traits—having the integrity and perseverance necessary to keep his promises.

Wilson's *Honor's Voice* won the Gilder Lehrman Lincoln Prize in 1999, given annually to "the finest scholarly work in English on Abraham Lincoln, the American Civil War soldier, or the American Civil War era." The premise of the book is that during the years 1831 to 1842, Lincoln developed the exemplary character traits that allowed him to succeed during his presidency.

In Wilson's eyes, the most important events that occurred during the transformative years was the impact on Lincoln of his becoming engaged to Mary Todd in the late fall of 1840; then breaking their engagement in early January 1841, to which she did not take kindly; his suffering a nervous breakdown after breaking his promise to marry her; and finally, his working through the emotional crises by deciding that the only honorable thing to do was to reconcile with and then marry her, which he did in November 1842.

Wilson labeled the almost two-year period between ending the engagement and having a small hurried wedding, "The Mary Todd 'Enbrigglement.'"[181] A woman who cooked and cleaned clothes for Lincoln during this time said his mindset was "an agony of remorse." A few days after breaking things off with Mary, Lincoln wrote a letter in January 1841 to his then law partner John Stuart and said, "I am now the most miserable man living.... To remain as I am is impossible; I must die or be better."[182]

After being in such a dangerously depressed, almost suicidal state of mind for over a year, Lincoln had an epiphany in the last half of 1842, tied to his ferocious ambition that he first expressed at age twenty-three, which he reiterated in the spring of 1841, saying in a letter to his best friend Joshua Speed that what gave him the desire to press on through the broken engagement crisis was the fact that as of then, he "had done nothing to make any human being remember that he had lived."[183]

Wilson then seized on Lincoln's use of a Latin phrase in one of his letters to Speed at the time: "*nolens volens*"—"whether willing or unwilling"—and the biographer then tied it together with Lincoln's epiphany that not only caused him to marry Mary Todd, but commit himself for the rest of his life to the proposition that he would *never* again break a promise: "Success was predicated on survival, and this meant learning to cope with what comes, *nolens volens,* whether willing or unwilling."[184] To demonstrate his renewed fearless commitment to press forward toward achieving his ambition no matter how difficult it might prove to be, in another letter to Speed written shortly thereafter, Lincoln said, "Our forebodings...are all the worst sort of nonsense."[185]

For Lincoln to regain his sensibilities and restore his emotional equilibrium, Wilson concluded that his subject knew he would *have* to restore his sense of honor, which could *only* come from fulfilling his original marriage promise to Mary. Lincoln counseled himself: "The remedy is clear: embrace the reality." In that context, Lincoln told Speed, "My old Father used to have a saying that 'If you make a bad bargain, *hug* it tighter.'"[186]

After getting engaged, Lincoln realized he had made a bad bargain in promising to become permanently connected in matrimony to Mary Todd. Despite that awareness, his epiphany drove him to "hug his bad bargain," reconcile with Mary, and marry her, even though he could see she was an emotional time bomb. Doing this, he could regain his honor and move forward in life committed to fulfilling his high ambition, with a renewed sense of self-confidence and no sense of guilt because somehow, some way, he had found the inner strength to keep his promise. This caused him to be that much stronger and more steadfast in keeping the difficult promises he would make in the years ahead about restoring the nation and liberating the enslaved.

Going forward after the "enbrigglement" with Mary, per Wilson's title, Lincoln made sure he kept his antennae *up* to hear "honor's voice," and "*from that time on,* Lincoln became known for his *resolution*.... His rock-solid ability to keep his resolves once they were made would undergird his performance as president. And that would make all the difference."

A. The Importance and Requirements of Keeping Promises

Before his death in 2012, life coach Stephen Covey sold tens of millions of self-help books, most notably *The 7 Habits of Highly Effective People*. When he netted out all his advice, and identified the most essential trait, he concluded: "Many times over the years people have asked if I had one idea that would best help people grow so that they could better cope with their problems, seize their opportunities, and make their life successful. I've come to give a simple four-word answer: 'Make and keep promises.'"[187]

Long before Covey arrived on the scene, Lincoln made and kept his promises through a process which had these essential elements:

(1) The matters which became the subject of his promises were so clearly supported by facts and moral truths that there was never a good reason for him to change his position.

  This part of his process required research, reflection, and sound judgment before Lincoln could finally reach a decision on what to promise.

(2) He necessarily had to determine that his promises were *achievable*, and not impossible—such that, in his eyes, no

obstacle could prevent him from keeping his promises. He would either overcome the obstacle or go down fighting to the end to get past it.

This part of his process required Lincoln to evaluate all the foreseeable factors in play that *might* prevent the fulfillment of his promises, and then decide that there *were* ways to prevail over them. His abundant confidence in his arsenal of talents gave him what he needed to succeed in making and keeping promises not attainable by anyone else. This commitment to achieving a desired result on occasion required him to go beyond prior legal or ethical boundaries because he believed that effectuating the promises was so important that he should do whatever was necessary to reach his goal.

(3) The final part of Lincoln's process was the belief that his promises constituted such an urgent imperative that achieving them should not be compromised by accepting a lesser good, but not great, outcome.

He made his choices among competing possible final outcomes through his dual powers of discernment and steadfast resolve.

Lincoln mastered all three of these requirements in making, keeping, and fully delivering upon his promises to reunite the nation and emancipate the enslaved. Mastery of this trait was possible because of his brilliant mind, his extreme self-confidence, his ferocious tenacity that prioritized success in achieving his goal, his unwavering moral compass, his high-road and empathetic emotional intelligence, and his rhetorical eloquence. In the Lincoln section of her superb book *Forged in Crisis: The Power of Courageous Leadership in Turbulent Times,* Harvard Business School Professor Nancy Koehn affirmed this ultimate trait of keeping promises because of Lincoln's having multiple virtues:

> Once he made a crucial decision, he saw it through, even when virtually everything around him seemed stacked against such a commitment. This adherence was not the result of stubbornness or self-righteousness. Rather, it came from the care that Lincoln exercised in making choices, including the slowness with which he acted when the stakes were high; from his growing depth as a moral actor; and from his sheer will to get up each morning and do what he could in service of his mission.[188]

B. Why Lincoln Had What It Took to Become the Ultimate Promise Keeper

Almost every Lincoln biographer works into his final product his subject's views on how his mind worked. Characteristically, Abraham Lincoln used metaphors:

> I am slow to learn and slow to forget that which I have learned. My mind is like a piece of steel—very hard to scratch anything on it and almost impossible after you get it there to rub it out.[189]

Here's how Lincoln explained the difference between his mind and his law partner Herndon's mind, after picking up Herndon's little knife with its short twin blades and his own large jack knife. He opened the short blades of the small knife and told Herndon:

> See here it opens quickly and at the point travels through but a small portion of space—but see this long bladed jack knife, it opens slowly and its points travel through a greater distance of space than your little knife. It moves slower but it can do more execution. Just so with these long convolutions of my brain. They have to act slowly—pass as it were through a

> greater space than shorter convolutions that snap off quickly.... [For this reason,] I am compelled by nature to speak slowly. I commence way back like the boys do when they want to get a good start. Then weight and speed get momentum to jump far.[190]

Yes, Lincoln *knew* he had been blessed with a brain that worked in a uniquely powerful way, such that he had the horsepower to remember and believe things permanently and to "jump far" with his thoughts. Donald decided that Lincoln's knowing this about himself from the time he was a young man gave him such "supreme self-confidence, that he believed he was at least the equal, if not the superior, of any man he ever met."[191]

One of Lincoln's first speeches was the Lyceum Address, given to a group of young men in Springfield in January 1838. It contained the following passage that inferentially spoke of Lincoln's perception of himself and what he might well be called upon to do in the future:

> *Towering genius* disdains a beaten path. It seeks regions hitherto unexplored.... It *thirsts and burns for distinction*; and, if possible, it will have it, whether at the expense of *emancipating slaves*, or enslaving freemen.[192] [author's emphasis]

Thus, Lincoln had the self-awareness to recognize that he *was* a towering genius who thirsted and burned for distinction, and, therefore, had the power to see and make promises about issues that lesser minds could not visualize as being achievable. To move forward in keeping his promises as he navigated his era's political minefield, Lincoln also possessed the emotional intelligence to know that to puff himself up with ego-fueled arrogance about his superior intellectual and moral powers would surely cause him to lose his appeal among those he sought to cultivate. Miller concluded, "His ego would *not* be stoked and enlarged from his rise from nowhere all the way to the supreme position, or inflated by the immense power that he held when he got there."[193]

This trait of unyielding self-confidence held in check by humility fueled Lincoln's upward rise as a political figure who had what it took to keep his campaign promises and get things done. According to Wilson, this combination was what drove his personal mandate of having "a noble destiny to fulfill."[194]

Because Lincoln retained virtually all of the information he learned *and* the moral conclusions he drew, Miller determined that his subject had "intellectual *and* moral self-confidence" and could push himself forward toward keeping his promises because he stayed vigilant about his positions in a mode of "deep conscientiousness."[195] Herndon said that Lincoln's extreme conscientiousness drove him to "express no opinion on anything until he knew his subject inside and outside, upside and downside.... When researching anything, he not only went to the root of the question, but dug up the root, and separated and analyzed every fibre of it."[196]

Thus, whatever Lincoln learned and/or decided about important issues was enhanced over time because he kept building on his knowledge and beliefs year after year. This steady growth deepened his knowledge and convictions through what Hay called the "process of cumulative thought." Koehn gave this explanation of how Lincoln's process of cumulative thought evolved on slavery:

> In struggling to make sense of American slavery and the politics surrounding it,...Lincoln aspired to be and then became *a leader*, building the structure of his thinking brick by brick, responding to the volatility of larger events, the political opportunities and exigencies he faced, *and* changes within himself. As conditions shifted and he evolved, he amended his judgment at times, all the while, observing, reflecting, and, ultimately, trying to get right with himself about the meaning of slavery and what he should do about his momentous issue.

> This is not to say Lincoln got it right from the beginning—far from it.... He made plenty of mistakes that exhibited many flaws...catering to the prejudice that most of his white contemporaries harbored toward blacks. Like Frederick Douglass, who frequently criticized him, we can view Lincoln's position on slavery in the 1850s as weak, even cowardly.
>
> We can see all this when we consider Lincoln...as a *human being* who grew—emotionally, intellectually, and morally—as he advanced along his journey. It flowed from Lincoln's ongoing commitment to better himself—inside as well as out...as a result of what he did to construct a cohesive, politically viable, and ethically grounded position on slavery.[197]

C. Lincoln's Political Strategy for Keeping Promises

If someone chooses to pursue a career in politics, he will not go far unless he wins elections. During Abraham Lincoln's life, the only people who could vote in elections were white men. To stay in their good graces, Lincoln knew he had to keep his finger on the pulse of what most of them believed, determine how best to communicate and attempt to persuade them to see the major issues his way, and prove to them he had what it took to achieve his goals despite the fractured "house divided" political arena of his time.

In one of his debates with Stephen Douglas in 1858, Lincoln asserted, "Public sentiment is *everything*. With public sentiment nothing can fail; without it, nothing can succeed. Consequently, whoever moulds public sentiment goes deeper than he who enacts statutes or pronounces decisions."[198]

In furtherance of his efforts to move the voting center toward his ultimate position, Lincoln was savvy enough to know he could make progress by building positive relationships with those in the newspaper business. In his perceptive book *Lincoln and the Power of the Press,* esteemed scholar Harold Holzer detailed Lincoln's constant efforts to build rapport with the media people of his era all over the country, stay in their good graces at least most of the time, and thereby keep his thoughts published front and center in the public's consciousness.[199]

Lincoln knew he couldn't mold the sentiments of most voters to where he wanted them to go by pitching to the body politic's outer extremes. The thrust of his message had to be directed to *the center,* and once he had created his bond with centrists, he believed he could move them toward greater enlightenment. Biographer David Reynolds, in his book *Abe: Abraham Lincoln in His Times,* zeroed in on his subject's strategy upon reaching the White House: "As president, Lincoln would teach the world that in a deeply divided time, the center is *everything*—the center, that is, with an eye always trained on pushing the nation in a strongly progressive direction."[200]

With this as his dominant political strategy, and having perfected its application in Illinois which was "a microcosm of the divided nation," with "sharp differences on slavery, with the southerners tending toward conservatism and northerners tending toward a more progressive view," Reynolds discerned that Lincoln "introduced a language that was uniquely forceful. It projected all the passion and principle of the Garrisonian abolitionists while avoiding their sensationalism."[201]

His efforts to begin molding the center toward what should be done about the slavery issue began in 1854 with his speech in Peoria shortly after Congress passed the Kansas-Nebraska Act. Reynolds explained Lincoln's credible approach to moving Illinois voters toward his way of thinking:

> The Peoria speech initiated his dramatic political rise and showed the tools he would use to refashion antislavery language. His three basic tools—history, humanity, and the Declaration of Independence as the nation's higher law—were standard antislavery ones, and Lincoln used them with special skill at Peoria.[202]

In making this pitch, Lincoln clearly recognized that, on the one hand, slavery was evil, but on the other hand, the Constitution allowed it to continue. He properly believed that he and everyone else in government lacked the power to have it abolished in the states where it was permitted, but he and the government *had* the power to prevent its movement into the Western territories which would soon want to join the nation as new states. As Lincoln sorted through his thoughts on how best to deal with the issue on which there were no clear answers, he reached into the hearts of the political center through his Euclidean-inspired logical reasoning and his unmatched eloquence that flowed from his knowledge of Shakespeare, the King James Bible, and history. Using that approach, as he figured things out before anyone else did, he guided those in the center with uniquely powerful words to the point where they would first embrace his conclusions and then he would move them toward supporting his future promises regarding how best to reunite the nation and deal with the evil institution of slavery.

D. Overcoming the Obstacles to Promise Keeping

It was Abraham Lincoln's successful cultivation of the center that allowed him to become the Republican presidential nominee in 1860 and then win the election in November. By February 1860, Lincoln had figured out how best to make his anti-slavery-expansion argument, honed through the Lincoln–Douglas debates in 1858, and finalized on February 27, 1860, in his Cooper Union Address in New York City, "the speech that made him president." At Cooper Union, he relied on his research of the Founding Fathers' intentions on the issue of slavery's expansion *and* the words contained in the Declaration of Independence, to support his position, *knowing* they were the gold standard for what had complete credibility and would inspire the country to act on the issue in a manner consistent with Lincoln's evolving thoughts. He concluded the speech with words of steadfast purpose about his unwavering intention to stop the expansion of slavery: "Let us have faith that *right makes might*, and in that faith, let us, to the end, dare *to do our duty* as we understand it."[203]

Regardless of his repeated statements to the effect that he only wanted to stop the expansion of slavery and *not* seek its abolition, seven Southern states decided that Lincoln's becoming president would inevitably move the country in an all-encompassing anti-slavery direction. So shortly after he was elected in November 1860, they seceded. This prompted his sterling but unsuccessful effort to reconcile with them in his First Inaugural Address, which was soon followed by the attack on Fort Sumter and the commencement of the Civil War.

In his book *Tried by War*, McPherson summarized how during Lincoln's presidency, it became increasingly apparent that the slavery issue was so all-consuming that it could *never be negotiated*:

> The question of national sovereignty over a union of all the states was nonnegotiable. No compromise between a sovereign United States and a separately sovereign Confederate States was possible. By 1864, Lincoln said the issue is distinct, simple, and inflexible. It is "an issue which can only be tried by war, and decided by victory."[204]

Just as a politician must do what it takes to win elections, a commander-in-chief must also do what it takes to win a war. Keeping his promise to preserve the Union meant Lincoln was *not* going to let it fall. Thus, soon after the war began, as the Confederate Army won almost every battle and six additional states seceded to join the CSA, as a matter of "military necessity," Lincoln played fast and loose with certain constitutional rights to keep the Union from collapsing, thereby *refusing* to allow rigid adherence to the Constitution to become, in essence, a suicide pact for the nation. In particular, he revoked the right to habeas corpus, arrested members of the Maryland legislature to keep them from voting to secede, shut down anti-war newspapers, and imprisoned political dissidents. *Absolutely nothing* was going to prevent him from winning the war and bringing the Confederate states back into the nation.

In his Second Annual Message to Congress in December 1862, Lincoln explained to the country why he was necessarily disregarding constitutional rights to achieve his goals: "The dogmas of the quiet past, are inadequate to the stormy present. The occasion is piled high with difficulty, and we must rise with the occasion. As our case is new, so we must think anew, and act anew."[205] In his book *Old Whigs: Burke, Lincoln & the Politics of Prudence*, political theorist Greg Weiner condensed Lincoln's thoughts and deeds on this issue into a nutshell: "Prudence understands when one must step temporarily outside the channels of normal law," but then to minimize his unconstitutional actions, the author injected, "Lincoln convened Congress as quickly as practicable to ratify his actions."[206]

In Lincoln's standard manner of conveying important ideas with metaphors, amid the thousands of amputations being performed on wounded soldiers during the war, here were his words on why winning the war and restoring the Union were much more important than adhering to every right contained in the Constitution:

> Was it possible to lose the nation, and yet preserve the Constitution? By general law, life *and* limb must be protected; yet often a limb must be amputated to save a life; but a life is never wisely given to save a limb. I felt that measures, otherwise unconstitutional, might become lawful, by becoming indispensable to the preservation of the Constitution through preservation of the nation.[207]

By late September 1864, in a letter to Quaker minister Eliza Gurney, while the Union army was finally beginning to gain some momentum, Lincoln explained why he had to do everything possible to win the war: "We shall nobly save, or meanly lose, *the last best hope of earth*."[208]

More game-changing than the extra-constitutional tactics, however, was Lincoln's decision to issue the Emancipation Proclamation. He knew this exercise of presidential power was extreme (and probably illegal), but he viewed it as essential to the war effort to gain needed momentum by expanding the war's purpose from merely restoring the Union and transforming it into a war for the liberation of Southern slaves.

In 2021, constitutional law scholar and Harvard Law School Professor Noah Feldman released his book, *The Broken Constitution: Lincoln, Slavery, and the Refounding of America*. In his book's Introduction, Feldman provided this explanation of how Lincoln, despite the oath he had taken at his inauguration, justified the Emancipation Proclamation. When it became clear that competing promises could not both be kept, he, as the nation's commander-in-chief, had to prioritize keeping the most important ones:

> Lincoln's act of emancipating enslaved people…marked the culmination of an extraordinary transformation in his beliefs about the meaning of the Constitution. He still purported to believe that slaves were private property, and that private property was protected by constitutional guarantee. Now, however, he allowed himself to develop an additional belief: [that] as commander in chief, he had the legal power to order the otherwise unconstitutional taking of the property of the citizens of states prosecuting the war of rebellion.
>
> In his First Inaugural Address, Lincoln told the public he was prepared to acknowledge the legal legitimacy of slavery if it would hold together the union. Emancipation represented a total reversal of this hierarchy of values…. By signing [the Proclamation], he was subverting the very Constitution that was supposed to provide the reason for going to war in the first place…and also re-forming the basic character of the Constitution….[209]

Regardless of Lincoln's discomfort over his constitutional violations, with the signing of the Emancipation Proclamation, he *knew* he was (at last!) fulfilling his life's ambition as he had stated it in 1832, 1841, and the early 1850s—to make himself "worthy of others' esteem" and to "make the nation better because he had lived." When he told his Cabinet in September 1862 that after winning the battle of Antietam, he was ready to move forward with the formal issuance of the Emancipation, his Secretary of the Navy Gideon Welles transcribed Lincoln's statement to them:

> I made the promise to myself and—(after hesitating)—*to my Maker* that if the Confederates were defeated, I would issue the Emancipation Proclamation. The rebel army is now driven out, and I am going to fulfill that promise.... I think the time has come now.[210]

McPherson gave this account of the drama when Lincoln signed the document:

> After shaking hands at the White House reception, Lincoln retired to his office with a few colleagues to sign the final copy of the Proclamation. His hand was so sore from three hours of social duty that he could scarcely hold the pen. He did not want to sign while his hand was still trembling, because "all who examine the document hereafter will say 'He hesitated.' That would not do, for I never in my life felt more certain that I was doing right than I do in signing this paper.... If my name ever goes into history it will be for this act, and my whole soul is in it." The president picked up the pen again, but his hand was still unsteady and he put it down. "The South had fair warning," he reflected, "that if they did not return to their duty, I should strike at this pillar of their strength. *The promise must now be kept*, and I shall never recall one word." Lincoln then picked up the

> pen once more and signed his name without a tremor. "That will do," he said.[211]

Shortly after the signing, his friend Joshua Speed came to visit, and Lincoln reminded him of the severe depression he had suffered two decades earlier (during the Mary Todd embrigglement), and of his disclosure at the time that he would gladly die but that he "had done nothing to make any human being remember that he had lived." Now, pointing toward the Emancipation Proclamation, he declared: "I believe that in *this* measure...my fondest hopes will be realized."[212]

After he signed the Proclamation on January 1, 1863, runaway slaves from the South immediately joined the Union Army and ended up supplementing and reinvigorating the troops by almost 200,000 soldiers. In furtherance of moving toward complete liberation of the enslaved, and treating them as equals, Lincoln again turned on his process of "cumulative thought" and brought it to a head when he gave the Gettysburg Address on November 19, 1863. Miller summarized the speech's importance:

> Lincoln gave what would prove to be his most enduring expression of his own (and, as he saw it, his country's) commitment to equality in his dedicatory remarks at the Gettysburg cemetery: American to the core, he understood his nation's distinctive self-definition...in universal moral truths that we hold in a creed. He...wrote not of a moral ideal the nation sought, nor of a principle that it served, but of a proposition to which it was dedicated: all men, as Jefferson had written, were created equal.
>
> The significance of reassuring that Jeffersonian phrase in November 1863 was to say that, for all the temporary contradictions in practice, in America's original aspiration, black persons were from the beginning, fundamentally equal to white ones.

> Lincoln then ended his remarks, after an eloquent recognition of the brave men who had consecrated the battleground, with a call to a high resolve, for "a new birth of freedom." A more inclusive freedom was to be born: a freedom linked to the equality to which the nation was dedicated.[213]

Lincoln's commitment to racial equality took on special meaning as he watched the formerly enslaved fight and die for the nation's "new birth of freedom" higher ideal. Reynolds encapsulated the promise the president intended to keep to the African American soldiers:

> On the guarantee of freedom for blacks who served in the military, Lincoln appealed to shared humanity: "[N]egroes, like other people, act upon motives. Why should they do anything for us, if we will do nothing for them? If they stake their lives for us, they must be prompted by the strongest motive—even the promise of freedom. *And the promise being made, must be kept*."[214]

From the time he signed it, Lincoln knew the Emancipation Proclamation was on shaky ground from a constitutional standpoint and would surely be challenged once the war ended. To guarantee that his promise of emancipation for the enslaved would be kept, the safest approach was the passage of a constitutional amendment that prohibited slavery. He successfully pushed the Thirteenth Amendment through two-thirds of the Senate in the spring of 1864 but couldn't get the requisite amount in the House.

In the November 1864 election, not only was Lincoln reelected, but Republicans in Congress upped their margin of majority. Despite that, Lincoln knew that to get two-thirds of the House to support the amendment would require the support of at least some Democrats. In January 1865, the arm-twisting necessary to persuade some Democrats to support the amendment began.

The three pages in Goodwin's *Team of Rivals* devoted to Lincoln's efforts to get the Thirteenth Amendment passed in January 1865 became the focal point of Steven Spielberg's film *Lincoln* that opened in November 2012.[215] Just as President Lincoln violated the Constitution to prevent being defeated in the war, as the film accurately showed, he also became much more flexible in his ethical conduct to get the votes in Congress that he needed to pass the amendment. To reach his goal, Goodwin said Lincoln "extended plum assignments, pardons, campaign contributions, and government jobs for relatives and friends of faithful members."[216] To expedite the vote prior to the arrival in Washington, D.C. of "Confederate Peace Commissioners" who would surely lean on wavering Democratic voters, Lincoln shaded the truth to make Congressmen believe that the so-called "Peace Commissioners" had not yet arrived in the nation's capital, even though he knew they were nearby. His semi-shady tactics worked and the constitutional amendment quickly passed in the House 119–56, reaching the necessary two-thirds margin with only three votes to spare before the Commissioners arrived.

With the Thirteenth Amendment's passage, Lincoln had kept and delivered on his promise to abolish slavery despite dozens of obstacles, none of which could block the tenacious, cunning, and indomitable president. When it was finally achieved, Lincoln received these words of praise to a crowd in Boston from his former antagonist, William Lloyd Garrison:

> And to whom is the country more immediately indebted for this vital and saving amendment of the Constitution than, perhaps, to any other man? I believe I may confidently answer—to the humble rail-splitter of Illinois—to the Presidential chain-breaker for millions of the oppressed—to Abraham Lincoln![217]

E. Keeping Promises by Refusing to Compromise

As of early 1865, Abraham Lincoln's top general Ulysses Grant had implemented a masterful strategy that made victory in the war a virtual certainty. Chernow described how Grant did it:

> Sheridan's successful rampage through the Shenandoah Valley, Thomas's demolition of Hood's army at Nashville, Sherman's conquest of Atlanta and Savannah—all formed part of the scheme Grant had envisaged when he became General-in-Chief. He had accomplished exactly what he had set out to do, interweaving his far-flung armies so they cooperated in a single strategy and moved with a common purpose, the result being that the Confederacy was sliced into ever smaller pieces. The only stalled part of his scheme was Virginia, but that effort had bottled up Lee and stopped his army from aiding embattled rebel forces in Tennessee and Georgia. Now Grant set his sights on finishing off the most fearsome Confederate army.[218]

After Lincoln's reelection, the inevitability of defeat led to mass desertions by Confederate soldiers who were often going days without food after their supply chain had been broken by Grant's tactics. The die was cast, and CSA president Jefferson Davis decided he needed to pursue a settlement strategy that might save face and get him at least some of what his constituents wanted. On January 29, 1865, Davis sent three emissaries to Grant with a letter seeking a meeting with the president. The three men knew that Davis sought an end to the war by which postwar there would be "two countries."

Lincoln met with the Confederacy's designated negotiators on February 3, 1865, in the saloon of the steamboat *River Queen* docked at Hampton Roads, only four days after Congress's passage of the Thirteenth Amendment. Chernow wrote: "Lincoln hoped the vote [on the amendment] would alert Southerners that their struggle to save slavery was now doomed.... [At the meeting,] he made clear he had three *non-negotiable* conditions: permanent restoration of the Union; an end to slavery; and no cessation of hostilities until all rebel forces were disbanded."[219] The conversation ended with no progress toward peace being made.

Weiner explained why Lincoln's being non-negotiable on the three points made such good sense:

> Lincoln recognized union as an ultimate value on which compromise was imprudent because it would lead to a process of infinite division: Disaffected subdivisions would be empowered to secede from the seceded states, and other subdivisions from them in turn, such that the idea of secession was, he said in his First Inaugural, "the essence of anarchy."[220]

Miller drew this conclusion regarding why the president's refusal to compromise became an essential element in his keeping promises:

> Max Weber, in the peculiarly affecting ending of the essay from which we have taken the concept of an ethic of responsibility, described the moment when a mature politician confronts that boundary situation of intrinsic goods and evils, calculates no longer, and says in the words of Martin Luther well known to his German audience: "*Here I stand: I can do no other.*"[221]

Lincoln "stood" on keeping his promises to restore the nation and free the slaves. He *knew* the only way he could fulfill them was by causing the unconditional surrender of the Confederate Army. He therefore ordered his troops to keep doing what it took until the enemy finally waved the white flag, and *then* he prevailed in getting what he wanted on all three of his non-negotiable issues, which were necessary to achieving his promised goal.

Abraham Lincoln's Flaws

Abraham Lincoln's flaws are a shorter section of this chapter compared to the other presidents profiled in this book. Why? Because he had so few of them. The first one worth noting was his having had a long-suffering troubled relationship with his father Tom Lincoln because his dad wanted him to stop "wasting his time" by reading books. Tom wanted his son to devote himself entirely to manual labor on the family's farm, to which Lincoln famously said in his later years, "My father taught me how to farm, but he didn't teach me how to love farming." Once Lincoln left home at twenty-two, he rarely saw his father again, and refused to visit Tom in his dying days. Adding insult to injury, he passed on attending his father's funeral. Thus, Lincoln did *not* get a passing grade on his Ten Commandments report card in connection with the commandment for people to honor their father (as well as their mother).

Himself a father to four sons—only two of whom survived him, and only the eldest Robert lived past childhood—for his second flaw, Lincoln was certainly kind and loving toward his children when he was around them, but as discussed previously, because he could only maintain sanity in his marriage by staying *away* from Mary as much as he could, he was often *not* around to attend to his boys' needs. Yes, while in their midst, Lincoln gave his sons "quality time," but there was definitely a major deficiency in his "quantity time."

Finally, during the early years of his political career, Lincoln did what Jefferson had done often—writing and having published "anonymous" attacks on his opponents. This practice came to an end in 1842 when one of his targets, James Shields, was so incensed by the attack in the local newspaper that he challenged Lincoln to a duel. To uphold his honor, Lincoln agreed to do it but fortunately the prospective combatants made peace before the actual broadsword duel began. The encounter caused Lincoln to stop his practice of publishing criticisms anonymously.[222]

Personal Application

You now know how Abraham Lincoln would have answered the following questions. How do *you* answer them?

- How do you typically respond when someone with whom you interact says or does something that disrespects you?

- When you evaluate people in deciding whether to employ or promote them, how much do you incorporate into the evaluation past instances of some level of personal conflict you have had with them?
- When someone working under you performs poorly on an assignment, do you criticize them privately or publicly?
- Before directing criticism toward someone, do you typically wait a while to cool off before communicating with them?
- Have you ever acted maliciously toward someone? If so, as you look back on the situation, do you think your conduct was appropriate?
- Have you ever been accused of being too harsh toward someone whose actions angered or disappointed you? Looking back, was that fair criticism?
- What is your attitude toward your competitors and/or adversaries? Is it grace-filled or hate-filled?
- Once you have prevailed over someone with whom you were competing, what is your attitude toward them? Sympathetic? Gracious? Or not?
- Are you involved in a binding business or personal relationship with someone who frequently manages to punch your buttons and set you off? If so, what is your strategy for improving how that relationship plays itself out going forward?
- Have you ever broken an important promise? If so, how did you respond to that failure?
- How much deep thinking and reflection do you give to an issue before you make a promise concerning it?
- Before making a promise, do you spend time evaluating whether you are truly capable of fulfilling it?

- Have you ever failed to keep a promise because an unexpected obstacle arose that prevented you from achieving your goal? If so, looking back, was that obstacle truly insurmountable?
- Have you ever gone far beyond your comfort zone in doing what it took to keep a promise? If so, do you regret going beyond your comfort zone?
- What is your level of due diligence before you make a promise?
- If fulfilling a promise requires the participation and cooperation of other people, how much time and effort do you spend cultivating your relationships with those people?
- Do you ever try to change someone's mind without changing his heart? If so, were you successful in changing his mind?
- When you are attempting to build support for an idea in your enterprise, do you seek to persuade those whose thinking is in the center or on the outer limits? Can you think of any reason why you would ever seek to cultivate a group that's not centered-thinking?
- How careful are you about word choice precision and tone when you are seeking to persuade?
- Have you ever had to compromise on a matter that was the subject of a promise you made? If so, looking back, was it prudent to compromise?

May the successful and esteemed leadership traits of Lincoln guide you in reflecting upon and answering these questions in the context of your ultimate leadership potential. There can surely be no greater role model for exhibiting best practices in leadership than our sixteenth president, Abraham Lincoln.

CHAPTER FOUR

HOW TO USE INFORMATION, EXPAND ONE'S DOMAIN OF POWER, AND BROKER RESOLUTION OUT OF CONFLICT—LIKE THEODORE ROOSEVELT

This book's premise is that the most important leadership traits of our eight greatest presidents can and should be implemented by those who seek to elevate their performance while leading an enterprise. The premise assumes that you operate in the same realm of human possibility as the presidents featured in each chapter. In some respects, this assumption goes out the window when addressing the potential application of Theodore Roosevelt's leadership traits to others because in many respects, he was superhuman—an apple, sui generis, compared to the oranges of his fellow men and women. For anyone to even think about following his footsteps would require a massive injection of high IQ brilliance, electric personality, and nonstop energy.

Over the last century and a half, those who knew Theodore Roosevelt (TR) personally and the historians who have studied his life have had loads of fun describing him. In his biography trilogy, Pulitzer-winner Edmund Morris quoted dozens of TR's peers who gave amazingly similar descriptions of the man's take-it-to-the-limit approach to life that made him dominate every arena he entered. Those who encountered him in person typically remarked that his manic pace reminded them of a "high-speed locomotive"—charged with the dual "voltage" of *joie de vivre* and "bulldog tenacity."

Along those same lines, in his book *The Wilderness Warrior: Theodore Roosevelt and the Crusade for America,* Douglas Brinkley quoted TR's peer, journalist William Allen White, who gave this depiction of Roosevelt as an unbridled force of nature: "There was no twilight and evening star for him. He plunged headlong snorting into the breakers of the tide that swept him to another bourne, full armed breasting the waves, a strong swimmer undaunted."[223]

These descriptions emanated from TR's complete lack of moderation in his activities, save and except for his being nothing more than a moderate drinker of adult beverages and rigorously faithful to his two wives. Morris provided a full panoply of details throughout his books in support of the proposition that whatever Roosevelt did, he did ferociously. When writing, TR wrote at a frenetic pace—often whipping out twenty-five letters in a morning and pouring eighty-three thousand words out of his pen in three weeks while creating a book.[224] When working on his cattle ranch in the Dakota Territory, he earned the respect of his fellow cowboys by riding a hundred miles a day, staying up all night on watch, and then going to work the next morning after consuming a big breakfast.[225] When he became the first president to campaign for election in 1904, he delivered thirty speeches a day from his train at whistle stops on his national tour, and got his energy up to present them by shadowboxing in the caboose.[226] In a tennis match on the White House court, he played ninety-one games in one day and celebrated his occasional good shots by shrieking, laughing, and hopping around on one foot.[227] With these types of extreme behaviors occurring routinely in Theodore Roosevelt's life, similar accounts, adjectives, and metaphors flowed repeatedly from the multitudes he encountered and never ceased to amaze.

Regardless of his uniqueness as a *homo sapiens,* there is still much to learn by "normal" people about effective leadership from TR's traits that allowed him to do what he did during his seven-and-a-half-year presidency, which began after William McKinley's assassination in September 1901, six months into his second term. Admittedly, Roosevelt served in the White House (the presidential residence *he* named) during a largely undemanding time when the country stayed out of wars and severe economic depression. Yet he had an incredible run of achievements that provides the basis for his being ranked as our fourth greatest president by historians in the most recent C-SPAN polls of historians—trailing only Abraham Lincoln, George Washington, and his cousin Franklin D. Roosevelt.

During his years in the Oval Office, in connection with his overall achievement of substantially expanding the powers of the president, Theodore Roosevelt:

- Settled the Great Coal Strike of 1902 on the verge of winter that threatened to put many Americans into a deep freeze and had the nation teetering on the brink of social revolution;
- Expanded and directed the Department of Justice to enforce anti-trust laws in the courts to lessen the power of monopolies that for decades had made wealthy people wealthier;
- Mediated an end to the Russo-Japanese War in 1905, while also resolving several lesser skirmishes around the world through hardball diplomacy that prevented wars;

- Became the instigator and driving force behind the American conservation movement;
- Arranged for the building of the Panama Canal;
- Substantially grew the US Navy, thereby triggering America's rise as a world power through his "Big Stick" diplomacy;
- Expanded presidential power to the point where the nation's executive branch moved past its legislative branch in the ability to get things done for the American people;
- Used his force of personality and mastery over the media to move the masses into line with his agenda through the platform of his "Bully Pulpit"; and
- Provided "Square Deal" fairness to the working poor by regulating railroad rates, successfully pushing through pure food and drug legislation, and lessening the power of trusts.

Brinkley encapsulated all these accomplishments in describing the big picture of TR's White House years in his interview with me in my earlier book, *Cross-Examining History*. His summation:

> Theodore Roosevelt created the modern presidency by using executive power in a new way that led America into the new century. He turned the office of president from being a lonely lighthouse into a citadel of direct action.... To be ranked in C-SPAN's top four while being president from 1901 to 1909 when America was not at war is simply amazing. With all his hawkishness and power bluster, he kept the United States at peace during his presidency.
>
> He defined the American centrist. By not being part of either the right or left paradigms, and by not being about politics first and foremost, he was able to look at what made sense for the whole country to go for-

> ward. For anyone who considers himself an independent-minded voter, he is the number one president. For those who want a political leader who can deal with circumstances from a pragmatic perspective, and who's a visionary and aspires to do what's right without worrying about the political consequences, TR shines mightily.[228]

TR's achieving what he did after the string of mediocre-to-bad presidents who followed Lincoln lifted America to new heights at home and abroad. Although his extraordinary capacity to absorb and use mass quantities of information to make good decisions, change hearts and minds through the immense power of his personality, and work at a torrid pace, pushed him far beyond the capabilities of the rest of the human pack, as shown in the remainder of this chapter, his three most important leadership skills *are* capable of being effectuated by those who pursue challenges while operating as mere mortals without having his super-human traits.

Leadership Trait #1: Never Stop Learning

A key to Theodore Roosevelt's success on multiple fronts was the fact that he made his decisions through the prism of a massive accumulation and synthesis of useful information that came to him daily from many sources, though mainly from the written word. *No one* read more than TR. He poured over dozens of newspapers every day while devouring one book after another. In her analysis of him, Goodwin said, "It is hardly an exaggeration to say that books were the chief building blocks of Theodore Roosevelt's identity."[229]

Turning dozens (and often hundreds) of pages daily brought TR sheer bliss because it allowed him to imbibe *new* information for which he had an unquenchable thirst. Morris determined that, "when Roosevelt was learning something new, he visibly *swelled* with pleasure and satisfaction,"[230] and because of his photographic memory,[i,231] he retained essentially all he read, meaning he had mass quantities of information implanted into his mind, available to guide him as he made decisions and plotted future strategies.

To hardwire knowledge into his brain, after reading about a subject, TR would then spend time reflecting on it, and he often deepened his thoughts by writing about it. He formalized this three-step reading/reflecting/writing approach while at Harvard in his college years. At that time, the only way to move armed forces around the world to address international strife was with a strong navy. Knowing how to maximize a navy's power required a thorough knowledge of naval history. Geoffrey Ward, in his book *The Roosevelts: An Intimate History*, recounted how "as an undergraduate, Roosevelt began writing a 498-page history, *The Naval War of 1812*, that would eventually influence a generation of naval planners."[232] Over the course of his life, TR wrote thirty-five books covering a wide range of subjects that showed the breadth and depth of his knowledge. Ward described TR's books as being about "*everything*—from bear hunting to Oliver Cromwell to what he believed to be the principles of Americanism."[233]

Although Roosevelt absorbed hundreds of varied subjects from his constant reading, he was *not* a dilettante about any of them; rather, he became an expert in every field he studied. When he decided he needed to understand Chaucer better, he read *all* of Chaucer's works in the summer of 1892, back-to-back.[234] When he wanted to go deeper into the life of his hero Abraham Lincoln on a beach vacation in 1902 while president, he read straight through the entire ten volumes of John Nicolay and John Hay's[ii] massive biography of their former

---

i His photographic memory was portrayed by Morris with this word picture illustration: "He astonished the diplomat Count Albert Apponyi by reciting, almost verbatim, a long piece of Hungarian historical literature. When the Count expressed surprise, Roosevelt said he had neither seen nor thought of the document in twenty years. Asked to explain a similar performance before a delegation of Chinese, Roosevelt explained mildly, 'I remembered a book that I had read some time ago, and as I talked, the pages of the book came before my eyes.'" See: Edmund Morris, *The Rise of Theodore Roosevelt* (Coward, McCann & Geoghegan, Inc 1979), 26.

ii Not coincidentally in 1902, John Hay was serving as TR's secretary of state.

boss.[235] No interruptions or distractions were permitted that might deflect his laser-beam focus when he was going deep on a subject.

After attending a White House dinner, British author H.G. Wells commented, after witnessing how TR shared his vast storehouse of knowledge with others, that the president's "range of reading is amazing. He seems to be echoing with *all* the thought of the time, with receptivity to the pitch of genius.... [He has] the most vigorous brain in a conspicuously responsible position in the world."[236] Wells's assessment was confirmed by a note Roosevelt wrote in 1906 to Henry Cabot Lodge's wife Nannie:

> Dear Nannie: Can you have me to dinner either Wednesday or Friday? Would you be willing to have Bay and Bessie also? Then we could discuss the Hittite empire, the Pithecanthropus, and Magyar love songs, and the exact relations of the Atli of the *Volsunga Saga* to the Etzel of the *Nibelungenlied*, and of both to Attila—with interludes by Cabot about the rate bill, Beveridge, and other matters of more vivid contemporary interest. Ever yours, TR[237]

Throughout his presidency, he put to work his readings *and* his remembrances of things learned from his conversations with the leading thinkers of his era, and together they provided the foundation for his successful foreign policy. In my previously mentioned interview with Brinkley, he gave this perspective on how Roosevelt formulated and implemented his foreign policy: "TR knew the world so well because he had a mind like a map. He knew every country and their leader. He spoke foreign languages. He had the bully pulpit of the American presidency, and with the full power of America behind him, he'd go to countries and say, 'Let's talk. Let's solve this problem.'"[238]

In line with Brinkley's perception, in his book *The Warrior and the Priest: Woodrow Wilson and Theodore Roosevelt*, historian John Milton Cooper Jr. gave this explanation of why TR operated so successfully in global circles:

> When he entered the White House, his scholarship and relationships with such intellectuals as Henry and Brooks Adams and the naval strategist Captain Alfred Thayer Mahan acquainted him with the latest thinking on America's international role. As a result, he was much better prepared in foreign affairs than any of his predecessors since John Quincy Adams.... Reading and reflection instilled in him a keen appreciation of the balance of power in international affairs and of his country's vital stake in certain aspects of that balance.[239]

This constant inputting of new information gained from what he read and the company he kept put TR in a position not only to grasp and make decisions about the present, but also, as his biographer Kathleen Dalton observed in her book *Theodore Roosevelt: A Strenuous Life,* his "reading omnivorously from an early age and using what he read, allowed him to look *into the future* to give his country new direction."[240]

As an example of how TR's extensive knowledge came in handy in moving people toward his desired future result, Dalton recognized that his successful mediation of the conflict between Japan and Russia in 1905, for which he received the Nobel Peace Prize in 1906, came about in part because of his having an encyclopedic level of information about the participants.

> Roosevelt demonstrated exceptional diplomatic skill and openness to new cultures and peoples in the negotiations. Although Tokyo's diplomats knew he supported Asian immigration restriction, they did not encounter in TR a bigot with a closed mind. It also helped that he had studied Japanese history and culture. Because of his long-standing admiration for medieval Europe and its legends of chivalry, it was not surprising that Roosevelt was drawn to the inter-

> twined Japanese traditions of service, honor, and high principle, and admired the classic Japanese samurai story of the forty-seven ronins.[241]

Being a lifelong learner steeped in knowledge about a wide variety of subjects empowered TR to have the necessary facts and figures ammunition at hand for confronting the challenges he faced as president. Those who aspire to be successful leaders can reach new heights by following his three-step information absorption approach of reading/reflecting/writing to maximize the impact of knowledge gained from a commitment to lifetime learning.

Leadership Trait #2: Boldly Expand in New Directions by Refusing to Be Limited by Conventional Wisdom or Others' Past Practices

Before Theodore Roosevelt entered the Oval Office in 1901, no president had ever attempted to settle a national labor strike, break up a monopoly, make an integrated effort to preserve nature, apply law equally to the rich and the working poor, or assert America's power over world order—and he advanced these causes in many instances despite them being in conflict with the leaders of his own Republican Party. The reason TR's predecessors failed to pursue such initiatives was because of their perception that, except for Lincoln's expansion of presidential powers during the Civil War, *Congress* (*not* the president) should be the instrument for moving the needle in pursuing the nation's priorities. If Congress failed to make something happen, then it was not supposed to happen.

Soon after becoming president, Theodore Roosevelt made it clear he had bold new plans for what the nation's chief executive could and should do to make America better. Having had success in achieving what he set out to do by breaking new ground for the responsibilities of a New York State assemblyman, US Civil Service commissioner, New York City police commissioner, assistant secretary of the US Navy, colonel in the US Army, and governor of New York upon reaching the White House, he followed his lifetime pattern of expanding what a person in leadership could address during his time at the helm. The following examples demonstrate the success he had by using that trait:

A. Mediating the Great Coal Strike of 1902

In her book *Leadership in Turbulent Times,* Goodwin covered the four presidents of whom she had written prior biographies: Abraham Lincoln, Theodore Roosevelt, Franklin D. Roosevelt, and Lyndon B. Johnson. The last one-third of her book presented a case study of each of them during a crucial time in their presidency to "show how their leadership fit the historical moment as a key fits a lock." For TR, she chose the Great Coal Strike of 1902 because it was "emblematic of the widespread mood of rebellion among the laboring classes in the wake of the Industrial Revolution,"[242] and provided the best example of his crisis management skills and his willingness to grow presidential power to prevent what many predicted could be "the most widespread and bloody civil disturbance we have known in our time"[243] had he not brought the strike to an end when he did.

In a nutshell, the crisis arose when the 147,000 members of the United Mine Workers went on strike because of low wages in May 1902. The resulting shortage of coal soon caused prices to quadruple, and the working poor (who couldn't afford the high prices) began stealing coal off trains, and anywhere else they could find it, to heat their homes. Goodwin pointed out that TR knew that "neither legal nor historical precedent warranted presidential intervention to manage any single aspect of the crisis."[244]

After the negotiation stalemate between the miners and mine operators had gone on for months, and winter loomed, President Roosevelt invited the leaders of both groups to the White House. There, he quickly recognized that they would surely remain deadlocked for the foreseeable future, and only bold action *by him* had any chance of breaking the impasse. Per his biographer Louis Auchincloss, after consulting with esteemed lawyer Elihu Root (who was then his secretary of war), TR accepted Root's advice that under the common law and Constitution, as president, he *arguably* (though *not* definitely) had the power to take over the coal companies, based "on the principle that any peasant has the right to take wood that is not his if necessary for the preservation of life in winter weather."[245] President Roosevelt then advised the parties that "if an accord was not reached, he would order federal troops to take over and run the mines as a receivership."[246] This threat of government takeover was sufficiently frightening for the coal companies' owners to agree to binding arbitration of the dispute's pertinent issues. Getting the dispute into an arbitration resolution mode was enough for the miners to call off their strike and go back to work.

Settling the coal strike marked a demonstration of Roosevelt's preferred strategy as president for bending people to his will through hardball diplomacy, regardless of their party affiliation. From his reading, he had come across the West African proverb: "Speak softly and carry a big stick." It resonated with him because it aligned with an approach he had often voiced as the best way to deal with conflict: "Don't hit till you have to, but when you do hit, hit hard."[247]

Goodwin pointed out in her narrative of TR's crisis management skills during the coal strike that Roosevelt's deep knowledge of history encouraged his decision to enlarge presidential power. A president like James Buchanan, who fiddled while the issue of slavery expansion burned up the country in the years leading to the Civil War, habitually resolved every doubt about whether to exercise power "in favor of inaction against action."[248] A president like Abraham Lincoln—whom TR was fresh on in 1902, having just read Hay and Nicolay's ten-volume biography—considered himself "the steward of the people,"[249] believing he had the clear responsibility "to do whatever the needs of the people demand, unless the Constitution or the laws explicitly forbid him to do it."[250] Roosevelt knew that as president, he *always* wanted to be in the business of mirroring Lincoln, and had no doubt that Lincoln would have *acted* to bring an end to the coal strike.

The Great Coal Strike of 1902 presented a clear national emergency that would *not* have been successfully addressed unless President

Roosevelt broke new ground and injected himself into the middle of it. In the letter he sent to the leaders of both sides in the dispute, he explained the basis for his firm decision to get involved:

> But that the urgency and terrible nature of the catastrophe now impending over a large portion of our people, in the shape of a winter fuel famine, and the further fact that as this strike affected a necessity of life to so many of our people, so precedent in other strikes will be created, and now *impel* me, after much anxious thought, to believe that my duty *requires* me to see whether I cannot bring about an agreement.[251]

Once the strike ended, and sufficient coal started getting mined and sold to people before the severe winter weather began, an outpouring of praise came to TR because of his fearlessness in taking on a new challenge that was clearly well beyond the dictates of conventional wisdom and/or what his predecessors would have done. The *New York Sun* recognized his having established a new precedent in presidential leadership: "Never before has a President of the United States mediated the contentions of capital and labor."

Hay, then his secretary of state, saw that bringing an end to the strike through the strong-armed compulsion of binding arbitration—with the arbitration panel ultimately awarding the workers a retroactive 10 percent pay raise and a reduced workload from ten to nine hours a day—resulted in TR's "readjusting labor-capital relations at the psychological moment and winning enormous personal success, too."[252] His ending of the coal strike emboldened him to seek other new areas where he could assert power for the remainder of his presidency, repeatedly using his great diplomatic skills as a mediator in bringing warring parties to a truce, which will be expanded upon later in this chapter's Leadership Trait #3.

B. Busting Trusts Through Aggressive Prosecution Under the Sherman Act

Another demonstration of Theodore Roosevelt's expanding the power of the presidency beyond past practices came with his decision to bust the trusts that had achieved a monopolistic grip on the American economy to the detriment of consumers. A "trust" is an entity that owned stock in several companies in the same business. The trust managed the companies together, thereby creating a monopoly. Typically, the business leaders who controlled trusts were strong financial supporters of Republican candidates. When TR became president, 65 percent of the nation's wealth was owned by trusts. J. P. Morgan controlled a trust that dominated American railroads; John D. Rockefeller had one that controlled oil refining; and Andrew Carnegie's assemblage of companies controlled the steel industry.

Upon becoming president, it did not take TR long to realize that the Republican majorities in both Congressional houses were *never* going to pass laws to reduce the power of the trusts, since big business (a.k.a., the trusts) controlled most senators and key leaders in the House at the time. To think Congress would proactively take action to reduce trusts' power was beyond illusory. The only potentially successful way for the president to deal with the monopolies would have to be by TR's going around Congress and having his administration's Department of Justice prosecute trusts in the courts under the Sherman Anti-Trust Act. The Act had become law in 1890, though none of the prosecutions brought under it had succeeded to date.

Relying on his Attorney General Philander Knox's advice concerning the likely effect of changes in the justices on the Supreme Court, and also recognizing the country's growing anger over the imbalance in power between the haves and have-nots, TR authorized Knox in February 1902 to prosecute a Sherman Act claim against a railroad trust named the Northern Securities Company, ran by J. P. Morgan, E. H. Harriman, and James J. Hill, that controlled three of the nation's largest railroads.

Just as TR saw the futility in watching idly while miners unsuccessfully negotiated against the coal company operators in the Great Coal Strike of 1902, he could also see that waiting on Congress to address the inequities of a trust-dominated economy would be equally ineffectual. Not wanting to waste a minute in seeking to right the wrong, he turned Knox loose, and through brilliant lawyering, the Department of Justice prevailed over Northern Securities at every step of the litigation from the trial court through the Supreme Court, where victory finally came down in a 5–4 decision. Again, Roosevelt was not going to let past practices or "conventional wisdom" prevent him from doing what had to be done to protect the best interests of *all* the American people—*not* just the best interests of the business leaders who controlled the Republican Party—as Congress and TR's White House predecessors had been doing for too long.

C. Instigating a More Active Foreign Policy

Another area where Theodore Roosevelt broke new ground as president was in America's foreign policy. Once the Civil War ended in 1865, as the nation dealt with the loss of 750,000 wartime fatalities and 1.6 million casualties over the three and a half decades between the war's end and the century's end, one national conclusion was reached: Americans had no desire to fight another war. Despite the entrenched national preference for isolationism, as assistant secretary of the navy in 1898, Roosevelt was instrumental in persuading President William McKinley to engage American troops and ships in the Spanish-American War. TR believed that commencing the war effort was in the nation's best interest because of the need to remove Spain from its occupation of Cuba and allow it to be independent, as a start at revitalizing the Monroe Doctrine, which almost a century before had sought to minimize Europe's influence in the Western hemisphere.

Famously, TR used the Spanish-American War as an opportunity to gain the battlefield experience he had always craved. Resigning his position as the navy's assistant secretary, he joined the US Army and organized and trained the Rough Riders in San Antonio, Texas. After the training ended, he arrived with his men in Cuba, where he achieved fame and glory for his courageous charge at the Battle of Kettle Hill in San Juan Heights. Upon returning from the war, his heroics in Cuba immediately elevated his political stature such that he was soon elected governor of New York in November 1898, and then was chosen as McKinley's vice-presidential running mate in the 1900 election.

Taking office after McKinley's assassination, TR believed that the United States—and *not* Europe—should dominate the Western hemisphere. This could only be done if our navy was strengthened, so he wasted no time in making that happen. In furtherance of that goal, he then authored the Roosevelt Corollary to the Monroe Doctrine, which explained why the US needed to act as a police enforcer in our half of the world and thereby heighten America's influence in the international order. In the aforementioned interview, Brinkley summarized the strategy behind the Roosevelt Corollary.

> If the international situation interfered with his objective for the United States, then he threw the rulebooks out. He wanted the Panama Canal built so he supported the idea of creating the Republic of Panama, thereby stripping the land away from Colombia, and letting Panama declare itself as its own country. Then he supported the American take-over of a zone in the middle of Panama where the canal was ultimately located.
>
> In a modern day context, the United Nations would have frowned on this, but TR was willing to jeopardize international relations in order to advance America's interest.... If Theodore Roosevelt drew a red line and anyone crossed it, that was it. There would be consequences and everyone knew it. We were ready, willing, and able to head to war. He believed that if people around the world knew our position and our military

> strength, they wouldn't cross the red line because they knew the Big Stick would be coming after them.[253]

Implementing his Corollary with the "big stick" US Navy at the heart of it, TR discretely used warships and the threat of America's military force to put out fires in the Dominican Republic in 1904 (arising from the claims of the country's European creditors), Venezuela (which was on the verge of war with Great Britain and Germany over unpaid debts), Panama (which needed to extricate itself from the clutches of Colombia, and thereby open the door to the construction of the Panama Canal), and Uruguay (which could preserve itself only by staving off a conflict between Brazil and Argentina).

In his foreign policy, as with the Great Coal Strike and Sherman Act trust-busting through court enforcement (along with his vast expansion of national parks, forests, and wildlife refuges), TR had no fear of breaking ground on new initiatives well beyond any perceived limitations on presidential power imposed by all his predecessors not named Lincoln, and also beyond the "conventional wisdom" of his time. In summary, he grew the presidency either to address ignored or otherwise unfixable domestic problems in need of urgent attention or to pursue foreign policy objectives that enhanced America's position in the world.

Following Roosevelt's example, if a leader of an enterprise sees something wrong and harmful going on, knows it hasn't been addressed before, and surely won't be addressed by the status quo's forces in play, then he needs to take it upon himself to act boldly and promptly in pursuing new initiatives that have at least some chances of solving the problem. This approach will surely expand the domain of his influence by setting a precedent for engaging in new arenas that would otherwise have continued their downward spiral, *but for* the exercise of proactive innovative leadership.

Leadership Trait #3: Use Every Tool in the Diplomat's Toolkit to Avoid War

In the immortal words of General William Tecumseh Sherman, "War is hell. You cannot qualify war in harsher terms than I will. War is cruelty, and you cannot refine it. Those who brought war into our country deserve all the maledictions a people can pour out."[254]

With these words, Sherman spoke pure blunt wisdom, though as Abraham Lincoln attested in his annual message to Congress in December 1864, when intractable opposition arises, some issues are "distinct, simple, and inflexible, and can only be tried by war and decided by victory."[255] Thus, the keys to being a successful leader in the midst of escalating conflict are: (1) knowing which issues can be resolved through diplomacy and which can only be addressed by war, and (2) having such superior diplomatic skills that war can be avoided as much as possible.

Consistent with his extreme approach to all aspects of living, in response to his lifelong embarrassment over his father's cowardice in paying for a substitute to take his place in fighting for the Union Army during the Civil War, throughout the first half of his adult life, Theodore Roosevelt relished the idea of engaging in battlefield combat. His dream came true at thirty-nine when he pushed the Rough Riders to victory in the Spanish-American War. In what he called "the crowded hour," and "the greatest day of my life," he led his men in the charge up Kettle Hill, killed a Spaniard with his pistol, saw men killed all around him, and miraculously avoided being killed as bullets whizzed all around him.

On that fateful day, though he saw first-hand what war was, fortunately for him and his men, their battle did not last long and it ended in victory. The triumph left TR with a more favorable impression of war than was held by those (like Sherman) who had fought in protracted wars, spent long stretches of time in battles, and witnessed deaths by the thousands. The positive experience of leading and surviving the action on a Cuban battlefield on one glorious victorious day never left Roosevelt's consciousness. For the rest of his life, although he acknowledged that the jingoism of his earlier years had been chastened by seeing deaths in Cuba, he still yearned for the opportunity to engage in more mano a mano combat if a war arose after diplomatic efforts seeking a peaceful resolution failed. Post-presidency, at age fifty-eight, he begged President Woodrow Wilson to permit him to lead a new group of Rough Riders to fight the Germans in Europe during World War I. To his credit, Wilson prudently rejected TR's problematic offer to serve.[256]

It is necessary to grasp Roosevelt's thirst for battlefield combat to appreciate that many of his greatest successes as president involved his using diplomacy to *avoid* war. Dalton determined that "*self-control* was the key to his presidency."[257] It allowed him to make the right choice as to "when to stand on principle and when to seek compromise in order to steer his country in a consistent direction."[258] Despite being a person whose preferred kneejerk response to conflict was belligerence, he consistently succeeded in stifling that impulse to commit his focus and energy on diplomacy. That fact demonstrates the high level of TR's powers of self-control.

Being a successful diplomatic mediator[iii] who negotiates compromise and achieves resolution between adverse parties requires a focused peacemaking temperament that communicates the best possible words and body language in an impactful tone to move the sides toward the point of settlement. Per that overview, the essential features in TR's success as a mediator, in Dalton's words, were that he "*took command* of the discussions without tact," and talked *and listened* to the parties until he located their "common ground."[259]

Goodwin agreed with Dalton's conclusions, saying, in her book *The Bully Pulpit,* that such talking *and* listening amidst parties at odds required TR as mediator to have "unusual powers of concentration, a rich cadre of ideas, and ruthless single mindedness," along with

iii As a commercial litigator in Dallas for more than four decades, I have served as a mediator in hundreds of cases, as well as represented parties in hundreds of lawsuits settled by other mediators. Thus, the comments made herein about what made TR such a successful mediator come from my first-hand experience in mediations which confirms that the tactics used by TR in his mediations are consistent with best practices in dispute resolution.

"warmth, unabashed intensity, and pluck of personality," all of which blended together and moved people to the goal line of resolution.[260]

Hay, TR's secretary of state, identified another essential trait in his boss's toolkit that fueled his success as a mediator: "the power to seize the psychological moment."[261] In negotiations, like almost every other activity in life, timing is crucial to success. Philosopher Carlos Castaneda described the "psychological moment" of perfect timing to act with maximum successful impact as occurring when "the cubic centimeter of chance pops out in front of one's eyes, and the leader *moves on it* because he is alert, and has the necessary speed and prowess to pick it up."[262] TR always knew *when* to move forward and *close* on a settlement in his mediations, as proven by his high success rate in getting his many challenging negotiations to close with a binding resolution.

Morris added another necessary trait possessed by Theodore Roosevelt that brought adverse parties into alignment in his mediations: his fearless and unyielding tenacity. In his book on TR's presidency, *Theodore Rex,* Morris quoted a well-known essay from a leading French commentator of his era, Leon Bazalgette, who recognized these essential traits in Roosevelt's diplomatic personality:

> He has only one limiting and devouring ambition, which is to move and convince. He has too much to say not to dispense altogether with artifices of style, too much faith and force to need anything else. He is a workman who puts the best of his energy into driving rivets. He *hammers out* understandings.[263]

With all these traits in play, using them as needed depending on who he attempted to persuade and what was happening in the negotiation, TR mediated with success through his diplomatic interventions into the Great Coal Strike of 1902; the end of the Russo-Japanese War in 1905; the Moroccan crisis (settled under the terms of a treaty signed at the Algeciras Conference of 1906 that brought Germany, France, Austria-Hungary, and Great Britain together on the issue of how Morocco should be policed); and at the Second Hague Conference in 1907 where, in Dalton's words, he "helped to make a voluntary Court of International Justice 'an operative force in history.'"[264] These major league achievements were brought about by a consummate Nobel Peace Prize–winning diplomat with the self-control and wisdom to resist the temptation to pursue warfare (and the hell that goes with it) and instead make peace by moving adverse parties to a successful negotiated compromise.

Those who lead organizations *know* that conflict is inevitable and arises often. It may be internal conflict among company personnel or external conflict with competitors or government entities. Prudent leaders address it quickly and decisively (or tries to "nip it in the bud") before it escalates into major disruption and/or litigation (i.e., lawsuits are the businessperson's war and the hell that goes with it). To put conflict into a mode of prompt resolution, the leader will have greater success if he prioritizes becoming a proactive mediator as soon as the conflict arises, and attempts to incorporate Theodore Roosevelt's previously described diplomatic traits into his own personal style of negotiation.

Theodore Roosevelt's Flaws

This section on the flaws of Theodore Roosevelt is somewhat longer than in this book's other chapters. There is a reason. There is *much* to learn about effective leadership not only by following other leaders' best traits but also by avoiding their worst traits. Thus, TR's flaws described in detail below should be given strong consideration by all who attempt to lead an organization.

Roosevelt's first major flaw that presents an instructive lesson for leaders was his lack of respect for the constitutional imperative of an independent judiciary guided by the rule of law to preside over society's disputes. This attitude of disdain for laws passed by legislators and cases addressed by the judicial system on occasion made him lose his moral bearings, causing him to fly off the rails after his presidency ended.

His ill-fated relationship with the law began when he dropped out of Columbia Law School as a young man because it seemed to him that those in the business of administering the law were more interested in following precedent than achieving justice. Later, as a federal civil service commissioner, New York police commissioner, and president of the United States—so, when he served in positions where *he* got to call the shots without any type of legal or judicial interference— Roosevelt operated from the vainglorious perspective that in his perfect world, justice was justice "because I did it."[265] Brinkley described Roosevelt's joy in creating desired results outside of legislative chambers and courtrooms when he described TR's creating legislation *instantly* to protect wildlife refuges during his presidency:

> [In a meeting with his advisers] Roosevelt asked, "Is there any law that will prevent me from declaring Pelican Island a Federal Bird Reservation?" The answer was a decided "No," the island, after all, *was*, federal property. "Very well then," Roosevelt said with marvelous quickness. "I Do Declare It."[266]

As president, however, when forced to operate *outside* the international mediation and wilderness preservation arenas where he had absolute power, TR often found himself frustrated by laws, rules, and statutes that restricted what he wanted to do, and vigilant lawyers and judges were always in place to make sure he obeyed them. His frequent bristling over laws, which slowed his progress, led esteemed Supreme Court Justice Oliver Wendell Holmes to conclude that President Roosevelt "didn't give a damn about the law."[267]

In fact, TR's preference was for a *dependent* judiciary who believed justice served its highest good when administered in accordance with *his* personal vision. In his biography of TR, Auchincloss pointed out that his subject expected any judge he appointed to do his best to carry out the spirit of the law *as interpreted by the party in power*, and his idea of a great constitutional lawyer was one who always agreed with him.[268]

Like most presidents, during his White House years, Roosevelt wanted federal courts to rule and the Constitution to be interpreted one way—his way. However, with an attitude *unlike* most presidents, when judges saw issues differently than he did, TR believed they were purposefully betraying his trust. Small wonder that after leaving the White House, as judgments and appellate opinions got rendered by various courts at odds with his desires, Roosevelt attempted to persuade the American electorate to vote for the repeal of those errant decisions and for the immediate removal from the bench of the judges who had authored the opinions. Fortunately, his crazed pitch for personal power over the rule of law was rejected by the American people, who took their cues on the issue from the leading constitutional lawyers and judges of the era.

Beyond his disrespect for laws and independent courts, an even greater flaw in TR arose from the fact that although his non-stop electric nature produced a steady stream of achievements, drama, and exhilaration, they also became so intoxicating that he lost his bearings because of his (1) belief in his personal infallibility and (2) presumably being spurred on by his lifelong frequently stated fear that (like his father), he would die at a young age. His staying constantly ramped up in a mode of passionate pursuits created such an exhausting lifestyle that it resulted in his self-destructing mentally, physically, morally, and prematurely after he left the White House, which led to the fulfillment of his fear of dying prematurely.

Upon completing his presidency at age fifty, TR had had a remarkable life, center stage, "in the arena,"[iv] as an East Coast scholar, Wild West cowboy, acclaimed naturalist, war hero, youngest presi-

iv A year after his presidency ended, at the Sorbonne in Paris, TR gave a famous speech where he praised "the man in the arena" (i.e., he praised himself), railing against critics who judge from the sidelines, and praising "the man who is actually in the arena, whose face is marred by dust and sweat and blood; who strives valiantly; who errs, who comes short again and again, because there is no effort without error and shortcoming; but who does actually strive to do the deeds; who knows great enthusiasms, the great devotions; who spends himself in a worthy cause; who at the best knows in the end the triumph of high achievement, and who at the worst, if he fails, at least fails while daring greatly, so that his place shall never be with those cold and timid souls who neither know victory nor defeat."

dent in American history, instigator of the Panama Canal, supreme mediator peacemaker, trust buster, resurrector, and expander of the Monroe Doctrine, champion of America's mighty navy *and* its national park and wildlife refuge system, and author of thirty-five largely acclaimed books.

And yet ... and yet ... after leaving the White House, for the remaining decade of his life, the prior glory and popularity TR had earned at home and abroad during his presidency went to his head, such that his outrageously egotistical comment upon leaving office became a self-fulfilling prophecy: "No man in American public life has ever reached the crest of the wave as I appear to have done without the wave's breaking and engulfing him."[269] With each successive year after his time in the Oval Office ended, his conduct became more problematic and progressively strange. Because of that, the waves inevitably broke and engulfed him into a personal decline that led to his early death.

In his book *The Wilderness Warrior*, Brinkley endorsed Johns Hopkins professor of psychiatry Dr. Kay Jamison's assessment of Theodore Roosevelt, which appeared in her book *Exuberance: The Passion for Life*.[270] Jamison presented TR as the poster child for both the bright and the dark sides of those with an exuberant personality, and her descriptions squared with Roosevelt's peaks in the White House and valleys post-presidency.[271]

According to Jamison, people with manic-depressive illness are more likely to be impulsive, utterly certain of their convictions, and susceptible to dangerous rushes of adrenaline. Although manic thought typically travels in a straight line when it first turns on, it later changes into chaotic thought as the mania progresses.[272] Rapid talking, marked by intentionally clicking one's teeth, biting off syllables with fervor, pounding a fist while making points, and consistently dominating (yes, hogging) conversations are traits of a manic personality, and all of them were characteristic of Roosevelt's verbal communications throughout his adult life.

Brinkley accurately summarized Jamison's findings on the exuberant manic-depression mindset as it applied to TR's personality, and how it led to his post-presidency decline:

> Roosevelt is Exhibit A for this condition. His set of symptoms—propulsive behavior, deep grief, chronic insomnia, and an all-around hyperactive disposition—demonstrate both the manic and the depressive phases of bipolar disorder. Too often, Jamison argued, people mistakenly thought manic depression meant despondence and withdrawal from human endeavors. Usually it does. But those afflicted with *exuberance*, she argued, go in the opposite direction; behaving as relentless human blowtorches who are unable to turn down their own flame. Diagnosing Roosevelt's medical condition more than eighty years after his death, Jamison claimed that the highs of the exuberance phase brought many wonderful gifts; but, she warned, there was also a sharp-edged downside. Living by throwing up skyrockets—as P.T. Barnum once put it—wore TR down to nothing. No sleep, for example, wasn't good for the heart or other vital organs. Only by exhausting oneself in physical activity—like climbing Mount Katahdin or ice skating on the Charles River in a winter storm—could allow an exuberant manic like Roosevelt to finally turn himself off.[273]

Early in his first TR biography, *The Rise of Theodore Roosevelt,* Morris provided a prophetic quote from novelist Henry James, in which James referred to Roosevelt as "a wonderful little machine that performs astonishingly, but is likely destined to be overstrained."[274] Morris later reaffirmed Adams' prophecy in his next book, *Theodore Rex,* with the same metaphor offered more than a decade later during TR's White House years. This time, the assessment of the downside of excessive exuberance came from the words of Irving Fisher, a fitness and nutritional expert of the era: "It is clear to me that the president is running his machine too hard.... In another decade or two...I would almost risk my reputation as a prophet in predicting that he will find friction in the machine, which will probably increase to almost the stopping point."[275]

In providing a compelling lesson for all who aspire to spend maximum time "in the arena," the life of TR can be compared to the finest Mercedes-Benz being steered by a brilliant but mad scientist, who is obsessed with keeping the gas pedal floored at all times, as the manic driver exhilarates in his own amazing achievement at navigating the glitzy car on a dizzying high-speed ride...for a while. But then the vehicle starts showing telltale signs of malfunction from being overused and abused, until it finally either crashes and burns or else collapses in a heap, long before the warranty period ends.

Yes, TR's life had a rise and a fall, both equally dramatic. His post-presidency decline manifested itself in a myriad of disturbing ways that surely accelerated the shortening of his life in accordance with his lifetime fear. Morris and others have described the following examples of TR as a man who lost control of himself in his final years:

- He stuffed himself three times a day with huge meals (his breakfast typically consisted of eating twelve fried eggs and drinking a gallon of coffee) and gained considerable weight.
- After being shot in the chest by an assassin in October 1912 while campaigning for president as the Bull Moose nominee, he insisted on giving a speech which lasted eighty minutes as blood flowed through his shirt and the right side of his body turned black. Morris riffed on Roosevelt's bizarre reaction to being shot, to the effect that TR's conduct in the immediate aftermath of the assassination attempt, one month before election day, was a statement to the voting public of the sincerity of his religious political movement: "This is my body, this is my blood. The mock-religious aura that had glowed around Roosevelt since he first stood at Armageddon had reached its grotesque climax."[276]

- Overweight and out of shape, Roosevelt took an extended trip to South America in 1914, where he nonchalantly confronted piranhas, anacondas, blood-sucking bats, and bloodthirsty pium flies, before contracting malaria, from which he never fully recovered.
- He repeatedly and publicly called President Wilson a "coward" for his delay in ordering American military forces to engage with our European allies in World War I.[277]
- When Wilson finally committed the United States to the war, though TR was sickly, tired, and old beyond his years at fifty-eight, he begged the president to allow him to organize a new regiment of Rough Riders to engage in battle on the European front.[278]
- When Wilson refused his offer to fight, Roosevelt pulled all his political and military strings to get his four sons onto the front lines of battle—where two were seriously wounded and his youngest son, Quentin, was killed. Auchincloss concluded that Roosevelt's efforts as an ill and elderly man to get to the trenches and have his sons rushed to the front lines of battle in World War I demonstrated his severe cognitive decline.[279]
- On the day he learned of Quentin's death, Roosevelt insisted on fulfilling a commitment later that day to give a speech to the New York State Republican Convention.

On Christmas Eve of 1918, knowing his days were numbered, Theodore Roosevelt told his sister Corinne that he had "kept the promise that I made to myself when I was twenty-one.... I promised myself that I would work *up to the hilt* until I was sixty, and I have done it."[280] Thirteen days later, he died, and his death certificate stated the cause of death as "an embolism of the lung, with multiple arthritis as a contributory factor," though in his third and final biography, *Colonel Roosevelt,* Morris strongly suggested that what really killed him was a broken heart caused by six months of deep grieving over the death of Quentin.[281]

Personal Application

Hopefully, the vivid depiction of Theodore Roosevelt's downward spiral/early collapse post-presidency presented in the "Flaws" section of this chapter has *not* sucked all the air out of the room, such that you can still place high value on TR's three dominant leadership traits as he used them to great effect during his presidency. Assuming that is the case, here are questions for consideration by those who want to evaluate themselves in the areas of lifelong learning, innovative channeling of leadership into important new areas previously unexplored, and timely effective diplomacy/dispute resolution.

You now know how Theodore Roosevelt would have answered the following questions. How do *you* answer them?

- In a typical year, how many books do you read aimed at understanding today's world affairs or the human condition? Do you always have a book going that you believe will truly advance your knowledge and consciousness?
- From how many sources do you follow the news each day?
- What do you do to retain what you read after you finish reading it?
- Do you have a circle of friends who often probe and advance your knowledge base?
- Do your social conversations focus more on ideas, subjects, or people?
- Do you frequently attend lectures (either in person or virtually) where you listen to experts speak on subjects of interest to you?
- What new subjects have you explored deeply in the last five years?
- Do you at least sometimes make time to write about what you've read?

- When you want to go deep to learn about a new subject, do you block out all distractions so you can give your full attention to it?
- When evaluating the areas of attention on which you should be focused in your leadership efforts, how much are you influenced by how your predecessors addressed these areas or how your peers look at these areas?
- Have you ever redirected your leadership efforts to address an unmet need that was ignored by your predecessors?
- If your predecessors in leadership failed to address a problem, does that inspire you to take it on as your personal responsibility?
- Is there an opportunity in your industry that to date your organization has largely ignored, but you believe has great potential for exploration and development? If so, do you have the tools you need to explore and develop that new avenue of opportunity?
- What are you doing to expand your turf?
- In the course of your time in leadership, how many times have you implemented a major new change in direction and/or initiative?
- When conflict arises in your organization, are you among the first to recognize it? When it does, how long do you let it fester, thinking it will somehow resolve itself without your assistance?
- When people are at loggerheads in your enterprise, do you intervene promptly and act as mediator?
- When it's time to negotiate or mediate conflict in your enterprise, do you bring a "big stick" to the table?

- What do you regard as your best traits as a mediator? How do they match up with Theodore Roosevelt's mediation talents described in this chapter?
- Do you take command of the conversations during mediation?
- Do you have an intuitive awareness of the "psychological moment" "cubic centimeter of chance" that kicks you into high gear when parties at odds are most likely to move forward and achieve closure on resolution?
- Do you give high priority to doing everything in your power to prevent conflict escalation?
- Do you understand why protracted litigation (the business-person's war) needs to be avoided, if possible?

May your having a deeper understanding of Theodore Roosevelt's three most important leadership traits covered in this chapter, your answers to the foregoing questions tied to these traits, and your awareness of his flaws give you greater success in leading an organization to new heights.

CHAPTER FIVE

HOW TO STARE DOWN ADVERSITY AND COMMAND PUBLIC SENTIMENT—LIKE FRANKLIN D. ROOSEVELT

With every changing of the guard at the White House, the last several C-SPAN presidential ranking polls have shown that when the time comes for leading historians to rank performance, Abraham Lincoln stands tall at the top of the list, and below Father Abraham are George Washington and Franklin D. Roosevelt (FDR), neck-and-neck, who battle for second and third place.

Each of the Big Three is recognized as the greatest American leader of his century. Washington led the country for two full terms from 1789–1797; Lincoln for one term and a month into his second term (until his assassination) from 1861–1865; and FDR for three terms and three months into his fourth term (until his death) from 1933–1945. We can all hope that a leader of their stature enters the Oval Office sometime in the twenty-first century—and the sooner the better.

Whereas Washington unified the thirteen colonies and set scores of sound precedents in moving the new nation forward at its inception; and Lincoln persevered as commander-in-chief to win the Civil War, thereby reuniting the United States, and in the process eliminated slavery; Franklin Roosevelt made his mark by leading the country through the Great Depression and most of World War II, while changing the size and role of government. FDR's New Deal programs attacked the Great Depression and advanced the social policy of the welfare state,[i] to the effect that our federal government would henceforth have the *duty* to provide aid to the hungry, jobless, and those with other dire needs.

Roosevelt wanted America's "forgotten" downtrodden people to navigate life feeling the support of their government, in hopes it would deliver to them two of the Four Freedoms he identified in his Third Inaugural Address: Freedom from Want and Freedom from Fear.[ii] To him, these freedoms could only be guaranteed by the government, and FDR supported his conclusion by saying that the New Deal "is as old as Christian ethics, for basically its ethics are the same. It recognizes that man is indeed his brother's keeper, insists the laborer is worthy of his hire, and demands that justice shall rule the mighty as well as the weak."[282]

---

i To make sure there is no misunderstanding about what the term means and how it's being used, this author relies on the Cambridge Dictionary, which defines "welfare state" as "a system paid for by taxes that allows the government of a country to provide social services such as healthcare, unemployment benefits, etc., to people who need them."

ii His other two "Freedoms" mentioned in the January 6, 1941 address: Freedom of Speech and Freedom of Worship.

Although Franklin Roosevelt's New Deal helped millions of down-and-out Americans get back on their feet, it did not restore the country to its pre-Depression levels of economic opportunity and low unemployment. Only the massive industrial buildup effectuated under FDR's insistent eye, driven by the need to increase the American war machine as World War II brought it into service, finally lifted the country out of its hard times and back to prosperity.[iii,283]

Regardless of FDR's inability to achieve all his domestic goals, once the war ended in victory four months after his death, the enlarged size and newly assumed duties of the federal government became locked into place for all time, for better or worse, which likely would not have happened but for Franklin Roosevelt's leadership.

Leadership Trait #1:
Fearlessly Stare Down Adversity to Inspire One's Constituents to Do the Same

What makes Franklin D. Roosevelt unique compared to every other president in American history is that he elevated himself to the country's most powerful leadership position, and then held it longer than anyone else, by overcoming the devastating setback of contracting the polio virus at thirty-nine, which caused him to lose the use of his legs for the last twenty-four years of his life. Despite the daily challenge of navigating his busy schedule with legs that could not support him, in time, he managed to regain and even enhance his political career's momentum, finally achieving his lifelong ambition to follow

iii To show how much the United States' military escalation invigorated the American economy in 1941, defense spending constituted 5.08 percent of America's GDP. By 1945, it constituted 37.19 percent of the GDP.

The 1940 GDP figures are from Louis Johnston and Samuel H. Williamson, "The Annual Real and Nominal GDP for the United States, 1789–Present," Economic History Services, March 2004. The 1945 GDP figure was calculated using the Bureau of Labor Statistics' "CPI Inflation Calculator," available at http://data.bls.gov/cgi-bin/cpicalc.pl. Defense spending figures are from Government Printing Office, "Budget of the United States Government: Historical Tables Fiscal Year 2005." See: 1940 GDP figure from Louis Johnston and Samuel H. Williamson, "The Annual Real and Nominal GDP for the United States, 1789–Present," Economic History Services, March 2004.

in his cousin Theodore Roosevelt's footsteps and serve as president of the United States. Once in the White House, *seemingly* unaffected by polio, he led the country with a Big Three elite level of distinction through two of its watershed events.

A. FDR's Initial Response to Polio

When physically vigorous, Franklin D. Roosevelt first learned he had contracted the crippling virus one year after he had been the vice presidential nominee on the Democratic ticket that lost to Warren G. Harding in the 1920 election.[iv] He was surely internally fearful of what the future held, though what he felt on the inside was *never* shown on the outside.[284] His private fear was not just tied to having to manage his life going forward with legs that no longer worked, but also his awareness that many Americans of his era mistakenly believed that polio adversely impacted the mind as well as the body.[285] Such a false conclusion could surely be devastating to a man who planned to spend the rest of his life running for top political positions no matter what his condition was.

Despite FDR's private reaction to the life-changing news, his wife, Eleanor, described his outward response: "His reaction was completely calm. His reaction to almost any great event was to be calm. If it was something that was bad, he just became almost like an iceberg and there was never the slightest emotion that was allowed to show."[286]

For the rest of his life, from time to time, FDR confided to his cousin and "closest companion" Margaret "Daisy" Suckley and a few others about the frustration and agony of dealing with lifeless legs,[v,287]

---

iv FDR's running mate, the Democrats' nominee for president in 1920, was Ohio governor James M. Cox.

v In a small gathering at the White House one night, FDR told Senator George Norris, "George, I am chained to this chair from morning till night.... You sit in your chair in your office too, but if something goes wrong or you get irritated or tired, you can get up and walk around.... I can't, I am tied down to this chair day after day, week after week, and month after month. And I can't stand it any longer. I can't go on with it." After that bit of private venting, the next day FDR was back to being his cheerful, driven self, seemingly oblivious to polio's impact on him. See: Doris Kearns Goodwin, *No Ordinary Time: Franklin and Eleanor Roosevelt: The Home Front in World War II* (Simon & Schuster 1994), 107.

but by the time he reached the White House in March 1933, any brief private feelings of fear over the prospect of living with polio were long gone, having served with it seamlessly during his powerhouse run as governor of New York from January 1, 1929 to January 1, 1933, and throughout his successful campaign for president in 1932.

In the seven years after he contracted the virus in 1921, FDR gradually accepted the fact that he would never be able to walk again without the aid of leg braces, a cane, and the uplifting support of another person. To get around without appearing to be an invalid, Roosevelt came up with a plan. His movement from place to place would occur in a dining room chair mounted on small wheels so it would not look like the standard bulky wheelchair used by everyone else with walking issues in those days (that had front wheels as big as bicycle tires). Upon entering a room, to remove all evidence of his disability, he would immediately be lifted from the wheeled chair onto a household or office chair with no wheels.[288]

When required to move short distances to reach a nearby destination without using his wheelchair, his valet would strap ten-pound metal braces onto FDR's legs, and he could then stand by holding on to someone and something (usually a cane).[289] To move forward in an apparent "walk," he leaned on his cane, gripped the arm of a strong person (usually one of his sons), and then would swing first one rigid leg forward and then the other by using his torso.[290] After putting down his cane and releasing his colleague's rigid arm support after the brief "walk," he would then grasp the lectern lightly (to prevent falling down) as he gave his speeches.[291] A rare exception to his practice of avoiding attention to his polio was during World War II when he approved of being rolled around military hospitals so wounded soldiers with lost limbs could see and think, "If President Roosevelt can do it, so can I!"[292]

In private, soon after polio hit, FDR aggressively exercised the top half of his frame to have the strength to effectuate his "walk" and assist his valets in shifting himself from his wheelchair to a regular chair and then later back to his wheelchair.[293] This necessary regimen aimed at building up his body above the waist had a side benefit. In photographs and newsreels, when sitting behind a desk, his robust arms and broad shoulders sent a clear message: This is a strong man.[294]

To enhance the effect of his command presence, Roosevelt made sure there were plenty of action photos taken of him while at the helm of his boat sailing in choppy waters and when catching large fish on his many excursions at sea.[vi,295,296] Unlike the public presentations of most "polios" (or sad victims of the virus), FDR projected himself to the world as a robust, eternally optimistic, and cheerful man—always smiling, eyes sparkling, cigarette holder tilted upward—a man who gave every appearance of having the world by the tail.[297]

As New York's governor for four years, despite his limited mobility, FDR demonstrated high energy and stamina, and performed all aspects of the job in a manner that earned him widespread acclaim.[298] He also cultivated a great relationship with the press corps to the extent they agreed not to photograph him when he was being moved around in his custom-made wheelchair.[299]

Having done all these things that allowed him to be the best possible political leader he could be (handicapped or not), first in New York and then as president, he stayed in a mode of beaming his contagious optimism while fearlessly taking on the challenge of turning the country around from the Great Depression and then leading it in World War II. With this effective approach in place that successfully minimized the appearance of his polio, Franklin D. Roosevelt embarked on what turned out to be a twelve-and-a-half-year run as president without *ever* letting most Americans grasp the extreme physical and logistical problems that he dealt with daily.

---

vi His biographer Robert Dallek reported that on a fishing trip in a whaleboat in 1935, FDR caught two sailfish weighing 119 and 134 pounds, and his battle to bring in the latter lasted almost two and a half hours. See: Robert Dallek, *Franklin D. Roosevelt: A Political Life* (Penguin Books 2018), 236.

B. FDR's Ultimate Response to Polio

Geoffrey Ward wrote the screenplay for Ken Burns's documentary *The Roosevelts: An Intimate History*. He also authored the coffee table book that accompanied the film,[vii] and has written three other books on FDR, one of which was a Pulitzer finalist. Ward has a special connection to his subject: he's lived most of his life with polio. When I interviewed him for my book *Cross-Examining History*, he provided unique insight on how polio affected Franklin D. Roosevelt in the White House:

> If you're going to understand Roosevelt, you've got to understand that when he wanted a glass of water, he had to find someone to get it for him; and if he wanted to pee in the Oval Office, somebody had to bring him a bottle. He was unable to dress himself. Polio affected every hour of every day. What he had was a serene sense of himself that polio could not diminish. Therein lies the great mystery. I've spent most of my life trying to figure out how the hell he maintained such serene self-confidence through it all, and stayed good-humored, and seemingly ready for anything, and I still don't know how he did it.[300]

Other leading Roosevelt biographers have marveled at their subject's stoic response to polio with the same awe and wonder as Ward. James MacGregor Burns drilled down on FDR's *refusal* to let polio be a hindrance while keeping a smile on his face.[301] Dallek said the president "*never conceded* to disability, and wore it with *nonchalance*."[302] Jean Edward Smith quoted broadcaster Ed Hill, who, upon witnessing FDR move around at the start of his first term, observed the new president's inspirational impact on the country: "If this man had the courage to lift himself by sheer willpower from the bed of invalidism, and

---

vii Ward has also written the screenplay and companion books for many of Burns' other notable films including *The Civil War, Baseball, Jazz, The War* (about World War II), and *The Vietnam War*.

had the determination and patience to make himself 'walk,' then he *must* have within him the qualities to lead the nation to recovery."[303]

Not only did Franklin Roosevelt find a way to win every election he entered after his legs became dysfunctional, he actually *used* his emotional response to polio to develop personality virtues he never had before. In his biography, Dallek used Frances Perkins'[viii] experience to describe the impression FDR typically made on others in his pre-polio years:

> Frances Perkins met him in 1910 at a party on the east side of Manhattan. She remembered that "there was nothing particularly interesting about the tall, thin young man with the high collar and pince-nez." She encountered him again the following year in Albany, where she was a social worker representing the Consumers' League. He impressed her then as "a supercilious snob who really didn't like people very much.... He had a youthful lack of humility, a streak of self righteousness, and a deafness to the hopes, fears, and aspirations which are the common lot." She saw him as an "awful arrogant fellow." Roosevelt told her years later, "You know, I was an awfully mean cuss when I first went into politics."[304]

Later, as he recovered from the "storm" of polio, FDR's personality changed for the better. Historian James Tobin wrote an entire book on Roosevelt's battle with the virus entitled *The Man He Became: How FDR Defied Polio to Win the Presidency*. In my interview with him for *Cross-Examining History*, Tobin summarized how the disability caused Roosevelt to become a more effective political leader:

> Before polio, FDR had a golden family background, the greatest name in American politics, a Harvard education, and success in politics and government. What he

viii Perkins later became the first female to serve in a presidential Cabinet, as FDR's Secretary of Labor for his entire presidency.

> didn't have was any kind of a common touch. What he could do in coming back from this terrible, devastating illness, was be someone who had had great difficulty and then surmounted it. His recovery from polio allowed him to present himself as a man of the people in a way he never could have done before.[305]

In addition to Tobin's assessments, Ward concluded that FDR's battle with polio gave him more patience and empathy.[306] Goodwin's work on her Pulitzer-winning FDR/Eleanor book *No Ordinary Time* led her to believe that his response to polio expanded his mind, sensibilities, concentration, humility, sympathy, and understanding.[307] Dallek quoted psychologist Alfred Adler for the proposition that defying polio "heightened FDR's optimism" because dealing with it brought on consistent "expectations of great triumph," which he usually fulfilled.[308] Eleanor Roosevelt said it best: "His paralysis taught Franklin what suffering meant, and it changed his voice and made it warmer. It melted listeners with its sincerity."[309]

Having the trait of facing major adversity with a positive attitude communicates in no uncertain terms that a leader possesses a sense of *total fearlessness*, and, therefore, real courage. In the words of Nelson Mandela, "Courage is *not* the absence of fear, but the triumph over it. The brave man is not he who does not feel afraid, but he who conquers that fear."[310]

This mindset of courageous unshakeability allows a leader to be a force for calming frightened constituents in times of trial and leads them to believe that the looming challenge they'll face together with their leader *will* be overcome. Eleanor again said it best about how her husband's ultimate lack of fear about his polio elevated the power of his leadership in her book *You Learn By Living*:

> You gain strength, courage, and confidence by every experience in which you really stop to look fear in the face. You are able to say to yourself, "I have lived

> through this horror. I can take the next thing that comes along." You must do the thing you cannot do.[311]

FDR confirmed Eleanor's thought in a conversation with one of his assistants during his presidency. The aide believed his boss's stated plan on some issue was impossibly audacious, and told him abruptly "You can't do that!" With a twinkle in his eye, FDR firmly replied, "I've done a lot of things I can't do."[312]

Leadership Trait #2:
Keep One's Finger on the Pulse of Constituents, and Never Get More than One Step Ahead of Them When It's Time to Change Their Opinions

When a leader loses the capacity to move his followers in the direction that he wants them to go, he stops being a leader. In politics, a candidate who cannot attract sufficient voters to win an election loses his right to lead in the future and soon gets pushed out to pasture.

Winning elections was Franklin D. Roosevelt's favorite sport. Burns observed in his book, *Roosevelt: The Lion and the Fox*, that when it came time to run for office, FDR "tried to win the election, *not* lay out a coherent philosophy of government. He had no such philosophy, but he knew how to pick up votes."[313] His willingness to change his position on issues to attract more voters caused Herbert Hoover to label Roosevelt as "a chameleon on plaid."[314]

He won four presidential elections decisively. In 1932, FDR received 81.36 percent of the electoral votes to unseat Hoover; in 1936, 98.49 percent in an unprecedented landslide that buried Alf Landon; in 1940, 84.56 percent that clobbered Wendell Willkie; and in 1944, when everyone *knew* they were voting for a dead man walking, 81.36 percent went his way in a dominant victory over Thomas Dewey.[ix]

---

ix In the four elections, his share of the popular vote was 57.4 percent in 1932, 60.8 percent in 1936, 54.4 percent in 1940, and 53.4 percent in 1944.

To win national elections for the right to lead huddled masses through the pitfalls of the Great Depression and then inspire those same people to go overseas and fight in a second world war at a time when many regarded America's participation in World War I as a mistake was a "Herculean task" greater than any undertaken by a president in our history. FDR not only took on the double-barreled task, he *loved* doing it because of his deep affection for the American people.

A. The Importance of a Leader's Knowing and Aligning Himself with Public Sentiment

Although Franklin D. Roosevelt's greatest political hero was his cousin Theodore, one of the main reasons he had so much success and made so few missteps throughout his White House years was because of his being a dedicated disciple of Abraham Lincoln. On the *necessity* for there being a steel chain connection between (1) a successful leader's sensibility to the needs of his constituents and (2) the ever-changing opinions of those he leads, Honest Abe weighed in on the subject at Ottawa, Illinois in 1858, in a debate with Stephen Douglas:

> Public sentiment is *everything*. With public sentiment, nothing can fail; without it, nothing can succeed. Consequently, *he* who moulds public sentiment goes deeper than he who enacts statutes or pronounces decisions. *He* makes statutes and decisions possible or impossible to be executed.[315]

In 1932, most Americans believed President Herbert Hoover had just not done enough to aid the poverty-stricken masses after the roof fell in on Black Tuesday, October 29, 1929. As the non-incumbent candidate, FDR promised that if elected, he would take prompt bold vigorous government action to arrest the downward economic spiral that paralyzed the country. Not surprisingly, Roosevelt annihilated Hoover on Election Day.

Upon taking office, the big question that had no clear answer was: Exactly what actions would the new president take to breathe life into the country? No pre-Hoover president had ever had to reckon with the levels of national unemployment, hunger, and poverty like FDR confronted when he took the oath on March 4, 1933. At that time, 25 percent of Americans (15 million people) were unemployed, with many so hopeless about their job prospects that they had stopped looking for work.[316] The efforts by Hoover, private enterprise, and charities to address the fallout had failed to make even a small dent in the situation.

As New York's governor throughout Hoover's presidency, before any other state's chief executive took action, FDR led the Empire State's government into an all-out effort to provide relief for his constituents. He achieved a measure of success in restoring hope for better days ahead.[317] What had worked in New York, however, could not be duplicated on a national scale to elevate the entire country with its hundreds of diverse raging needs. For the first time since the nation's founding, America's ideals of self-determination and rugged individualism were under threat. Unlike some European countries that had already moved toward becoming welfare states, most Americans had a fixed belief that *each person* was responsible for getting himself out of his ditch, and, therefore, the government should *not* provide charity. Roosevelt then had no prior model for comprehensive relief programs to follow as to what should be done to affect a national economic turnaround.[318]

B. The Road Taken by FDR After Being Sworn in to Maintain the Approval of Public Sentiment

Knowing the basis of his decisive victory in 1932, and mindful of public sentiment like no president since Lincoln, yet having no clear plan in mind for taking the necessary action to confront the Depression, Franklin D. Roosevelt proceeded to do what he was elected to do: TAKE VIGOROUS ACTION ASAP, NO MATTER WHAT!

Beginning with his First Inaugural Address, he made it clear that a new day had arrived in America: "A day of national consecration," when there would be "nothing to fear but fear itself," because the

American people under FDR's leadership would realize that our people's "true destiny is not to be ministered unto but to minister to ourselves and to our fellow men," with a new awareness of "our interdependence on each other," where people "sacrifice for the good of a common discipline, and would be bound as a sacred obligation with a unity of duty hitherto evoked only in time of armed strife," recognizing that "the emergency at home *cannot wait* on international economic readjustment."[319]

Roosevelt then said in the second part of his Address that if Congress was slow or nonresponsive to his electoral mandate to attack the Depression aggressively, then by golly he would just start signing Executive Orders to move things where they needed to go. His words:

> It is to be hoped that the normal balance of legislative and executive authority may be wholly adequate to meet the unprecedented task before us. But it may be that an unprecedented demand and need for undelayed action may call for temporary departure from that normal balance of public procedure.... In the event that the Congress shall fail [to act], and in the event that the national emergency is still critical, I shall not evade the clear course of duty that will confront me.[320]

In committing to take executive action when necessary in a national emergency, FDR was guided by Abraham Lincoln who took such measures early on during the Civil War. In particular, only sixteen days after the war started at Fort Sumter, Lincoln revoked the constitutional right to the writ of habeas corpus in the area between Washington, DC and Philadelphia to prevent the takeover of the nation's capital by the Confederates. When challenged on the constitutionality of his action, Lincoln answered, "By general law, life and limb must be protected, yet often *a limb must be amputated to save a life*, but a life is *never* wisely given to save a limb."[321]

FDR was ready to follow his hero's lead and, if necessary, do what had to be done in the way of pruning limbs to save the life of the country in the Great Depression, *regardless* whether he had Congressional approval. Why? Because public sentiment in March 1933 *demanded* big, bold, fast government action to address the national economic malaise, and would allow *no excuses* for a failure to act caused by a slow Congress. Whereas Lincoln justified the constitutionality of his unilateral unlimited wartime maneuvers as a matter of "military necessity," FDR believed he had the power to take executive action as a matter of "brother's keeper" necessity which was absolutely *required* by "a stricken nation in the midst of a stricken world."[322]

For his first major action item, on March 6, 1933, his third day in the White House, Roosevelt responded to a national run on the banks in which customers had pulled out their cash and planned to hoard it in mattresses until they believed their money would be secure on deposit. He attempted to stop the run by closing the nation's banks and calling it "a bank holiday." Three days later, at FDR's urging, Congress passed the Emergency Banking Act, which provided insurance to bank depositors.[323]

The new president then spoke to the American people (with his polio-warmed empathetic voice) in a national radio address on March 12, 1933, in what became his first Fireside Chat. Using a calm conversational tone, his clear words regarding why he had done what he had done succeeded miraculously in restoring the public's trust in the banking system.[324] When banks reopened the day after his radio message, the panic stopped. Having regained their confidence by trusting in what FDR had said, the American people proceeded to redeposit their funds into local banks all over the country within the next few days.

C. No Fear of Failure in Pursuing Legislative Agenda

Franklin D. Roosevelt was great in knowing, responding to, and shaping public sentiment to support his goals during his presidency, and he did the same with Congressional sentiment. Burns believed that "the classic test of greatness in the White House has been the chief executive's capacity to lead Congress—whether it be by bulldozer or finesse."[325] During his First Hundred Days in office, seeking to keep the promises he had made in his Inaugural Address, FDR got fifteen major bills passed in Congress to address the immediate needs of millions of destitute Americans. Most of the legislation succeeded in achieving its intended purpose (most notably, the establishment of both the Civilian Conservation Corps and Tennessee Valley Authority, the Farm Relief Act, and the Securities Act of 1933), though some of the new initiatives sputtered and did not last long.[326]

The programs that were duds, however, such as the National Recovery Act, did not slow down FDR's mojo or lessen his magical capacity to maintain the approval of the national public sentiment. In his second Fireside Chat two months into office on May 7, 1933, he explained his unshakeably optimistic perspective with this sports metaphor:

> I do not deny that we may make mistakes of procedure as we carry out the policy. I have no expectation of making a hit every time I come to bat. What I seek is the highest possible batting average, not only for myself but for the team.[327]

After hearing the Chats on the radio and seeing their government come alive like never before in response to their dire circumstances, during FDR's first term, the American public came to believe that they now had a president who listened to them, was eloquently sensitive to their needs, and was working as hard as he could to provide them with a measure of sustenance in their blood-spattered corner of the ring as the uphill fight for a better life continued.

The operative word for FDR's national Depression recovery strategy was "experimentation," as the New Deal became "a laboratory for economic learning." He specifically used that word to tie his untested initiatives to what public sentiment demanded:

> We have new and complex problems. We don't really know what they are. Why not establish a new agency to take over the new duty rather than saddle it to an old initiative?... The country *needs* and, unless I mistake its temper, the country *demands* bold, persistent *experimentation*. It is common sense to take a method and try it. If it fails, admit it and try another. But above all, *try something*.[328]

Historian Richard Hofstadter confirmed why experimentation was the most prudent approach for Roosevelt to take: "The nation was confronted with a completely novel situation for which the traditional, commonly accepted philosophies offered no guide. An era of fumbling and muddling-through was inevitable. Only a leader with an experimental temper could have made the New Deal possible."[329]

Mindful of the passionate public sentiment that had fueled FDR's landslide victory in 1932, and how committed he was to responding to it with full force, maximum speed, and executive action, Congress cooperated with the new president on most of his emergency programs during the First Hundred Days, thanks in large part to the way he interacted with them. In her book *These Truths: A History of the United States*, Jill Lepore said, "Roosevelt met with legislators *every day* of the first hundred days of his administration."[330] Biographer Jean Edward Smith gave this assessment of why FDR's dealings with Congress during the First Hundred Days were so successful:

> After eight years as Assistant Secretary of the Navy, working with Josephus Daniels and observing his easy relations with Capitol Hill, Roosevelt had an unparalleled understanding of how to deal with Congress. He knew how to stroke the members, how to play to their vanity, and how to accommodate their needs. "No president ever approached the prerogatives of the legislative body with more scrupulous attention to

> detail," said John Gunther, one of Washington's most astute observers.[331]

During his Second Hundred Days, with his confidence soaring, FDR maintained his strong response to the public's needs by keeping the pressure on Congress in an urgent but professional manner, as described by Burns:

> No longer was he squeamish about putting the lash to congressional flanks. Now he was bluntly telling congressional leaders that certain bills *must* be passed. Administration contact men ranged amid the legislative rank and file, applying pressure. Late in the afternoon they would report back to the President. When they mentioned a balking congressman, the big hand would move instantly to the telephone; and in a few moments, the President would have the congressman on the wire, coaxing him, commanding him, negotiating with him. To scores of others, Roosevelt dictated one- or two-sentence chits asking for action. He and his lieutenants, worked late into the night, acted in close concert with friendly leaders on Capitol Hill, and stayed one or two jumps ahead of the divided opposition.[332]

By the end of his first term, Roosevelt had at least partially succeeded with his New Deal programs by reducing national unemployment from 25 percent to 17 percent. Nonetheless, he had not cut joblessness as much as he had hoped, per his 1932 campaign promises. Given these facts, FDR provided the American people with an even more eloquent expression (than he used in his second Fireside Chat) of why hitting less than 1.000 with his recovery programs didn't bother him at all and should not bother anyone else, when he gave his acceptance speech at the National Democratic Convention in Philadelphia in June 1936:

> Governments can err, Presidents do make mistakes, but the immortal Dante tells us that divine justice weighs the sins of the cold-blooded and the sins of the warm-hearted on different scales. Better the occasional faults of a Government that lives in a spirit of charity than the consistent omissions of a Government frozen in the ice of its own indifference.... To some generations much is given. Of other generations much is expected. This generation of Americans has a *rendezvous with destiny.*[333]

Through his first two terms, in line with the demands of public sentiment, FDR focused almost entirely on domestic policies aimed at bringing present relief and future hope to Americans. During his second term, however, he made two major mistakes in evaluating the public's perspectives on two key issues that took some wind out of his sails. First, overconfident after his landslide reelection victory in 1936, and beside himself with disappointment after having twelve of his New Deal initiatives struck down as unconstitutional by the Supreme Court in the last eighteen months of his first term, Roosevelt attempted to pass the Judicial Procedures Reform Bill of 1937. This bill sought to "pack" the Supreme Court with additional justices who would be more inclined than the existing nine to uphold the constitutionality of FDR's experimental government relief programs.[334]

In this instance, he missed the boat on gauging public sentiment, as most Americans believed that such a material change in the Court would be unconstitutional. Many who had supported him enthusiastically since his 1932 election became concerned that their beloved White House leader had enjoyed so much popular success during his first term that it had gone to his head, and had twisted off to the point that he now had aspirations to lead the country more as a dictator than a president. After his plan for changing the court crashed and burned in Congress, FDR accepted his fate[335] (lesson learned!), and in no time was largely forgiven by his constituents for attempting to go a bridge too far in pursuing his recovery agenda. Surprisingly, soon after the court-packing plan tanked, the Supreme Court began looking more favorably at FDR's programs and the justices never again held that a New Deal program was unconstitutional.[336]

In Roosevelt's other major second term mistake, he rejected John Maynard Keynes's advice (provided in accordance with Keynes's ground-breaking book *The General Theory of Employment, Interest and Money* that had come out in 1936) to pursue deficit spending as a means of funding his costly New Deal programs. Instead, he decided to cut government spending in a tone-deaf effort to balance the budget.[337] His mistake in missing the fact that public sentiment favored the need to fund potentially helpful relief programs *over* the need to balance the federal budget brought down the markets and elevated unemployment.[338] It did not take FDR long to recognize his error and correct his ill-conceived economic policy the following year.

D. FDR's Process for Staying Connected to Public Sentiment

Regardless of the bumps in the road that came from twice misreading public sentiment in 1937, Franklin D. Roosevelt *never* lost his commitment to drill as deep as he could on the task of assessing the status of public opinion on the day's leading issues, and then most of the time he responded in a manner aligned with it.

To keep himself well-positioned to receive a steady stream of reliable information about the public's views, and gauge where "the middle" was in the overall sentiment (knowing that little is gained by listening to people with extreme positions on opposite ends of the spectrum), Franklin Roosevelt held a record number of press conferences in his office throughout his presidency, where he listened to reporters from all over the country as much as he spoke to them;[339] periodically canvassed the country on train and car trips (Burns noted that FDR modified his remarks in every town where he spoke "as he caught the rhythm of the crowd");[340] and per Dallek's assessment, was pleased that his wife Eleanor traveled constantly "on buses and trains, as an ordinary citizen, without Secret Service agents" and would then report back to him on what she had learned in places where his position and polio wouldn't let him go.[341]

Regarding Eleanor's importance to her husband's information gathering on public sentiment, FDR's postmaster general James Farley said, "On matters of social conditions...economic, racial, religious... which affected the mass of the people in the country or a particular section of a certain community, President Roosevelt had complete faith in her judgment and ability to observe."[342] The same conclusion was reached by his secretary of labor, Frances Perkins, who remembered that, "In a Cabinet meeting, President Roosevelt took pride in announcing: 'My Missus says they have typhoid fever in that district,' or 'My Missus says the people are leaving the Dust Bowl in droves because they haven't any chance there,' or 'My Missus says that people are working for wages way below the minimum set by NRA in the town she visited last week.'"[343]

In her book *Leadership in Turbulent Times,* Goodwin gave a historian's perspective on Eleanor's importance as a public sentiment information–gatherer for FDR:

> More than any other source, Roosevelt counted on Eleanor to provide "the unvarnished truth." He called her his "will o' the wisp" wife, for she traveled hundreds of thousands of miles around the country, spending weeks and months at a time talking with a great variety of people from every region, listening to complaints, examining New Deal programs, amassing an anthology of stories. Each time she returned, she arranged "an uninterrupted meal" with her husband so the anecdotes would be "fresh and not dulled by repetition." Roosevelt had absolute trust in the dependability and accuracy of her observations.[344]

On top of what he saw and heard first hand, no one paid more attention to opinion polls than Franklin Roosevelt.[345] Furthermore, no one before him ever fully explored where public sentiment appeared to be at any given moment as he did by listening to the many diverse political positions that existed among Congressmen and Senators—be they progressive Republicans, independent Republicans, Southern Democrats, Northern Democrats, or anyone else. In fact, for a while during his first two terms, Roosevelt's most disruptive antagonists were some of his fellow Democrats.[346]

By voraciously taking in so many perspectives to maximize his awareness of public sentiment's nuances, FDR became a full-service information clearinghouse. He used his spongelike memory to retain the details as to what the various factions were thinking, while always searching for a clearer picture of what he should do and say that would mesh with what the most Americans "in the middle" on an issue wanted their president to do and say, as *together* they faced the greatest economic crisis in American history.[347]

E. His Approach to Leading Public Sentiment in a Different Direction When Necessary

Yes, Abraham Lincoln, "public sentiment is everything," but it is also fickle, shifts with the tides, and sometimes is off the mark. Despite this inconvenient truth, a successful leader must emulate Franklin D. Roosevelt and *stay fixed* on monitoring the thoughts of his constituents rigorously, recognizing how frequently their sentiments change. Failing to stay abreast of changes in perceptions risks falling out of step with the largest bloc of the middle, where elections are won or lost, and thereby reduces the odds of a leader's staying in power when the next election comes around.

Having said that, a prudent leader knows that his highest and best role when he acts for his constituents goes well *beyond* serving as a rubber stamp for what they want in a particular moment on a particular issue; rather, a great leader aspires to be someone who, when necessary, actually *leads* public sentiment away from ill-informed, poorly considered positions to a more enlightened perspective that will provide a better long-term outcome on a particular issue.

FDR knew Lincoln had done this type of leading by moving *one step ahead* of his constituents on the slavery emancipation issue as the Civil War dragged on. Lincoln started with his original position upon becoming president in 1861 that he only wanted to stop the expansion of slavery into the West, and ultimately ended with successfully emancipating all slaves throughout the country by the passage of the Thirteenth Amendment that he pushed through the Senate in April 1864 and the House in January 1865.[x]

Consistent with his hero's example, beginning in the last part of his second term, FDR recognized he would *have* to follow Lincoln's "one step ahead" course in guiding the American people to a different perspective on the major foreign policy issue facing the nation at the time. As of 1939, the dominant sentiment among the masses was *stuck* in the post-World War I mindset, whereby most Americans wanted the country to keep doing throughout the late 1930s and into 1940 and 1941, what it had been doing since Woodrow Wilson's demise.[348] Specifically, they wanted their government leaders to maintain a policy of isolationism and remove America from activities abroad, despite the fact that with each succeeding month as FDR's second term came to an end, Adolf Hitler and Benito Mussolini were aggressively attacking and, in most cases, conquering one nation after another in the Eastern Hemisphere with every intention of taking over the world. Lepore properly identified the consequence of the nation's isolationist mindset: "American indifference *emboldened* Germany. 'America is no danger to us,' Hitler said. 'Everything about the behavior of American society reveals that it's half Judaized, and the other half Negrified.'"[349]

To understand *why* our nation's being stuck in an isolationist mindset was becoming increasingly dangerous, set forth below is a chronology of what the Berlin-Rome-Tokyo Axis did in the way of international aggression from 1938 to 1941, by acting on the premise that America's desire for isolationism tied FDR's hands and would keep the United States on the sidelines:

---

x Ratification of the Thirteenth Amendment by the required three-fourths of the states was not completed until December 1865, eight months after his death.

March 1938: Germany annexed Austria.

April 1938: Italy conquered Ethiopia, while Germany took one-third of Czechoslovakia (called Sudetenland).

March 1939: Germany took the remaining two-thirds of Czechoslovakia.

September 1939: Germany took Poland, and England declared war on Germany.

March 1940: Germany bombed a naval base near Scotland.

April 1940: Germany took Denmark and Norway.

May 1940: Germany took Belgium, the Netherlands, and Luxembourg.

June 1940: Italy declared war on and soon defeated France.

July 1940: German U-boats attacked merchant ships in the Atlantic.

August 17, 1940: Hitler ordered a blockade of the British Isles.

September 7, 1940: Germany began the London Blitz.

September 18, 1940: Italy invaded Egypt.

September 27, 1940: Japan joined the Axis with Germany and Italy.

October 7, 1940: Germany entered Romania.

October 28, 1940: Italy invaded Greece.

April 1941: The Berlin/Rome Axis invaded Yugoslavia.

June 1941: Germany invaded the Soviet Union.

August 20, 1941: The German siege of Leningrad began.

> September 4, 1941: A German submarine attacked the US destroyer USS Greer with the intent to sink it, though facts were murky regarding whether the attack might have been provoked.
>
> September 17, 1941: German troops took Kiev.
>
> December 1941: Japan bombed Pearl Harbor.

As this escalation of aggression and conquests mounted, Hitler (Germany's leader since 1933) grew his army from five hundred thousand in 1935 to over six million by 1940, while American troops that year had only five hundred thousand men. It meant that the United States military forces in 1940 were smaller than the armies of Belgium, Holland, Portugal, and Switzerland.[xi,350,351]

Under these circumstances, if President Roosevelt wanted to act in accordance with a prudent public sentiment, he knew he'd have to *change* the sentiment to where it was...prudent!—to the extent that it broke free from where it had been since the end of World War I, and started supporting the need for America to contest and ultimately defeat its increasingly powerful Axis enemies. If FDR *failed* to change the outdated, stuck-in-place isolationist public sentiment, he knew he would go down in history as the president who fiddled while the prospects for freedom around the world burned, and his beloved nation would likely sustain ultimate defeat and destruction *on his watch*. Furthermore, time was of the essence in getting the public sentiment changed. If President Roosevelt moved too slowly, England might well fall to Germany and give Hitler control of the entire European continent, which would have made defeating the Axis that much more difficult to accomplish.

---

xi After FDR succeeded in breaking the nation out of its stuck isolationism mindset, from 1940 to 1945, American troops rose to over 12 million, over two-thirds of which were in the US Army. By the end of the war, the US Navy had 7,601 ships—more ships than were in the navies of all other countries combined. See: National WWII Museum, "Research Starters: US Military by the Numbers," nationalww2museum.org; "Ship Force Levels 1917–Present," history.navy.mil.

So *that* was the big, fat, juicy pickle FDR found himself in at the end of his second term as he faced the thorny issue of whether to break new political ground by seeking a third term for president in 1940, which would necessarily require his taking on the responsibility of being *not* just a rigorous public sentiment *follower*, but rather a public sentiment *changer* in charge of doing what it took to motivate Americans to throw off their outdated commitment to isolationism and move forward full force on the international front to stop Hitler from taking over the world.

Once he made this assessment, the heavy-lifting question for FDR became: Exactly what should he say and do to change American public sentiment as the world's future hung in the balance? Just as he had done when implementing his New Deal programs to lessen the Great Depression's impact, he faced the isolationism question knowing there were *no* existing ideas or strategies that made wrestling with his constituents on these world-changing issues simple or easy. Franklin Roosevelt's response to this question had two parts.

FIRST PART:

> **To move public sentiment, a leader must (a) craft messages that contain words powerful enough to be taken to heart by those who hear them, (b) deliver those words with authentic sincerity and dramatic flair at times when his listening audience is at its largest size, and (c) time his communications in sufficiently spaced intervals for his messages to resonate fully within his constituents' consciousness.**

Franklin D. Roosevelt had first shown his ability to move public sentiment toward his way of thinking by using head-snapping words while campaigning for president on April 7, 1932, in a radio address. On that occasion, he moved the national movement of Depression-era victims solidly behind his candidacy by calling them "*the forgotten*, the unorganized but *indispensable* units of economic power," and explaining why the "*forgotten man* [was] at the bottom of the economic pyramid."[352] BINGO! His two simple words touched millions of hearts. FDR moved the multitudes' sentiments because he not only *remembered* but *cared deeply about* the Great Depression's "forgotten man" who had been suffering miserably ever since Black Tuesday. From that radio address on, referencing the "forgotten man" became his favored way of moving Americans his way as their preferred candidate.

When Roosevelt became his party's presidential nominee that summer at the Democratic National Convention in Chicago, he did two things no one in his position had ever done before. He traveled to Chicago by airplane *and* he arrived at the convention to deliver his acceptance speech in person. Knowing his appearance was "unprecedented," he capitalized on it in his speech, again using words that penetrated instantly to the roaring crowd:

> The appearance before a National Convention of its nominee for President, to be formally notified of his selection is *unprecedented* and unusual, but *these are unprecedented and unusual times*.... In doing so, I broke traditions. Let it be from now on the task of our Party to break foolish traditions...I pledge you, I pledge myself to a *new deal* for the American people. This is more than a political campaign. It is a *call to arms*.[353]

Up close and personal for all the convention delegates to see and for all Americans to hear on the radio and read about and see photos of in their daily newspapers and weekly *TIME* magazine, using new buzzwords "unprecedented times," "new deal," and a "call to arms" that together struck a major chord, all of a sudden, FDR moved sentiments throughout a hurting nation comprising millions of "forgotten men" who now realized that they had found a bold eloquent presidential nominee willing to come where the action was, and speak words they fully grasped and had been *yearning* for years to hear a candidate say. And this strong-from-the-waist-up dynamic man appeared ready to *lead* the movement they wanted led by rejecting the status quo and doing something new and better with maximum urgency once he got elected and sworn into office.

Keeping the flow of the public's election sentiments solidly behind him, Franklin Roosevelt opened his presidency by telling Depression-ravaged Americans in his First Inaugural Address, "First of all, let me assert my firm belief that *the only thing we have to fear is...fear itself*."[354] These immortal words came across as the roar of a lion injecting confidence into his pride, assuring the fearful that the current storm could *and would* be weathered with FDR at the ship of state's helm. *He* darn sure was not afraid of the future. *They* should not be either!

Roosevelt's well-chosen words that flowed from his calm powerful voice beamed across the airwaves with Barrymore-like dramatic force, projecting his having the capacity to move mountains, which that day's dire economic conditions demanded. Like Lincoln, FDR had a high level of self-confidence in the power of his strongest words to change hearts, and his track record at doing it kept getting better.

After his First Inaugural Address, Franklin Roosevelt's most important follow-up public presentations to the masses where he attempted to move the needle on public sentiment were his twice a year Fireside Chats on the radio (the infrequency of which made each Chat more anticipated—i.e., FDR knew that in public speaking, more often than not, *less is more*), his annual State of the Union addresses, his speeches to the Democratic National Convention every four years, and his subsequent Inaugural Addresses. *These* were the centerstage opportunities for the President of the United States to either speak firmly but gently or roar like a lion—depending on the circumstances—and thereby ring the bell for Americans to start embracing their president's position, as FDR stayed mindful of Lincoln's rule of persuasion that a person will not change his mind until he changes his heart.

On these select occasions, which called for his most stirring oratory, Roosevelt knew he would have the ears of most of the American people, and that they would stop what they were doing and listen to what he had to say. They would then read and further digest his powerful words the next day in their local newspaper. Each opportunity for FDR to deliver a powerful message to the multitudes was precious, and he knew that to maximize each speech's impact required his using the most memorable words in the most penetrating manner to impact each listener and cause him to start questioning and begin moving *away* from his existing beliefs and *toward* where Roosevelt wanted him to go.

Thus, prior to 1939, FDR had had a great run as a powerhouse communicator to the American people, using words filled with snap, crackle, and pop resonance delivered by his warm dramatic voice. To enhance the impact of it all, America knew that the messages they heard from the White House came from a man who on every day of his presidency confidently chomped at the bit for the privilege of putting the responsibility of dealing with the nation's most important issues on top of his massive shoulders.

Because of these factors, biographer Smith marveled at how in every opportunity he had to persuade the multitudes, Roosevelt rose to the occasion with "an uncanny ability to say the right thing at the right time to the right audience."[355] Novelist Saul Bellow agreed with Smith's assessment, noting that because of FDR's grasp of public sentiment and his sincere empathy, "the secret of his political genius was that he knew *exactly* what the people needed to hear…and they affirmed the rightness of his tone and took assurance from it."[356]

From 1939 to 1941, President Roosevelt used all these rhetorical skills to get the nation unstuck from its outdated isolationist foreign policy. In those three years, per Smith's and Bellow's evaluations, FDR delivered exactly the right words at the right times to bring about the desired change in public sentiment. He achieved his goal when isolationism died a quick death on December 7, 1941, after the Japanese bombed Pearl Harbor. Immediately thereafter, Americans locked arms in total unity with *pro*-foreign war sentiments, ready for their commander-in-chief to pull out all necessary stops and send American soldiers abroad to defeat the despised enemies.

Here were Roosevelt's strongest words that moved the nation's public sentiment away from isolationism and toward internationalism, step-by-step, during these three critical years:

- Knowing that the key to changing American minds about isolationism was for the people to *recognize* the dangerous threat on the horizon as Hitler picked up speed in taking over more countries in Europe, FDR delivered a Fireside Chat on September 3, 1939, at a time when according to Dallek, "an opinion survey showed a 50–50 split among Americans on the choice of isolationism vs. internationalism."[357] That night, Roosevelt told Americans that the reasons Congress had passed the Neutrality Acts (which prevented the United States from exporting "arms, ammunition, and implements of war" to foreign nations at war), in effect since 1935, were now worthy of *reconsideration*:

> "You must master at the outset a simple but unalterable fact in modern foreign relations between nations. When peace has been broken *anywhere*, the peace of all countries *everywhere* is in danger. It is easy for you and for me to shrug our shoulders and say that conflicts taking place thousands of miles from the continental United States, and, indeed, thousands of miles from the whole American Hemisphere, do not seriously affect the Americas—and that all the United States has to do is to ignore them and go about its own business. Passionately, though we may desire detachment, we are *forced* to realize that every word that comes through the air, every ship that sails the sea, every battle that is fought, *does affect* the American future.... This nation will remain a neutral nation, but I cannot ask that every American remain neutral in thought as well. *Even a neutral has a right to take account of facts. Even a neutral cannot be asked to close his mind or his conscience.*"

- When Italy declared war on France on June 10, 1940, FDR delivered a Fireside Chat that very evening, and told Americans:

> "On this tenth day of June, 1940, *the hand that held the dagger has struck it into the back of its neighbor*…. In our American unity, we will pursue two obvious and simultaneous causes: we will extend to the opponents of force the material resources of this nation, and at the same time we will harness and speed up the use of those resources in order that we ourselves in the Americas may have equipment and training equal to the task of any emergency and every defense…. Signs and signals call for speed—*full speed ahead*."

- Throughout 1940, while steadily ratcheting up his warnings about Hitler, Roosevelt repeatedly assured Americans that he would *not* send our boys to fight in a foreign war, though initially he inserted the caveat "unless under attack." By October of that year, fearful that Willkie was gaining on him as he sought a third term because of Willkie's claim that regardless of what FDR said, he would definitely be sending American soldiers abroad into war, Roosevelt removed the caveat, explaining to his speechwriter, "It's not necessary. If we're attacked, it's no longer a foreign war."[358]
- In his Fireside Chat on December 29, 1940, to which 70 percent of Americans listened,[359] after making the unpopular decision among isolationists to send fifty American destroyers to England to be used by Winston Churchill in opposing Hitler's forces, and having made it without Congressional approval, advocating a policy he artfully called "Lend Lease" (though it was essentially a giveaway to the Brits), here were FDR's ringing words that justified his actions as commander-in-chief in response to the rising threat of Hitler:

> "My friends, this is not a fireside chat on war. It is a talk on *national security*…. Never before since Jamestown and Plymouth Rock has our American civilization been in such danger as *now*…. Some of

us like to believe that even if Britain falls, we are still safe because of the broad expanse of the Atlantic and the Pacific.... If Great Britain goes down, the Axis powers will control the continents of Europe, Asia, Africa, Australia, and the high seas—and they will be in a position to bring enormous military and naval resources against this hemisphere.... *We must be the great arsenal of democracy*. For us, this is *an emergency as serious as war itself*...."

Congress proceeded to approve his Lend-Lease Program in March 1941, which essentially nullified the Neutrality Acts, after having also approved his call for a peacetime draft in September 1940 to begin increasing the size of American armed forces.

- In his State of the Union Address on January 6, 1941, after again criticizing the folly in anyone believing that a world dominated by Hitler could result in a world where people enjoyed freedom, FDR gave his eloquent vision for ideals worth fighting for in the future that needed to be protected both home and abroad:

  "In the future days, which we seek to make secure, we look forward to a world founded upon *four essential human freedoms*. The first is freedom of speech, and expression—everywhere in the world.

  The second is freedom of every person to worship God in his own way—everywhere in the world.

  The third is freedom from want—[to] secure to every nation a healthy peacetime life for its inhabitants—everywhere in the world.

  The fourth is freedom from fear—which, translated into world terms, means a worldwide reduction of armaments...anywhere in the world.... This is no

> vision of distant millennium. It is a definite basis for a kind of world attainable in our own time and generation. That kind of world is the very antithesis of the so-called new order of tyranny which the dictators seek to create with the crash of a bomb."

- For his Fireside Chat on May 27, 1941, FDR again spoke of continued German aggression, and Dallek described the president's chosen words on this occasion as "all but a declaration of war," since he declared what was happening abroad as "an unlimited national emergency." His high points:

> "The pressing problems that confront us are military and naval problems, in a Nazi-provoked world war for world domination.... The war is approaching the brink of the Western Hemisphere itself. It is coming very close to home.... Anyone with an atlas (and) anyone with a reasonable knowledge of the sudden striking force of modern war knows that it is stupid to wait until a probable enemy has gained a foothold from which to attack.... We have, accordingly, extended our patrol in north and south Atlantic waters.... It is well known that the strength of the Atlantic Fleet has been greatly increased during the past year, and that it is constantly being built up.... We must be willing to fight if necessary to keep the Nazis from gaining a foothold in the Americas. In the meantime, it is imperative to ensure the delivery of Lend-Lease supplies to Britain.... Shall we now...hesitate to take every single measure necessary to maintain our liberties? Our people and our Government will not hesitate to meet that challenge.... I have tonight issued a proclamation that an unlimited national emergency exists and requires the strengthening of our defense to the extreme limit of our national power and authority."

With each of these public messages broadcast nationwide, while always promising *not* to send American soldiers into foreign wars, Roosevelt slowly but surely, one step at a time, moved American public sentiment *away* from isolationism and *toward* internationalism. After the Japanese joined the Berlin-Rome Axis in September 1940, with FDR knowing (per Dallek's book) that "only a more overt and substantial attack would unify the nation in agreeing to war,"[360] it was only a matter of time before an Axis member attacked American troops. When it inevitably happened, FDR knew it would make it easy for him to finally pull the trigger on declaring war against the attacker with full public support behind him.

Roosevelt's following this "best-time-to-declare-war" plan matched Lincoln's Civil War strategy at Fort Sumter, South Carolina, in April 1861, where he *waited* for the Confederates to attack the Union fort *first,* knowing it would cause the American response to the unprovoked attack to be strong and unified, thereby allowing him as commander-in-chief to immediately ramp up the nation's war effort and sustain it until the war was won.

Hitler did not fire the first shot at the United States; rather, it came from his Axis partner, the Japanese, and with that attack, Pearl Harbor became the Fort Sumter of World War II. In his message to Congress the day after the bombing, FDR again chose exactly the right words to inspire public sentiment going forward to support America's war effort to defeat the Axis:

> "Yesterday, December 7, 1941—*a date that will live in infamy*—the United States was deliberately attacked by naval and air forces of the empire of Japan....
>
> No matter how long it may take us to overcome the premeditated invasion, the American people in their righteous might *will win through to absolute victory...*
>
> With confidence in our armed forces—with the unbounding determination of our people—*we will gain the inevitable triumph—so help us God*."

Three days after FDR's speech, on December 11, 1941, Hitler declared war on the United States, meaning all parties on all fronts were now committed to participating in a full-scale world war. Roosevelt's stirring words in his speeches after war was declared proceeded to spur America's massive and amazingly quick war production effort.

Thanks to his consistently good judgment, charisma, eloquence, optimism, work ethic, and skills as an information clearinghouse, which had all been used in the past to take charge of American public sentiment, Franklin D. Roosevelt brought the same sentiment-shaping skills into the international arena in his dealings with foreign leaders during the war. For the next three and a half years (until his death on April 12, 1945), he became the world's most effective military strategist and international statesman.

SECOND PART:

> **When the time is right to change the sentiments of constituents to a mindset different from where they are, move forward to effect changes—but never more than one step ahead of them.**

It is one thing to have the gift of word precision eloquence and a powerful empathetic voice with perfectly modulated tone to fit the occasions when there will be maximum audience engagement. It is something else to have the sense of *optimum timing* in knowing exactly *when* to communicate constituent sentiment-changing words. Franklin D. Roosevelt said on more than one occasion, "I can't go faster than people will let me go,"[361] but he knew from having studied Abraham Lincoln's approach to ending slavery that people would follow him so long as he stayed only one step in front of them with his stated position on the issue at hand. A message that is two or more steps ahead of people's mindset is simply too hard to grasp and support.

The sequence of FDR's public remarks delivered in the context of what was going on in the United States and around the world in the 1939 to 1941 time period, as covered previously in this chapter, is the best evidence of his perfect timing in knowing when and how to move public sentiment to where it needed to go from where it had been, step-by-step, as events unfolded in the war abroad.

To confirm the accuracy of this conclusion, without exception, FDR's leading biographers are unanimous in believing that his capacity to locate exactly *where* public sentiment was and *when* he had the best opening to change it incrementally but permanently, was the foundation of his political genius. His approach provides the perfect example for leaders in all arenas to know how and when to make their most impactful statements and press forward steadily (but not *too* quickly) with their most important objectives, assuming that, at all times, they have maximized their awareness of their constituents' sentiments.

Here is what the top historians said in their wrap-ups at the end of their books on what made FDR such a stellar leader:

- Goodwin in *No Ordinary Time*: "His success in mobilizing the nation rested on his uncanny sensitivity to his followers, his ability to appraise public feeling, and to lead the people one step at a time. More than any prior president, he studied public opinion…and this gave him a magnificent sense of timing. He understood when to invoke the prestige of the presidency and when to hold it in reserve, when to move forward and when to pull back."[362]

  In *Leadership in Turbulent Times*: "The reciprocal connection between Roosevelt and the people he served lay at the heart of his leadership."[363]
- Burns: "It was his sensitivity to people in all their subtle shadings and complexities that stamped him as a genius in government."[364]
- Dallek: For his "touch of genius…Roosevelt had an uncanny sense of the country's shifting national mood and a talent

for articulating it in the most perilous of times—depression and war."[365]

- Smith: "Roosevelt's speeches and press conferences of December 1940 and January 1941 deepened America's understanding of what was at stake. Buoyed by his unprecedented third-term mandate, FDR *assumed command of public opinion* as he had done during the First Hundred Days in 1933."[366]
- Beschloss: "Had Franklin Roosevelt bowed to the polls in 1940, he would not have dared to push public opinion toward aiding Britain while trying to win a third term. On the eve of that election year, when Gallup asked Americans what problem was "most important," forty-seven percent—by far the largest number—had said, "Keeping out of war." But Roosevelt knew that, especially in crisis, a President's job is not to follow the public but lead it. Part of his genius was framing events like the fall of France [i.e., "the hand that held the dagger has struck it into the back of its neighbor"] for Americans in ways that advanced his cause. Another part was his *feline sensitivity* to how far he could change people's minds at a given time."[367]

Franklin D. Roosevelt's Flaws

As was true of Abraham Lincoln, Franklin D. Roosevelt was not a good husband or a consistently available father. His marriage got off to a bad start because he allowed his mother Sara to dominate all aspects of his household and family life, with his wife confined to being a mere bystander in her own home. Eleanor Roosevelt's superb biographer David Michaelis provided this global assessment of FDR's attitude toward the women in his life:

> All but three years of his life, FDR remained unchangingly attached to his mother. With women, the essential bond was always with an adorer. He would have

> shrunk without women needing to come to him and sit at his feet. The core of each relationship was about *his* primacy, not what he did for the other or others. The relationship was not that of his concern or affection repaid by their adoration but of the adoration of the irresistibly affectionate and sincerely concerned but *not* deeply loving Franklin Delano Roosevelt.[368]

Relations between husband and wife became irreparably damaged when Eleanor learned of her husband's love affair with her social secretary Lucy Mercer from 1917 to 1918. Although they did not divorce over it, from the time Eleanor came upon their love letters in FDR's suitcase when he returned from a trip abroad in 1918, thereafter, except for Eleanor's being helpful to her husband's polio recovery team from 1921 to 1928, they led largely separate lives in parallel camps. Their son James described their marriage as "an armed truce that endured until the day he died."[369]

Remarkably, wanting to give her father at least some joy amid the stress of managing the war effort, and knowing of her parents' long-time intimacy disconnect, their daughter Anna became a facilitator in rekindling FDR's friendship with Lucy during the last years of his life, being careful never to let Eleanor know when they got together.[370] In fact, Lucy was with him at his Warm Springs retreat on the day he died. Eleanor became understandably resentful when she arrived in Georgia and learned of Lucy's presence at his death, especially when she found out that her own daughter had facilitated their prior meetings.[371]

As a father, totally obsessed with finding a way to resume his political career after he contracted polio, and upon doing that, then becoming totally consumed with being the governor of New York and then president of the United States, FDR had little time for parenting and meeting the emotional needs of his five children who reached adulthood.[372] The five of them had eighteen marriages, and his four sons often found themselves in trouble during their school years.[373] Later, after reaching adulthood, his sons took several jobs with high salaries for which they had no qualifications on the implied (or perhaps stated) promise that their employers would have access to their father.[374]

Because of Roosevelt's "impenetrable" personality, which featured what his speechwriter Robert Sherwood artfully called "his heavily forested interior,"[375] there was limited emotional connection between FDR and any family member because they all found him impossible to know on a deep personal level.

With regards to Roosevelt's leadership flaws, using many examples, Burns criticized his refusal to engage in long-term strategic planning.[376] He acknowledged but did not apologize for this trait because he believed that planning anything more than six months in advance was imprudent since pertinent facts inevitably change and hence void the assumptions on which the long-term plans were based. Burns also addressed his subject's lack of creativity as a leader in that Roosevelt was not a good idea generator; he was a good synthesizer of other people's ideas.[377]

In his Roosevelt biography, Dallek focused his criticisms on (1) FDR's seeking to overreach and exercise essentially absolute power over the country when he pursued his ill-fated court-packing effort;[378] (2) his inhumane and unconstitutional decision to inter 120,000 Japanese-Americans in concentration camps after the bombing at Pearl Harbor;[379] (3) his reluctance to be proactive in helping Jews escape the Nazis during most of World War II, other than by creating the War Refugee Board in January 1944 (whose Executive Director John Pehle acknowledged at the end of the war that the Board's results in saving Jews from the Holocaust was "too little, too late");[380] and (4) his refusal to support an anti-lynching bill in Congress for fear of damaging his relationships with many Southern Senators and Congressmen.[381] During his over twelve years of presidency, FDR never advocated any civil rights legislation,[382] although, under duress, he signed an Executive Order in 1941 that prevented racial discrimination in the hiring of workers in defense industries to prevent a march on Washington by several thousand African Americans that was being organized by A. Philip Randolph, the leader of the Brotherhood of Sleeping Car Porters. Smith corroborated Dallek's criticisms on all these issues, as did Goodwin.[383]

Had Franklin Roosevelt been present to read his biographers' criticisms, he likely would have responded to them as he did to a young man who visited the White House while in the nation's capital for a youth conference in June 1940, and had the audacity to start taking potshots at the president. Here was FDR's reply that day to the tactless attacks on his performance, as described by Burns:

> "Young man, I think you are very sincere. Have you read Carl Sandburg's *Lincoln*?"
>
> No, the young man had not.
>
> "I think the impression was that Lincoln was a pretty sad man." FDR went on, "because he could not do all he wanted to do at one time, and I think you will find examples where Lincoln had to compromise to gain a little something. He had to compromise to make a few gains. Lincoln was one of those unfortunate people called a 'politician' but he was a politician who was practical enough to get a great many things done for this country. He was a sad man because he couldn't get it all at once. And nobody can.
>
> "Maybe you would make a much better President than I have. Maybe you will, some day.
>
> If you ever sit here, you will learn that you cannot, just by shouting from the housetops, get what you want all the time."[384]

Personal Application

Here are questions for consideration by those who want to evaluate themselves in the areas of handling adversity; and absorbing, processing, and shaping constituents' sentiments.

You now know how Franklin D. Roosevelt would have answered these questions. How do *you* answer them?

- Identify the absolute worst setbacks that have ever happened to you—be they a health crisis, a family crisis, a business/job crisis, or any other type of crisis.
- Did you respond to the crisis with fear?
- Assuming you were fearful (for at least a little while, because, presumably, you are a normal human being), *how long* were you fearful?
    - How did your fear manifest itself?
    - What actions did you take to combat your fear?
- As you confronted your adversity, do you think those around you saw fear in your eyes?
- As you faced your adversity, and processed its likely impact on your life, did you quickly devise an approach to dealing with it that minimized the appearance of how fearful/anxious you were?
- What ultimate impact on your temperament and philosophy of life did dealing with the adversity have on you? Did dealing with it impact either your natural optimism or natural pessimism? If so, how?
- Can you now look back on your life and recognize some good things that happened to you because of the setbacks you suffered? Articulate the good things that happened with each setback.
- Do you believe that the way you handled your adversity inspired those around you to deal with their present or subsequent setback in a bolder, less fearful way?
- As the leader of an organization, how much do you seek to know and understand the sentiments of those below you?

- If you now are leading (or want to lead) an organization, what are you doing (or what would you do) to gain meaningful feedback from those under you about their thoughts on the issues facing your enterprise?
- Assuming you did *something* to gather and monitor the sentiments of others in your organization (which I hope is a safe assumption), how often did you do it?
- After gaining information about the sentiments of those in your organization on key issues, how did you use it?
- If there were times when you gained information about the sentiments of others in your organization and decided that their consensus opinion was imprudent, what did you do to change the flawed sentiment?
- When trying to change sentiments among those below you by means of making a speech or some type of presentation, how much time do you spend choosing the most impactful words for your remarks?
- Before giving such a presentation, how many times do you revise the text and/or rehearse it either in front of a mirror or some small group?
- Before giving such a presentation to change the sentiments among those below you in the enterprise's chain of command, did you examine your organization's calendar of events, and decide upon the best possible time and place for delivering your message to have maximum attendance and engagement?
- Do you speak to your colleagues about the major issues facing your organization too often, too rarely, or with just the right frequency?

May having a deeper understanding of Franklin D. Roosevelt's two most important leadership traits, your answers to the foregoing questions tied to these traits, and your awareness of his flaws give you greater success in leading your organization to new heights.

CHAPTER SIX

HOW TO ORGANIZE AND LEAD A STAFF, REAP DIVIDENDS WITH PATIENCE, AND PLAY HARDBALL WHEN NECESSARY—LIKE DWIGHT EISENHOWER

"My place in history will be decided by historians. And I don't think I'll be around to differ with them."

Dwight D. Eisenhower

In 1962, Arthur Schlesinger Sr. reached out to seventy-four of his fellow historians and asked them to rate American presidents from best to worst. Among the thirty-one considered,[i] Dwight D. Eisenhower tied with Chester Alan Arthur for twenty-first place, one notch ahead of Andrew Johnson, who at the time was the only president to have been impeached. Twenty years later, the *Chicago Tribune* resumed the practice and received input from forty-nine leading historians. Because Eisenhower's presidential papers were released for public viewing beginning in 1973, scholars knew more about him than they had two decades before, and the results of their poll shocked the history world by having Eisenhower leapfrog over twelve of his White House peers, moving him up to ninth place.

In the twenty-first century, C-SPAN has continued the ranking business and has now done it four times, gathering 150 historians' opinions[ii] whenever a president leaves the White House. In 2000, Eisenhower stayed in ninth place; in 2009, he moved up to eighth; and in 2017 and 2021, he was rated fifth best (trailing only Abraham Lincoln, George Washington, and the two Roosevelts). His 1962 tied-for-twenty-first-place colleague, Chester Arthur, now ranks thirtieth, and the much-maligned Johnson is currently viewed as the second worst[iii] president in history.

How to account for this seismic shift in appreciation for Eisenhower by those who are supposed to know how to evaluate presidential performance? Let's start with why Eisenhower, or Ike, ranked so low in 1962. Answer: As part of America's frenzied overreaction to the October 1957 announcement that the Soviets had launched into space their Sputnik satellite, pundits (most notably Joseph Alsop of

i Only thirty-one of the thirty-four presidents were ranked in 1962. William Henry Harrison and James Garfield were not ranked because they both served such short periods of time, and John F. Kennedy was not ranked because he had been in office only one year at the time.

ii C-SPAN asks historians to rank presidents in the following categories: public persuasion, crisis leadership, economic management, moral authority, international relations, administrative skills, relations with Congress, vision/setting an agenda, pursued equal justice for all, and performance within context of times.

iii Lincoln's predecessor, James Buchanan, finished last in 2017 and 2021.

the *Washington Post,* Walter Lippmann of the *New York Herald Tribune,* and Richard Rovere of *The New Yorker*) and Democratic Party leaders (mainly Senators John F. Kennedy, Lyndon Johnson, and Stuart Symington—all of whom planned to run for president in 1960) succeeded in crafting a false claim (though believable to many at the time) that Eisenhower's seemingly relaxed style of leadership had caused America to be on the short end of a "missile gap," and, thus, the United States was on the verge of losing its status as the most powerful nation in the world.[385] JFK would later learn that it was the Soviet Union who was on the short end of a missile gap.[386]

In addition to this politically driven canard, Eisenhower's low ranking in 1962 was also impacted by the capture of Francis Gary Powers in May 1960, when his American U-2 spy plane flew over the Soviet Union's airspace, took pictures of their missiles, and was then shot down.[387] At first, Ike and the CIA denied having knowledge of the espionage mission (thinking "plausible deniability" would give them a way out of the nightmare scenario), but they soon had to come clean and admit they had planned the mission when Premier Nikita Khrushchev announced that the Soviets had captured Powers and found his photos, which made it clear that the United States had intentionally violated the flight restrictions over enemy territory.[388] The incident caused Khrushchev to cancel the Soviets' participation in the Paris Peace Summit scheduled two weeks later, and it became a black mark on American credibility at a time of increasingly tense global relations.[389]

Because of the bogus-but-believed Sputnik/missile gap scare tactics, the ugly truth about the U-2's activities, and the self-inflicted lost opportunity to turn down the Cold War heat in Paris, Eisenhower's otherwise highly successful two-term presidency ended in a trough. Assessments of his presidency continued to go downhill in the last half of 1960 as Americans looked at the upcoming election and faced the choice of voting for dogged dour Richard Nixon (coming off an eight-year run as Ike's vice president) whom the media despised, or eloquent Hollywood handsome John F. Kennedy whom the media adored, along with his promise of a "New Frontier" for America.

Throughout the 1960 election year, as Democrats and the press bashed Eisenhower and claimed Nixon would be no better than Ike, their message resonated to many who thought the time had come for the old likeable war hero (Ike turned seventy that year) to retire to his farm in Gettysburg, Pennsylvania, and allow the country to move forward with new blood (at age forty-three, Kennedy aspired to be the youngest president ever elected). When JFK won in a squeaker, Eisenhower's hopes for the continuation of his domestic and foreign policy agendas under Nixon died on the vine.

With that assessment of why Ike was ranked so low in 1962, let us flip the switch and understand why he ranks so high today. In his book, *The Age of Eisenhower*, esteemed historian William I. Hitchcock put into a nutshell his subject's stellar eight-year performance:

> His approach to international affairs was masterful... bringing about an armistice in the Korean War, declining to bail out France in its colonial war in Indochina, using economic pressure to compel Britain and France to halt their ill-conceived invasion of Egypt in 1956, and initiating America's space program. His foreign and security policies combined restraint and vigilance in equal measure...and achieved a remarkable record of Great Power stability and the absence of large scale conflict.
>
> He also gets high marks for his stewardship of the economy—GDP increased 60 percent; he balanced three budgets and came close on five others; he found a way to expand defense spending, boost the minimum wage, limit inflation, widen Social Security, and invest in infrastructure. He rightly deserves to be known as one of the shrewdest managers of the nation's economy.
>
> Finally, he's received superlative marks for his moral authority. His administration was remarkably free of

> scandal, and Ike held himself to the highest standard of personal conduct befitting the most honored office in the country. In the 1950's, he was a model of loyalty, dignity, and decency, and the American people knew they had lived in the presence of greatness.[390]

To get the benefit of a first-hand impression of Eisenhower's presidency, his Undersecretary of Labor and later his Director of the US Information Agency, Arthur Larson, gave this perspective on his former boss's extraordinary foreign policy as measured against his predecessors and successors, in his book aptly titled *Eisenhower: The President Nobody Knew*:

> In the same stormy modern world that saw the Second World War under FDR, the Korean War under Truman, the Bay of Pigs invasion under JFK, and the Vietnam War under LBJ, President Eisenhower closed out one war, the Korean War, and carried his country through eight difficult years without any war, large or small, and without any loss to Communist aggression.[391]

Considering America's subsequent failed wars in Vietnam, Afghanistan, and Iraq, in his book *Eisenhower in War and Peace,* Jean Edward Smith gave the tightest explanation for Ike's being recognized as a Top Five president due to his unique skill as a peacemaker and peacekeeper: "After he made peace in Korea [in July 1953], *not a single American died in combat for the next eight years*."[392]

Having reviewed these glowing evaluations of Eisenhower's presidential performance after recognizing why it took a while for his greatness to be appreciated, the question at the heart of every chapter in this book now rears its head: *How did he do it?*

Leadership Trait #1: Active Engagement with a Well-Oiled-Machine Organization

Dwight Eisenhower started his military career at West Point in 1911, then served continuously through both world wars, and rose to the positions of five-star general in the US Army and Supreme Allied Commander in Europe. After orchestrating the D-Day invasion, aided by the Soviet's success in the East, he led the Allied effort in Europe from the West and secured Germany's unconditional surrender in May 1945. He hung up his uniform when he stepped down as NATO's Supreme Commander to run for president in June 1952.

Ike's decades of military service branded into his DNA the fact that leadership of a large enterprise is most likely to succeed when talented people are selected for positions worthy of their talents and integrated into a well-designed chain of command; responsibilities and expectations are clear; substantive interaction occurs often and seamlessly; and the guy at the top lets those below him call their shots and leaves for himself the most important shots, which he calls after synthesizing the flow of information received from reliable sources.

Eisenhower's aspirational plan for optimum organizational structure in the White House was foreshadowed by an incident during his military career that provided a strong indication of how his extraordinary management skills as a general could be transferred to his presidency, as described in Fred Greenstein's book, *The Hidden-Hand Presidency,* which was released in 1982 and triggered the rise of Ike's ranking. The incident occurred shortly after America entered World War II, when Eisenhower was leading the Allied campaign in North Africa. A group of senators had accompanied Secretary of War Henry Stimson on a trip to Ike's headquarters. Shortly after arriving, they asked how major responsibilities were assigned in the emerging war effort but received little information in response except a vague comment about "the mystery of leadership."[393]

Years later, in his book on Eisenhower's war years, Pulitzer-winning historian Stephen Ambrose gave his direct *unmysterious* answer to the senators' question: "Cunningham commands the naval forces, Tedder commands the air forces, and Alexander commands the grand forces. What in the hell did Eisenhower command? He commanded Cunningham, Tedder, and Alexander [all esteemed British military leaders]—and did it by holding weekly meetings with the three officers, having frequent casual conversations with them individually, acting as referee to settle their inter-service disputes, and above all by the force of his personality."[394]

In his presidential memoirs, Eisenhower explained how his underwhelming impression of FDR's and Truman's administrative organizations during the war impacted his thoughts on how best to construct a team when his time came to serve in the Oval Office:

> For years I had been in frequent contact with the Executive Office of the White House and I had certain ideas about the system, or lack of system, under which it operated. I wanted to organize the White House for *efficiency*.... Organization cannot make a genius out of an incompetent, but on the other hand, disorganization can scarcely fail to result in inefficiency and can easily lead to disaster.[395]

In managing the presidency's moving parts, Ike organized his staff as he had done in the war, delegating major responsibilities to those whom he trusted while knowing it would reflect poorly on him as a leader to hoard power. On this subject, he liked to quote Helmuth von Moltke, leader of the German army more than a half century before: "Centralization is the refuge of fear."[396]

Greenstein recognized Eisenhower's "preoccupation with organization" and how "some of his organizational innovations became central components of the modern presidency, including the provision for a White House Chief-of-Staff, National Security Advisor, and Congressional Liaison Office.[397] The approach engaged his colleagues in a continuing process of policy deliberation and coordination, and wielded them into a cohesive team."

A. The Cabinet: Titans and Sounding Boards

Success in leading the executive branch usually begins when a strong president-elect selects a Cabinet whose members have the professional horsepower to run their assigned departments, show a willingness to collaborate with colleagues, and above all, commit to providing a bulwark of good counsel and full support for the guy in charge. Decades before social consciousness elevated the importance of diversity as a necessary component for an organization's having a broader based perspective, Dwight Eisenhower's Cabinet was described by Hitchcock as a group that had at least some divergence in their political slants, but overall "felt and looked much like a corporate boardroom," made up of "a small, dynamic coterie of men with shared experiences, ideals, values, and ambitions," who "had developed a network of influence and corrections," and most definitely were "*not* brought in for their diversity or heterodox ideas."[398]

To find the right people for his Cabinet, many of whom he had never met before, Eisenhower relied on the recommendations of two men: his wartime colleague and close friend General Lucius Clay and Herbert Brownell, former chairman of the Republican National Committee.[399] Clay said Ike's preference was to have "people who were *exceedingly competent* and on whom he could count to run their departments"[400]—that is, just as General Eisenhower didn't want to run the naval force, air force, or ground forces in North Africa, President Eisenhower didn't want to run the State Department, Justice Department, or Treasury Department in Washington, DC.

For secretary of state, he chose John Foster Dulles, partner at the Wall Street law firm of Sullivan & Cromwell; for attorney general, he selected Brownell, a partner at the New York law firm of Lord Day & Lord, who had impressed him throughout the campaign; for secretary of defense, he picked Charles Wilson, CEO of General Motors ("What's good for General Motors is good for the country!"); for secretary of the treasury, George Humphrey, head of M. A. Hanna Company, a Michigan-based multinational steel, plastics, and banking conglomerate; for secretary of interior, former Oregon governor Douglas McKay; for secretary of commerce, Massachusetts banker

Sinclair Weeks; for secretary of agriculture, Ezra Taft Benson, a leader of the Mormon Church; and for postmaster general (who had a multitude of patronage jobs to fill), Arthur Summerfield, outgoing chair of the National Republican Committee and a successful car dealer in Michigan. None had prior experience in Washington, were professional politicians, or came from academia, but all of them were self-made; like-minded in purpose; and ready, willing, and able to lead their departments.[401]

The Cabinet had regularly scheduled meetings with the president on Friday mornings[iv,402] and attendance was mandatory. To ensure that everyone stayed engaged, per Smith, "they were *not* permitted to raise matters that pertained solely to their own departments."[403] From start to finish, Ike set the tone at the meetings with his electric presence and unique power to convey his authority. On the one hand, he pushed the team to share their thoughts while coming together in consensus toward his treasured "Middle Way" in addressing the day's issues. On the other hand, throughout the meetings, it was the president who drew the lines, made the decisions, and issued the orders.[404]

Although Eisenhower called his Cabinet a "policy body," Greenstein determined that this did *not* mean it "was a policy-*making* body;" rather, it was a policy "sounding board" and at their meetings Ike treated them "as general statesmen, not simply as defenders of departmental positions," although the statesmen never forgot who was commander-in-chief.[405]

As the head of the Congressional Liaison Office (discussed later in this chapter), Wilton "Jerry" Persons attended Cabinet meetings. Here was his description of how Eisenhower stoked the weekly discussions among his top lieutenants: "He hit fungoes out there just to see what would happen. He directed questions to each person around the table, and everyone was free to contribute his thoughts on any subject, regardless of his responsibilities."[406] State Department policy

---

iv In his two terms, Ike averaged thirty-four Cabinet meetings a year, which meant the Cabinet met almost every Friday except when the president was traveling or ill. See: Fred I. Greenstein, *The Hidden-Hand Presidency: Eisenhower as Leader* (Johns Hopkins University Press 1982), 113.

planning director Robert Bowie also attended many Cabinet meetings and witnessed how the president deepened the discussions by showing "an uncanny ability to enter directly and forcibly into a debate *without squelching it*."[407]

In her instructive book *How Ike Led*, international political consultant Susan Eisenhower said that for her grandfather's Cabinet, he insisted on unbiased input and a spirit of camaraderie, believing it was more important to "get good people to join his administration than be concerned with someone's political orientation—*as long as they could be counted on to join his Middle Way*."[408] For his process at meetings, just as Ambrose said Ike had done with his wartime commanders, Susan determined that in the White House, he "would elicit the views of the subordinates, referee their debates, listen for new perspectives, and then make his own decision as the supreme decider and strategic leader."[409]

When differences of opinion arose, he did not bully anyone, though Clay said Ike would "test a man's strength of belief and his logic, and require those with conflicting thoughts to prove their case," as he moved them toward his ultimate objective: "unity of purpose."[410] Thus, his method in fulfilling the Cabinet's potential involved choosing people of the highest caliber who flourished in leading their respective departments while abiding under his authority; and making sure they stayed in a mode of brainstorming solutions to problems while holding fast to collaboration, compromise, and conciliation as their guiding principles.

Just as top classical musicians enjoy performing under a dynamic symphony conductor whose genius is evident and control is absolute, so it was for Cabinet members at meetings led by Dwight Eisenhower. Not only did he show them "a quick mind and a strong and vigorous personality," per White House staff secretary Andrew Goodpaster,[411] but he also dazzled them with his sheer brilliance, using what seasoned diplomat George Kennan recognized as Ike's "intellectual ascendancy over every man in the room."[412] Yes, life is good in an organization's top echelon when every person in leadership positions believes that the boss *is* the smartest guy in the group.

Through this interpersonal dynamic, per Greenstein, Eisenhower used Cabinet meetings as "his bully pulpit."[413] By the time they ended, members *knew* they had played a part in making history, having seen how the boss advocated, argued, questioned, and listened to them before all the information gained from their discussions jelled in his mind, at which point he announced his decision on the issues they had covered.

Greenstein noted how the sessions elevated the group's *esprit de corps* because "Eisenhower knew advice-seeking was an effective tool for winning the willing support of those he consulted, even though he might not take their advice."[414] Cabinet members surely reveled in alpha male bliss knowing they had not only been "in the room where it happened," but provided input when major policy was proposed, discussed, debated, and determined by the world's most powerful leader. Furthermore, Ike's grandson David Eisenhower, author of two books on his grandfather (one a Pulitzer-finalist), recognized that "including all in discussions greatly minimizes the possibility that a leader's decisions will be subverted by an insider dissenter."[415]

Based on his personal experience, Bradley Patterson, deputy secretary of state during most of Eisenhower's presidency, who later published, *The President's Cabinet: Issues and Answers* expanded upon Greenstein's point:

> Nothing can equal the impact on a group of Cabinet officers of hearing the President, *in person*, deliver private remarks about his own decisions and priorities, his disappointments of the past, and his hopes for the future. Coming from an emphatic and articulate man like Eisenhower, often with some purple language added, Cabinet remarks by the Chief Executive carry a strength and an indelibility which the senior most White House aide cannot duplicate.[416]

B. The National Security Council: Shaper of Foreign Policy

Smith contrasted how, unlike his Cabinet, Eisenhower's National Security Council actually *set* his foreign policy and in the international realm *was* "his principal tool for governing."[417] Empowering the NSC to have this crucial role in his administration was a dramatic change from Harry Truman's presidency where the Council played such a small role in addressing international relations that Truman rarely bothered to attend their meetings.[418]

Eisenhower saw the Council's potential value immediately and put it to work right off the bat. Throughout his presidency, their meetings occurred every Thursday morning with Ike at the head of the table. He met with the NSC fifty-one times in his first twelve months as president. Over his two terms, the Council had 366 meetings, and the president led 329 of them.[419] Members included Robert Cutler, Ike's top assistant in the 1952 presidential campaign who was chosen for the newly created position of National Security Advisor[v]; Secretary of State John Foster Dulles; CIA head Allen Dulles; Secretary of Defense Wilson; Secretary of the Treasury Humphrey; and those who held the positions of Chairman of the Joint Chiefs of Staff and the Atomic Energy Commission and Directors of the Bureau of the Budget and the Office of Foreign Assistance.

Hitchcock revealed how in the early summer of 1953, after being in office a few months, Eisenhower made it clear that he wanted the NSC to *make* policy when he gave them the task of preparing "a top-secret document that articulated America's grand strategy for the global Cold War."[420] After the Council completed their assignment, they delivered a report on July 16, and Eisenhower promptly rejected it—for being too conventional in how it addressed America's potential confrontations with the Soviet Union.[421] The document showed that NSC members were stuck in a World War II/Korean War mindset of ground war as the most likely scenario for engagement in the Cold War.[422] Ike unabashedly sent them back to the drawing board, saying

---

v The position was originally called Assistant to the President for National Security Affairs.

he wanted a new report that reflected "more strategic patience, resilience, and vigilance."[423]

The Council produced its second "Basic National Security Policy" position paper in October 1953. This time around, Eisenhower accepted it because it contained a sentence that guided Ike's thoughts throughout his presidency: "In the event of hostilities, *the United States will consider nuclear weapons to be as available to use as other munitions*."[424] This statement of world-changing policy was the secret sauce behind Eisenhower's eight years of success in his diplomatic maneuvering. It became known as the "New Look" (invoking a popular term in the 1950's fashion scene) and was at the heart of Evan Thomas's book on Eisenhower's foreign policy, *Ike's Bluff*.

In essence, beginning in the first year of his presidency, Ike and his National Security Council had their way in saber-rattling stare downs abroad by successfully *bluffing* the threat to use nuclear weapons. The strategy made America's foes blink and then back down all over the world. He used it to dodge one Cold War landmine after another—in the Korean War in 1953; the First Formosa Strait Crisis (Quemoy and Matsu) in 1954 to 1955; the Suez Crisis in 1956; the Second Formosa Strait Crisis in 1958; and the Berlin Crisis in 1958 to 1959.

Unlike the collegial sounding board culture of Eisenhower's Cabinet meetings where members covered a broad scope of issues by catching the "fungoes" hit to them by the president and throwing them back with opinions freely expressed while having little or no skin in the game, Greenstein perceived that at the NSC:

> The operating procedures for framing and conducting discussion were at once more formally elaborated and more conducive to fostering pointed discussion of disagreements over genuinely consequential issues.... It was the mandate of the National Security Advisor (who served as the Chairman of the NSC Planning Board) from Eisenhower to make sure that differences were brought into the open and clearly stated.[425]

Council meetings were more intensely focused on hot button issues than Cabinet sessions because they followed a tight agenda, set and refined, per Greenstein, at "twice-a-week, three hour-long working sessions of the NSC Planning Board comprised of the senior policy advising officers in each of the constituent departments represented in the NSC."[426] As with the Cabinet, the NSC's final decisions were made by the president but only after he had discussed and debated the issues on a much more heated confrontational basis with the Council's members[427]—that is, during the NSC meetings, Eisenhower and his Council smashed line drive rockets at each other—not fungoes.

A good example of how the NSC operated took place in 1954 when it debated whether American troops should supplement French troops in France's Vietnam War as the turning point battle at Dien Bien Phu raged. Smith wrote:

> At the meeting of the National Security Council on April 29, 1954, Eisenhower *laid down the law*. There would be no intervention in Vietnam [even though Secretary of State Dulles wanted it to happen]. For almost two hours, Eisenhower waged a one-man battle against the members of the NSC, all of whom advocated coming to France's rescue.... The President: "To go in unilaterally to Indochina or other endangered areas would amount to an attempt to police the whole world. If we attempt such a course of action, we would lose all our significant support in the free world."[428]

Thus, in organizing and leading his administration in the critical foreign policy arena during the height of the Cold War, Eisenhower brought into the room his top guns—the guys with the most skin in the game for handling the most critical responsibilities in the event of conflict abroad—and he then went eyeball-to-eyeball with them over what America should do in confronting potentially world-changing events. To ensure the process was thorough, efficient, and timely, Ike and the Council rigorously maintained their weekly meeting schedule and discussed issues in line with a well-planned agenda. The fruit of this adroit organizational process was Eisenhower's superior foreign policy track record as described in this chapter's introduction.

C. Lobbying by Cabinet Departments and the Congressional Liaison Office: Moving Mountains in the House and Senate

In addition to his Cabinet and National Security Council, another organizational component of Eisenhower's administration that was critically important to his success as president was what he put into place to maximize his working relationship with Congress. Per his biographer Michael Birkner, the effort allowed him to function as "legislator in chief,"[429] and it included a lobbying staff within each Cabinet department who collaborated with the Congressional Liaison Office (CLO), a group no prior president had thought to create, that was responsible for pushing through Ike's highest priorities in Congress.[430]

Stephen Hess worked in the White House as a speechwriter during Eisenhower's presidency. In his 2012 article for the Brookings Institute, "What Congress Looked Like from Inside the Eisenhower White House," he gave this explanation for how the Capitol Hill lobbying load was shared between the departments' staffs and the CLO:

> The modus operandi for dealing with Congress was to let the departments do the heavy lifting, which helped keep down the size of the White House staff and insured that lobbying was done by experts in substance, rather than simply experts in lobbying. It also kept the President out of the line of fire. The departments' lobbyists had the day-to-day contact with Congressional committees and took responsibility for getting legislation pertinent to their department passed. The CLO conducted a major assault on Capitol Hill only once or twice a year on the "presidential" issues.[431]

All lobbying efforts in Eisenhower's administration had to deal with the challenge that in six of his eight years at the helm, the Democratic Party controlled both houses of Congress, though on some issues, Ike had tougher dealings with Republicans than Democrats. Smith wrote: "His principal adversaries throughout his tenure as president were not Democrats but the calcified wing of the Republican Party, which continued to live in the shadow of Calvin Coolidge and see communists under every rock."[432]

Regarding the newly created CLO, which led the lobbying effort on the issues most important to Ike, Susan Eisenhower explained its purpose: "to assure steady, ongoing communications with members of the House and Senate, and make members of Congress, including Democrats, partners on the most critical issues that needed to be addressed."[433] On key issues, the boss's order to the CLO was: "If a congressman or senator, Republican and Democrat alike, called to talk to the president, he or she should be put straight through."[434]

For its first five years, the CLO was led by "Jerry" Persons, who had worked with Eisenhower as the War Department's chief lobbyist during World War II and later served on his NATO staff. In between his military assignments, Persons worked as a lobbyist in the nation's capital. In his book *Eisenhower the President,* White House Staff member William Ewald described Persons as: "a genius in assessing the aims of Congress, and a man of no individual philosophical bent: Whatever Eisenhower wanted—left, right, or center, Persons would deliver."[435] Cold War historian Chester Pach Jr. offered a similar opinion of Persons, calling him "a master of diplomacy and compromise, whose staff proved adept at the delicate task of exerting influence without bruising egos on Capitol Hill."[436]

Birkner explained that "one of Persons' responsibilities at the CLO was to ensure Ike knew the specifics—and the political implications—of bills heading for his desk. If that meant calling in experts, he would do that."[437] Persons's elevated stature in the pecking order of Eisenhower's White House was proven by the facts that he attended the weekly Cabinet meetings. After Ike's heart attack in 1955, a committee of six men took over the president's duties until he recovered. Persons was one of the six.[vi,438]

The schedule and organization for the extensive lobbying efforts in the Eisenhower administration were set up such that every Saturday, the lobbyists from the Cabinet departments gathered at the White House and met with the CLO. During Persons' years on the job, his top lieutenant was Bryce Harlow, who succeeded his boss in 1958 when Persons replaced Sherman Adams as White House Chief of Staff. Harlow's top aide during his three years of leading the CLO was Clyde Wheeler, who had previously led the lobbying staff at the Department of Agriculture. Wheeler explained how the Saturday meetings went under Harlow's leadership:

> Bryce went around the room and asked each of us who we had been talking to on the Hill, who was backing our programs, and who was against us. He always let us have our say before smoothly setting out the Eisenhower agenda and how it affected each agency. After our Saturday meeting, he would prepare a detailed agenda for the president to use in his weekly meetings with Republican congressional leaders.[439]

Thanks to the synchronization among the Cabinet departments' lobbyists, the CLO, and the president, and despite the stacked deck of Democrats and Old Guard Republicans in Congress at the time, Eisenhower largely succeeded in having the executive branch work with the legislative branch to achieve his most important goals. The collaboration worked because in Ike's dealings with Congress, Harlow observed that the president set his tone "more to induce than demand."[440]

Eisenhower also gained rapport on Capitol Hill by being transparently bipartisan, and thereby above the fray, as proven by his behind-

---

vi The other five were Vice President Nixon, Secretary of State Dulles, White House Chief of Staff Adams, Attorney General Brownell, and Treasury Secretary Humphrey. See: William I. Hitchcock, *The Age of Eisenhower: America and the World in the 1950s* (Simon & Schuster 2018), 281.

the-scenes leadership in bringing down Republican senator Joseph McCarthy (described later in this chapter); his active participation in defeating the Bricker Amendment in 1954, a measure pushed by isolationist Republicans who sought to limit the commander-in-chief's capacity to make agreements with foreign countries;[441] his bringing together a coalition of Republicans and Democrats to support the Interstate Highway Act and the St. Lawrence Seaway;[442] his making a point of hosting every member of Congress for a meal at the White House at least once a year;[443] his having frequent late afternoon cocktails with Democratic Speaker of the House Sam Rayburn and Senate Majority Leader Lyndon B. Johnson;[444] and his supporting some of Franklin D. Roosevelt's social welfare programs, especially Social Security, which Eisenhower succeeded in expanding.[445]

Another necessary component of Eisenhower's staying on top of the executive-legislative dynamic was making sure that the bills he deemed truly objectionable never became law. In his two terms, he vetoed 181 bills and only two of them were overturned, an amazing 97.3 percent success rate given that the opposing party-controlled Congress during most of his presidency and his own party always had a coterie of Eisenhower antagonists.[446]

As Eisenhower observed the effectiveness of the talented people in his Cabinet, National Security Council, departmental lobbyist teams, the CLO, and throughout his administration, and saw how seamlessly they performed under the watchful eye of White House Chief of Staff Adams, while giving him the respect for his authority and support he needed in all aspects of his presidency, he surely beamed when he made this diary entry after his first year in office, putting into words an observation that would hold true through his terms:

> I have had a good many years of experience in selecting people for positions of heavy responsibility, and I think the results so far achieved by this Cabinet and by other close associates, justify my conviction that

> we have an extraordinarily good combination of personalities. I think the individuals in the Cabinet and other offices like each other. At least, I can detect no sign of mutual dislike among the group. I know that I like them all; I like to be with them; I like to converse with them; I like their attitude toward their duty and toward governmental service.[447]

The way Eisenhower executed personnel selection, delegation, supervision, and interaction among those in his administration provides a model for all leaders who aspire to have an effective support structure. Not surprisingly, it matched how he had led the world's largest military force as Supreme Allied Commander in World War II.

To summarize, any leader who seeks the highest level of performance from a large organization can learn from these aspects of Ike's approach:

- Choose strong competent people and put them in the right place to maximize their talents; give them the freedom to do their jobs without interference; and make sure they are committed to collaboration, compromise, and conciliation—such that they are not afraid to advocate views that conflict with others yet they stay in a mode of civil discourse, and are willing to yield to the authority of the person on whose desk the buck stops;
- Adhere to a schedule of frequent meetings guided by rigorously planned agendas that keep discussions on track and substantive; and
- Preside over the process with energy, optimism, respect for others, and a willingness to share the floor to inspire the open expression of views, while always striving to build a consensus-driven "middle way" solution that will ultimately be embraced in a way that supports the person with ultimate authority.

Leadership Trait #2: **Exercising Patience to Reap Major Dividends**

Anyone who has ever led an organization in a time of crisis has heard voices urging him to move "Faster, Faster, Faster!" Despite those voices, a wise leader knows "Haste Makes Waste."

Dwight Eisenhower did not order the D-Day invasion until he believed every aspect of the operation was exactly where it needed to be and the enemy was in its most vulnerable position. Greenstein determined that Ike "personally made the decision [about when to invade Normandy] *at the latest possible time* that would still permit implementation."[448] He maintained this commitment to patience throughout his presidency regardless of how much advisors and critics pressed him to move faster, and it invariably rewarded him with the desired outcome.

Like Theodore and Franklin Roosevelt, Eisenhower chose for his presidential role model Abraham Lincoln, a leader of wisdom and patience, virtues that usually go hand in hand. Through his extensive dealings with Eisenhower, Larson witnessed his boss's "prodigious knowledge of Lincoln life and writings."[449] That being the case, Ike surely knew that on the patience front, in the years of Lincoln's political career that preceded his presidency, although he lost several elections, he nonetheless persevered until finally grabbing the brass ring In November 1860.

In line with Ike's knowing Lincoln's patient career path, Thomas gave this overview of Eisenhower's patience during his military career to the effect that though his walk up the ladder was slow, he stayed with it:

> At the beginning of Eisenhower's presidency, he invoked "honesty of purpose, calmness, and *inexhaustible patience*" as "the principles by which I try to live" in a letter to a friend who was fretting about Senator Joe McCarthy's capturing the headlines. Tempered by delayed gratification—denied combat in

> World War I, held back in Washington by General Marshall at the outset of World War II—Ike was long practiced in swallowing his ambition and disguising his guile. His patience, in public at least, was nearly "inexhaustible."[450]

Eisenhower was also aware that during Lincoln's presidency, he'd shown patience throughout the Civil War: waiting for the Confederates to fire the first shot at Fort Sumter; giving his generals ample time to prove whether they had what it took to lead the Union army before he replaced them; delaying the Emancipation Proclamation's issuance until after his troops won a major victory; and waiting to make his big push with Congress on the Thirteenth Amendment until after the war's tide had turned and he had been elected to his second term.

To show Ike's awareness of Lincoln as the leader he most wanted to emulate, Thomas revealed that Eisenhower "closely studied Lincoln's elliptical style—in particular his ability to command headstrong political rivals and balky generals with a mixture of *patience*, firmness, and cunning"... such that Ike regarded Lincoln as "the master of men" who "by guile and *patience*, and a subtle mix of moral, mental, and physical strength bent to his will some outsize figures."[451] His hero worship of Lincoln was so all encompassing that early in Ike's presidency, he painted his hero's portrait in his second floor studio at the White House, and at his Gettysburg farmhouse, the only framed picture in his office was of Lincoln, and a small bust of the Great Emancipator sat on the television in his glassed-in porch.[452]

To explain how he stayed confident about the pace of his decision-making, Lincoln famously said "I am a slow walker, but I never walk back."[453] Eisenhower took that statement to heart and made it his goal as well. In fact, connecting dots, just as Ike's organizational genius made its way into his toolkit by reason of his long military career, his Job-like patience came from his lifelong desire to lead like Lincoln.

A. Prevailing Over Joe McCarthy

During his White House years, nothing demonstrated Dwight D. Eisenhower's patience and authority more than how he handled Senator Joseph McCarthy, the scoundrel who promulgated the Red Scare. For the last three years of his presidency, Ike's predecessor Harry Truman used a direct approach and publicly attacked "Tailgunner Joe," and it totally failed to bring down the young senator after he had burst on the scenes with his headline-grabbing speech to the Women's Republican Club of Wheeling, West Virginia, on February 8, 1950. In his bogus pronouncement that day, McCarthy claimed he had a list of 205 men employed in the State Department "who have been named as members of the Communist Party and members of a spy ring." Truman's strong retorts to the false allegations only increased the demagogue's influence,[454] such that by the time Eisenhower was inaugurated in January 1953, McCarthy's popularity was soaring among a sizable bloc of Americans, especially after getting a bump from his 1952 reelection as a senator from Wisconsin.

Historian David Eisenhower noted the political realities in play as his grandfather devised a necessarily deliberate plan to end McCarthy's reign of influence. Before receiving the Republican nomination for president in 1952, Ike had had no prior political affiliation, as demonstrated by the fact that President Truman offered to step down as commander-in-chief in 1948 if Eisenhower would agree to be the Democratic nominee (and have Truman as his vice president). Once Ike decided to pursue the presidency as a Republican in 1952, many GOP leaders believed him to be too bipartisan and not conservative and isolationist enough to align with their views of the party's essential identity.[455]

In the context of those facts, and given that McCarthy was a Republican, for Eisenhower to have pursued the Wisconsin senator immediately after being sworn in would have raised questions to some about his loyalty to the party. Attempting to bring down McCarthy at the start of his presidency, according to David Eisenhower, "would have vindicated GOP critics who believed Ike to be a Democratic Trojan Horse—which he most definitely was not—and would have resulted in a loss of authority for him in the short term," given that during the first two years of his presidency, Republicans held the majority in both the House and Senate.[456]

Per David Nichols' fine book *Ike and McCarthy: Dwight Eisenhower's Secret Campaign Against Joseph McCarthy*, at the outset of his presidency, Eisenhower's "simple approach to dealing with McCarthy was: *ignore him*—at least in public."[457] To make sure he stayed disconnected from McCarthy, the president *never* said the senator's name in public. Ike explained why his approach was sound (and Truman's approach backfired): "Never get in a pissing match with a skunk."[458]

Early on, McCarthy attempted to disrupt Eisenhower's White House. In late February 1953, a month after Ike was sworn in, McCarthy opposed the president's choice of veteran diplomat Charles "Chip" Bohlen to become the US ambassador to the Soviet Union, and attempted to assassinate Bohlen's character with unsubstantiated innuendo. Unfazed, using his stellar lobbying team, Ike worked behind the scenes with senators from both parties and got Bohlen confirmed 74–13.

For his next effort at disturbing the Eisenhower administration, on March 27, 1953, McCarthy made a surprise announcement to the national media that he had succeeded in negotiating a trade agreement with several Greek shipping magnates that required them to cease doing business with communist countries. Making such an international commerce deal was within the jurisdiction of the government's executive branch and, therefore, *not* within the purview of a senator acting unilaterally. When McCarthy announced the alleged deal, Eisenhower immediately arranged a meeting between the senator and Secretary of State Dulles, who told McCarthy in no uncertain terms that he needed to abide by the separation of powers. The shipping deal soon disappeared.

As the tension between McCarthy and Eisenhower grew, the president's closest advisor, his brother Milton, urged him to go public with his thoughts on the senator. Brother Dwight refused: "I would not demean myself or the presidency by getting in the gutter with him."[459] Nichols described how Ike "instinctively understood that treating McCarthy as inconsequential would drive the senator into self-destructive behaviors."[460]

McCarthy's bogus spiel focused on the need to locate and remove the alleged multitudes of communist sympathizers who worked for the government. Though the senator's claims were not supported by credible evidence, Eisenhower knew that, in fact, there were at least *some people* in the federal government whose activities were treasonous and, therefore, they needed to be identified and fired. Again, seeking to lessen McCarthy's stature without attacking him directly, Eisenhower ramped up his own government effort to ferret out communists, and made it clear to the public that taking responsibility for "internal security" was the job of the commander-in-chief and his attorney general—and, thus, by inference, *not* the duty of a crackpot senator.

Throughout Ike's first year in office, McCarthy (presumably seeking to promote himself for a presidential run against Eisenhower in 1956) kept making front page news with his scare tactics. In time, Eisenhower got tired of playing defense so he began strategizing on how he could get ahead of the senator's fabricated publicity-driven agenda.

An errant McCarthy tactic which Eisenhower foresaw was the senator's attempt to generate headlines by using his Congressional subpoena power to compel members of Ike's administration to testify before the senator's committee. Knowing McCarthy would use a public hearing to browbeat and slander his aides, in early 1954, to get ahead of his adversary, Eisenhower directed Attorney General Brownell to do what it took, within the law, to allow those in his administration to be able to assert executive privilege as the basis for not having to testify and thereby get the senator's subpoenas quashed. Brownell proceeded to win the privilege fight, and thereby succeeded in denying McCarthy the opportunity to attack the president's aides with his false claims.

Also in early 1954, the Eisenhower White House played offensive "hidden-hand" hardball when it directed the US Army's legal team to investigate McCarthy and his chief advisor Roy Cohn in their efforts at pressuring the Army to provide favorable treatment for their Red Scare crony David Schine. Evidence soon came to light confirming that Schine received such preferential treatment and it ultimately became critical information that brought down McCarthy.

On June 9, 1954, McCarthy finally crashed and burned on national television when he was humiliated for his slanderous attacks on innocent people by lawyer Joseph Welch, Special Counsel to the US Army. The setting for the takedown was the Army-McCarthy hearings in which the senator, as Chairman of the Senate Committee on Government Operations and its Subcommittee on Investigations, was purportedly investigating whether an army dentist with alleged communist tendencies had been promoted at the US Army's facility at Fort Monmouth, New Jersey. In his biography, *Ike: An American Hero*, Michael Korda gave this vivid word picture of the image Joe McCarthy presented on national television during the Army-McCarthy hearings: "His heavy 'five o'clock shadow,' his sweaty face, his wild accusations, his menacing eyebrows, his beady eyes and guilty expression, all too clearly an alcoholic on a rampage."[vii,461] On December 2, 1954, after debating the issue for four months, the members of US Senate censured Senator Joseph McCarthy by a vote of 67–22.

In summary, it took eighteen months of patient, slow-but-sure, defensive and offensive "hidden-hand" tactics by Eisenhower to demonstrate his having authority over McCarthy and thereby move the Senate to bring down their depraved colleague. Hitchcock gave this assessment of how Ike's patience and strategy was instrumental in bringing about a good ending to one of the most shameful episodes in American history:

> The president played his hand well, supervising the accumulation of evidence in [the Army's chief lawyer John] Adams' dossier [of McCarthy's pressure tactics

vii In May 1957, at the age of forty-eight, McCarthy died from acute alcoholism. See: Michael Korda, *Ike: An American Hero (Harper Collins 2007), 680.*

> to get preferential treatment for Schine] and wielding executive privilege like a drawbridge, swiftly pulled up to stop the attacking hordes.... Ike had approached McCarthy as an experienced prizefighter might have assessed a hard-punching brawler: he played rope-a-dope until McCarthy, exhausted and out of ideas, lowered his guard. Then Eisenhower struck him with a powerful series of jabs.[462]

Eisenhower's successful disposition of McCarthy came to pass because of a plan that, per Lincoln, involved evaluating all the pertinent circumstances, walking slowly but never backward, and bringing his efforts to a successful conclusion by giving the government's biggest dope enough rope to hang himself.

B. Patience Rewarded on Other Fronts

Dispensing with McCarthy was not the only instance where Eisenhower's patient strategic handling of a knotty problem produced the desired outcome during his presidency. Among the most notable of other situations where Ike's emulating Lincoln's patience led to stellar results were the following:

- **The First and Second Formosa Strait Crises:**

When asked in a 1954 press conference about whether he might use atomic weapons against the Chinese to protect the islands of Quemoy and Matsu, the world's greatest bluffer replied, "For a man to predict what he is going to use would exhibit his ignorance of war. *You just have to wait* and that is the kind of prayerful decision that may some day face a president."[463] Eisenhower proceeded to wait, bluff the Chinese about his willingness to use nukes, and hold on to the islands not once but twice (in 1954–1955 and in 1958) without firing a shot. Hitchcock on Formosa One: "The saber rattling had the desired effect.... Eisenhower tried his best to pursue his broader goal of containment while avoiding war."[464] Hitchcock on Formosa Two: "After rejecting the stark choice between nuclear war and appeasement…, he retrained the generals and his secretary of state, calmed his allies, and showed that the United States would not be bullied. It was a quiet and terribly important victory for the president."[465]

- **Civil Rights:**

Eisenhower's efforts to advance civil rights during his presidency took place *long before* the moral compasses of Senators John F. Kennedy and Lyndon B. Johnson kicked in on the need to start taking action to remedy racial injustice. As Ike confronted the locked-in prejudice of the Jim Crow mentality, he knew Southern states were nowhere close to being ready to peacefully accept the Supreme Court's holdings in the 1954 and 1955 *Brown v. Board of Education* decisions, Rosa Parks's refusal to leave her seat on the front row of a city bus, or the lunch counter and bus boycotts that combined to kickstart the Civil Rights Movement in the 1950s. Susan Eisenhower explained the dangerous can of worms her grandfather faced in deciding how best to move the country forward on racial issues:

> Avoiding the prospect of violence was a key concern. Emotions were highly charged, and *Brown* overturned the daily lives of at least two generations of Americans. Until 1954, Southerners embraced the 1896 Supreme Court ruling in *Plessy v. Ferguson* which made "separate but equal" the law of the land. "To expect a complete reversal of these habits and thinking in a matter of months was unrealistic," wrote the ever-pragmatic president.[466]

Knowing there would likely be violence when efforts to integrate schools moved forward in accordance with the new Supreme Court opinions, and believing "gradualism" was the only way to minimize the violence, Eisenhower patiently pursued a "Middle Way" of "walking slow but never backward" on his actions in furtherance of Civil Rights. As key steps in the walk forward, he desegregated the District of Columbia in 1953 and America's armed forces in 1954;[viii,467] appointed racially enlightened judges throughout his presidency; worked closely with Attorney General Brownell in 1957 to get the first Civil Rights Act passed since Reconstruction (though it did not end Jim Crow); and after the leaders and people of Arkansas failed to obey the law, sent in the US Army to enforce the court-ordered integration of Little Rock's Central High School in September 1957 (as will be described later in this chapter). He did all these things while publicly empathizing with Southerners about the challenge of accepting court-ordered changes in their way of life.

- **Khrushchev's Berlin Ultimatum:**

Soon after becoming the Soviet's first secretary of the Communist Party, Khrushchev thought the time was right to end American, British, and French support of West Berlin, located in the heart of East Germany. To achieve that, in November 1958, he issued an ultimatum for the three western nations to reach an agreement with the Soviet Union and both German countries that achieved his desired result within the next six months. If they failed to make such a deal on that timetable, Khruschev warned that the Soviets and East Germany would do what it took to take over West Berlin.

In response to the ultimatum, Eisenhower took a firm but patient approach in cultivating a closer personal relationship with Khrushchev. Their relationship somehow grew warmer despite Ike's making it clear at the outset that the United States would go to war if necessary to protect West Berlin. Through the president's extended use of his quietly dynamic personality, the Soviet leader decided it would be prudent to let his deadline pass without taking any action.

What brought about the turnaround? Though negotiations took place during the six months, they did not materialize into an agreement on Berlin. Nonetheless, Khruschev withdrew his ultimatum after Ike

viii On July 26, 1948, President Truman signed into law the desegregation of the armed forces, though he failed to make sure it was fully implemented. Eisenhower was the president who made sure the law was obeyed. See: Susan Eisenhower, *How Ike Led: The Principles Behind Eisenhower's Biggest Decisions* (Thomas Dunne Books 2020), 247.

invited him to the United States and rolled out the red carpet during the Soviet leader's thirteen-day trip to America in September 1959 where among other things, he and the president visited New York City (and addressed the United Nations), Hollywood (where he met Marilyn Monroe, Elizabeth Taylor, and Frank Sinatra), Eisenhower's home in Gettysburg, and finally Camp David, where at a final meeting with the president, Khrushchev expressly abandoned the ultimatum. Hitchcock on the impact of Eisenhower's successful patient process in softening Khruschev and ultimately getting him to buckle: "He reestablished his dominance over world affairs and found a way to defuse the Berlin crisis without showing any sign of bending under pressure."[468]

Evan Thomas told the story in *Ike's Bluff* about how one day at the White House in January 1958, Eisenhower welcomed Robert Frost as his visitor. The poet had just released a new book and wanted the president, as his long-time fan, to have a copy. Frost inscribed it with this statement: "The strong are saving nothing *until they see,*" to which the president responded, "I like this maxim, perhaps best of all." Thomas wrote:

> Eisenhower had retained an unusual capacity for a man of such large ego (and being president had not deflated his ego), *to wait and see—to resist the pressure to act merely for the sake of action or for political reasons.* It was a quiet, confident kind of masculinity.[469]

As a military leader and then as president, Dwight Eisenhower knew that impatience often brings on disaster while patience usually produces a good outcome. Whether facing dishonest demagogue Joe McCarthy, hostile Cold War adversaries (where nuclear warfare always loomed as a possibility and pursuing conventional warfare would likely produce a no-way-out quagmire), or a racially divided nation unwilling to embrace Civil Rights, Ike consistently addressed complex problems during his presidency "with all *deliberate* speed"[ix,470] and never went backwards, consistent with the historic words that he was instrumental in getting into the Supreme Court's second *Brown v. Board of Education* opinion and with Lincoln's words on the best way to lead when unexpected challenges arise that take time to grasp before determining the best strategy for moving forward.

Leadership Trait #3: Play Hardball When Necessary

Continuing with the theme of Dwight Eisenhower's wartime leadership foreshadowing his presidential leadership, in her book, granddaughter Susan told the story of how at the end of the European portion of World War II, shortly after the surrender documents were signed, the Supreme Allied Commander had a brief meeting with German Army chief of staff Alfred Jodl and other Nazi leaders. Ike asked if they understood the terms of what had just been signed and they said "Yes." He then said that if they failed to adhere to them, he would hold them personally responsible.

The next day, Eisenhower learned that some German units were still fighting. He immediately had Jodl and the other German leaders arrested and imprisoned until all the fighting stopped.[471] From then on, Ike made it his mission to have the leading Nazi war criminals aggressively prosecuted and to film and publicize the full extent of the Germans' atrocities so that the whole world would know then and forever what evil things the Nazis had done.[472]

The lesson of Susan's story: If anyone ever thought about crossing a line drawn by Dwight Eisenhower, he should proceed at his own peril because once the line got crossed, Ike would not hesitate to reach into his bag of retaliatory weapons, pull out the strongest, and use it

ix Evan Thomas's research for *Ike's Bluff* led him to conclude that it was President Eisenhower who inserted into his Attorney General Brownell's amicus brief the argument that desegregation should be effectuated "with all deliberate speed." Thus, Ike's chosen words ultimately became the most important part of the Supreme Court's holding. See: Evan Thomas, *Ike's Bluff: President Eisenhower's Secret Battle to Save the World* (Little, Brown and Company 2012), 247.

with overwhelming force. Consistent with that lesson, on his desk in the Oval Office, Ike kept a plate engraved with the Latin phrase: "*Suaviter in modo, fortiter in re.*"[473] During his years in the White House, many visitors saw the plate who did not know Latin, and had to ask for a translation. My guess is that the president responded with a slight smile and a twinkle in his eye: "Gently in manner, strongly in deed." No brag. Just fact.

As long as people behaved themselves and operated within Eisenhower's instructions and expectations, he was a "got your back" ally. On the other hand, as shown by his response to the recalcitrant German leaders after their surrender, he became an unleashed tiger toward anyone who disobeyed or double-crossed him—and during his presidency some people learned that lesson the hard way.

A. The Suez Crisis of 1956

Throughout World War II and the decade that followed, on the short list of America's closest allies were England, France, and Israel. Even good friends, however, sometimes get out of line and the three nations did exactly that in the Suez Crisis of 1956. Henry Kissinger set the stage for what happened in his book *Leadership: Six Studies in World Strategy*:

> In 1954, Gamal Abdel Nasser had taken over Egypt, deposing General Muhammad Naguib, who two years earlier had replaced the monarchy. Nasser created a nationalist regime that increasingly moved toward Soviet economic support and armed itself with Soviet weapons, In July 1956, he nationalized the Suez Canal, which had been under French and British ownership. Britain was thus faced with the end of its preeminence in the region, and France with the prospect that an emboldened Nasser might redouble his support for insurgent nationalists in its own North African possessions, especially Algeria.[474]

As tension grew over who would ultimately control the Suez Canal, Eisenhower decided the best policy for the United States was to stay neutral—that is, let Egypt have the canal—and he told British prime minister Anthony Eden that England and France should *not* try to retake it. Eden assured Eisenhower he would not pursue such action and a diplomatic settlement was his preferred method for dealing with the situation.

As Ike soon learned, Eden's statement was a total lie. Unbeknownst to Eisenhower, Britain, France, and Israel had entered into a written agreement on October 24, 1956, whereby they joined forces to take back the canal from Egypt. Michael Korda explained their plan:

> The British and French collaborated on a plan in which they encouraged the Israelis—who were infuriated by terror attacks from [Egypt's] fedayeen fighters (the 1950s equivalent of suicide bombers) crossing the Sinai from Egypt into Israel—to attack the Egyptian army in the Sinai and advance toward the canal. At that point, the British and French would intervene militarily to "protect" the canal; Nasser would fall; and the canal would be back in Anglo-French hands.... It was felt that Prime Minister Eden would have no trouble in bringing Eisenhower, his old comrade in arms, around once the seizure of the canal was a fait accompli.[475]

Five days after the agreement was signed, to commence the joint effort, the Israeli army invaded the Sinai Peninsula and began moving toward the canal.

When Ike learned of the three nations' pact and subsequent invasion, realizing he'd been double-crossed by Eden, he went from "gently in manner" to "strongly in deed" in a nanosecond. Kissinger explained why the president prioritized maintaining peace in Egypt over supporting America's long-time allies: "The Eisenhower administration, viewing the Cold War as an ideological contest for the allegiance of the developing world, was transfixed by fear that the Soviet Union would use the occasion to coopt the Middle East."[476]

Believing the three countries' actions would permanently drive Egypt into the Soviet Union's camp in the Cold War, Ike gave the following order to Dulles: "Foster, you tell them, Goddamnit, that we're going to apply sanctions, we're going to the United Nations, we're going to do everything there is so we can stop this thing."[477]

True to his word, he did exactly that. His explanation for playing hardball to nullify the plans of America's former allies: "How could we possibly support Britain and France if in doing so we lose the whole Arab world?"[478] In rapid-fire sequence, he took the following actions:

- Instructed America's UN Ambassador Henry Cabot Lodge to file a motion in the UN Security Council seeking an immediate ceasefire and the removal of Israeli forces from Egypt; and when British and French vetoes blocked the motion, Lodge appealed it to the UN's General Assembly who approved it 64–5.
- Refused to use America's influence to restore the supply of oil to Western Europe after it was interrupted by the Israeli intervention.
- When British and French troops landed on Egypt's coast on November 5, Britain's pound went into freefall. To strengthen it required an infusion of dollars which the US had done in the past, when needed, to bail out the Brits. This time, however, when the call for help came, Ike said he would *not* grant Britain's request for dollars unless they removed their troops from Egypt.
- When Soviet Premier Nikolai Bulganin threatened to aid Nasser by bringing their troops into the conflict, and possibly even use their nuclear weapons to help Egypt defeat the three enemies, he invited the US to join forces with them. Eisenhower not only rejected the offer, he told Bulganin that if the Soviets entered Egypt, American forces would do the

same and oppose them. Nuclear war between the two most powerful nations in the world became a real possibility. Not wanting to start World War III, Bulganin blinked in the staredown with Eisenhower and stayed out of the conflict.

- On November 5, 1956, Election Day in the United States, because of Britain's inability to cope with the financial pressure Eisenhower applied by refusing to loan them dollars, Eden announced that the Brits were ready to agree to a ceasefire. When Ike insisted that they withdraw their troops from Egypt *immediately*, and Eden hesitated, Ike threatened to impose even harsher economic sanctions that "would drive the pound down to zero."[479] Eden caved and withdrew his troops immediately, and soon France and Israel followed suit. Two months later, the totally humiliated Eden resigned as Prime Minister.

Eisenhower came out of the Suez Crisis with a landslide election victory (57.5 percent of the popular vote and 86 percent of the electoral votes, winning forty-one of the forty-eight states) and the overwhelming approval of the American people who praised him for his handling of the crisis even though his decision to oppose Britain, France, and Israel was criticized by Truman and Ike's 1952 and 1956 presidential opponent, Adlai Stevenson. In his book *Eisenhower 1956: The President's Year of Crisis—Suez and the Brink of War*, Nichols explained why he believes Eisenhower's approach was the right move at the right time:

> Eisenhower's confrontation with his World War II allies, Britain and France, required a level of courage that's hard to fathom especially in the face of fierce criticism from the Democrats in the midst of a presidential election campaign.... Throughout the crisis, he played a major role in ushering in the post-imperial era in the Middle East.

> His paramount concern was that a Suez-type crisis might escalate into a nuclear holocaust. If that had happened, he foresaw that Americans would be "digging ourselves out of ashes, starting again..." He said in his final campaign speech on November 1, 1956: "We believe that the power of modern weapons makes war not only perilous—but preposterous. The only way to win World War III is to prevent it." By any standard, his was a virtuoso presidential performance—an enduring model for effective crisis management.[480]

Though some critics have challenged the conclusion that America's response to the Suez Crisis was ultimately prudent, the bottom line as far as this book is concerned: Eisenhower's handling of it demonstrated how a strong leader responds when anyone (friend or foe) double-crosses him—that is, with such overwhelming force delivered to the offender that it makes others realize they should not even think about crossing the line for fear of provoking the same level of wrath.

B. Little Rock in 1957

On May 17, 1954, Eisenhower's presidency changed in a flash when the Supreme Court handed down its landmark unanimous opinion authored by its new Chief Justice Earl Warren in the case of *Brown v. Board of Education of Topeka*. In *Brown*, the court overruled the 1896 *Plessy v. Ferguson* decision that held public school segregation was deemed to be protected by the Constitution as long as the quality of education was equal in white and black schools. At last, with the *Brown* decision, after fifty-eight years of *Plessy*'s nonsense, the Court acknowledged reality and recognized that when schools were segregated, the caliber of education provided to white and black students was inherently unequal, and, thus, a violation of the Fourteenth Amendment's Equal Protection Clause. As important as the 1954 *Brown* decision was, it still left open two big questions: What *methods* should be used to implement school integration and what was an *appropriate timetable* for putting the races together in classrooms?

A year later, the questions were answered when the Supreme Court handed down its *Brown II* decision on May 31, 1955, another unanimous decision authored by Warren, in which the Court held that (1) the acceptable method for integrating public schools would be determined by the federal district judge having jurisdiction over each school, and (2) integration of the schools should be achieved "with all deliberate speed."

This chapter's previous section was devoted to Ike's leadership trait of patience, and how he had success with it in his handling of Joe McCarthy, the Formosa Strait Crises, Khruschev's Berlin ultimatum, and Civil Rights. Regardless of how much Eisenhower's strides forward in Civil Rights exceeded those of his predecessors, African American leaders on the order of Martin Luther King Jr. and Jackie Robinson decried Ike whenever he endorsed the need for patience in the battle against Jim Crow. They sure sang his praises though, when he showcased his trait of "playing hardball when necessary" on September 24, 1957, and sent the US Army's 101st Airborne Division into Little Rock, Arkansas, to enforce Judge Ronald Davies' federal court order to integrate Central High School.[481]

As was his practice on other fronts, Eisenhower's personal commitment to Civil Rights was "hidden hand" and his Lincoln-inspired pace for making good things happen was by "walking slowly, but never walking back" to advance the status of African Americans. As an early example of his commitment, in March 1942 (four months after Pearl Harbor), Australian leaders made a plea for help to the Allied forces when it appeared their continent was about to be attacked by the Japanese. At the time, American military regiments were still segregated. To protect the Land Down Under, Ike sent troops to Australia that included a division of African American soldiers. When the Aussie leaders objected that their laws prohibited the importing of Negroes into their country, "Hardball Ike" responded with words to the effect, "Okay, if that's the way you want it, then you won't get any American support at all. Good luck with the Japanese." The Australians immediately withdrew their objection and accepted the black troops.[482]

The best book on Eisenhower's position on civil rights over the course of his presidency is David Nichols's *A Matter of Justice: Eisenhower and the Beginning of the Civil Rights Revolution* released in 2007.[483] It corrected many of the falsehoods perpetrated by earlier historians who had criticized Ike's racial positions, presumably due to their lack of information since the papers of Max Rabb, Eisenhower's Chief White House aide on Civil Rights, were not made available to the public until 2006.[484]

Returning to a point made earlier about Ike's organizational prowess, Eisenhower always sought to lead his administrative team and the entire nation toward the "Middle Way" to be able to achieve "unity of purpose." His becoming president while Jim Crow laws were still in effect and for the first year and a half of his White House years when *Plessy*'s "separate but equal" holding was still the law of the land, meant that from the moment he was sworn in, Eisenhower presided over a nation that was almost as deeply divided in its racial attitudes as it was when Lincoln became president in 1861.

Amid such a wide breadth of deeply held conflicting feelings among Americans, as President Eisenhower tried to calm the discord and find a middle way that the American people could accept, he acknowledged a basic problem in human nature, "You cannot change people's hearts merely by laws." Mindful of Lincoln's evolving journey almost a century before when Father Abraham dealt with the politics of slavery, Ike knew that changing hearts takes time—"slow walking" time—with the hope that over the course of the time-consuming process, there would be "no walking backwards" and "Middle Way" progress toward some measure of "unity of purpose" that could be achieved on racial equity and justice. He knew it wouldn't be easy—and it wasn't.

Before embarking on the particulars of what happened in Little Rock in 1957, Eisenhower's playing Civil Rights hardball in Arkansas should be processed on the front end by recognizing the challenge that confronts any student of history who tries to pass judgment on the decisions and mindsets of leaders from prior generations. To engage in a "long after the fact" evaluation with some measure of fairness toward the leader under the microscope, at least in the opinion of this writer, requires appraising his words and deeds *not* by using *today's* level of social consciousness, but on where the needles of the population's moral compasses rested *at the time the leader had his days in the arena*. Using Nichols' words as the basis for evaluating Ike's track record on Civil Rights during his presidency, "We must try to see the world as the men and women of the 1950s saw it."[485]

Having laid the predicate for fairness in historical objectivity, here were the pertinent facts that led to Eisenhower's playing hardball when it was necessary by ordering US Army troops into Little Rock to implement the integration of Central High School on September 24, 1957:

- Shortly after being reelected in November 1956, Eisenhower and Attorney General Brownell decided that 1957 would be the year for them to push forward a Civil Rights bill focused on addressing the fact that at the time, largely because of poll taxes, literacy tests, and outright intimidation in many communities, only 20 percent of African Americans in the United States were registered to vote.
- June 1, 1957: After extensive negotiations, the House of Representatives passed Ike's Civil Rights bill by a margin of 286–126. It created a Civil Rights Section in the Department of Justice and established a Civil Rights Commission charged with the responsibility of investigating and correcting unconstitutional violations of Civil Rights. The House bill also gave the attorney general the right to (1) enforce constitutional protections associated with Civil Rights, meaning the AG could get court orders for the integration of public schools, and (2) pursue civil contempt lawsuits

seeking damages against anyone who violated a federal court order which involved Civil Rights.

- June 19, 1957: At a press conference, Eisenhower stated that the reason he had pressed forward with the Civil Rights bill was because after *Brown II,* he had been asked: "Do I contemplate sending the Army into the South to enforce this decision?" Since the prospect of taking such action was so distasteful to him, Ike said he favored Civil Rights legislation because it provided "moderation and the development of a plan that everybody of good will could support."[486]
- August 29, 1957: The Senate passed the Civil Rights bill 60–15 (thirty-seven Republicans and twenty-three Democrats supported it, while fifteen southern Democrats opposed it) after extensive negotiations led to its being watered down from the House version. During the negotiations, on July 16, Eisenhower said at his press conference, "I can't imagine any set of circumstances that would ever induce me to send federal troops into any area to enforce the orders of a federal court, because I believe the common sense of America will never require it."[487] To get the bill passed by the Senate, Majority Leader Lyndon B. Johnson strong-armed Ike into removing the attorney general's enforcement powers.[488]

  On the same day the Senate passed the Civil Rights bill, Arkansas state court judge Murray Reed (appointed by Governor Orval Faubus) signed an order that enjoined the integration of Central High School in Little Rock. The next day, federal judge Ronald Davies signed an order that nullified Judge Reed's order.[489]

- September 2, 1957: With school scheduled to open the next day, Faubus ordered his state's National Guard to Central High School to prevent its being integrated.[490]
- September 3, 1957: Considering his enforcement power having been stripped from the Civil Rights bill by LBJ and

the Democratic senators, Attorney General Brownell advised the president that the federal government could intervene in Little Rock only if federal judge Davies signed an order that requested such intervention.[491]

- September 4, 1957: Arkansas National Guardsmen prevented nine African American students from entering Central High School, while a crowd outside the school screamed racist epithets at the adolescents.[492]

  On that same day, US Army chief of staff Maxwell Taylor ordered the Army's 101st Airborne Division to begin training in riot control and prepare for deployment to Little Rock.[493]

- September 5, 1957: Faubus sent a telegram to Eisenhower blaming the federal government for the ugly confrontation the day before.[494] Ike responded: "When I became President, I took an oath to support and defend the Constitution. The only assurance I can give you is that the Federal Constitution will be upheld by me by every legal means at my command."[495]
- September 7, 1957: Judge Davies denied the Little Rock School Board's motion to vacate his order of August 29, 1957.[496]
- September 9, 1957: Eisenhower signed into law the Civil ights Act of 1957, the first such legislation since Reconstruction in 1875. Nichols gave this tight summary of the impact of that Act:

  > It contained enduring provisions. Fifty years later, the Civil Rights Commission and the Civil Rights Division in the Justice Department still exist. While part three [of the bill, that had passed in the House], designed to give the Attorney General authority to file suits to protect all constitutional rights, including school desegregation, had been jettisoned [by the Senate], it laid the groundwork for stronger legislation in the 1960s. Weak

> as part four [of the bill] protecting voting rights was, it authorized the Justice Department to seek civil, not just criminal, federal court injunctions against discrimination in voting, and persons cited for contempt could still be prosecuted under the criminal provisions. Most important, the congressional barrier to Civil Rights legislation had been breached; and never again could Southern segregationists guarantee blockage of legislation to protect the rights of African-Americans.[497]

- On the day the bill became law, Judge Davies asked Brownell to have the federal government intervene in the case before him in Little Rock.[498] Relying on the *Brown II* holding, in his pleading that brought the US Department of Justice into the lawsuit, the attorney general sought an injunction to prevent the Arkansas National Guard from stopping the integration of Central High School.[499] Judge Davies scheduled the hearing on Brownell's injunction application for September 20.
- September 14, 1957: After the president accepted Faubus's invitation to have an in-person private meeting to discuss the Little Rock crisis, they met in Newport, Rhode Island, where Eisenhower was vacationing. Ike's hardball ultimatum to Faubus at the meeting: "In any area where the federal government has assumed jurisdiction and this is upheld by the Supreme Court, there can be only one outcome: the state will lose." After he delivered the message, Eisenhower said, "I definitely had the understanding that Governor Faubus would go back to Arkansas and act within a matter of hours to revoke his orders to the Guard to prevent re-entry of the Negro children to the school."[500]
- September 15–19: Faubus failed to revoke his prior order and Eisenhower seethed, believing the governor had violated the deal they had made in Newport.

- September 20, 1957 (a Friday): At the conclusion of the injunction hearing before Judge Davies, the judge ordered Faubus to cease and desist from stopping the integration of the high school.[501] Later that day, Faubus announced that he would comply with the federal court order. He then dismissed the National Guard from the school, which violated Eisenhower's instructions at their Newport meeting to *keep* the National Guard at the school, but have them there to *protect* the black students' *entry* into the school.[502]
- September 23, 1957 (a Monday): A mob of 1,500 local racist citizens arrived at the high school and sought to prevent black students from entering, which resulted in a three-hour riot.[503] Little Rock's school superintendent called the Justice Department and asked for federal assistance to stop the violence. That afternoon, the mayor of Little Rock sent a telegram to the president telling Eisenhower it was Faubus who had organized and inspired the mob to do what they had done.[504]

  An hour after receiving the mayor's telegram, White House Press Secretary James Hagerty read a statement from the president to the media: "The federal law and orders of a United States District Court implementing that law cannot be flouted with impunity by an individual or any mob of extremists.... I will use the full power of the United States including whatever force may be necessary to prevent any obstruction of the law and to carry out the orders of the Federal Court.... It will be a sad day for this country—both at home and abroad—if school children can safely attend their classes only under the protection of armed guards."[505]

  Two hours later, the White House issued a public proclamation titled "OBSTRUCTION OF JUSTICE IN THE STATE OF ARKANSAS: Now, THEREFORE, I, Dwight D. Eisenhower, President of the United States, under and by virtue of the authority vested in me by the Constitution...do command all persons engaged in such obstruction of justice to cease and desist therefrom, and to disperse forthwith."[506]

- September 24, 1957: Despite the president's proclamation of the day before, the mob refused to cease and desist from blocking entry to the school. At 9:16 a.m., Eisenhower received a telegram from Little Rock's mayor that said, "The immediate need for federal troops is urgent. The mob is much larger in numbers at 8 AM than at any time yesterday.... Situation is out of control and police cannot disperse the mob. I am pleading to you as President of the United States in the interest of humanity, law and order, and because of democracy worldwide to provide the necessary federal troops within several hours. Action by you will restore peace and order and compliance with your proclamation."[507]

  Shortly after noon that day, Ike signed an order for federal troops to be sent to Arkansas. His words to Attorney General Brownell: "In my career I have learned that if you have to use force, use overwhelming force and save lives thereby." By late afternoon, 1,000 US Army soldiers arrived in Little Rock.[508]

  At 9:00 p.m. that night, President Eisenhower spoke to the nation on television from the White House to explain why he had ordered the troops to Arkansas. His key justification: "Mob rule cannot be allowed to override the decisions of our courts." His final words: "One nation, indivisible, with liberty and justice for all."[509]

- September 25, 1957: Federal troops dispersed the mob at the school, and then the soldiers escorted the "Little Rock Nine" black students into Central High School.[510]

  That same day, Eisenhower told *TIME* magazine editor John Steele that sending federal troops into Little Rock, "was the hardest decision I ever had to make, except possibly D-Day. But

> it was the only thing I could do. It was a question of upholding the law—otherwise you have people shooting people."[511]

When the crisis ended and school integration had been achieved, pollsters reached out to the nation for feedback on the president's handling of Little Rock. Nichols reported that the leading poll showed that "68.4 percent of the country (77.5 percent outside the South) approved of the president's action in sending troops into Little Rock, but in the South, 62.6 percent of the people disapproved."[512]

Jean Edward Smith's assessment of Ike's handling of Little Rock:

> Eisenhower took the most divisive issue to confront American society since the Civil War and moved it toward a solution with as little rancor as possible. At the time, that satisfied neither those who sought immediate integration everywhere, nor those rabid segregationists who opposed any change anywhere. In the long run, Ike's course proved correct. His moderation carried the day. Had he not acted and sent the 101st to Little Rock, every white racist from Manassas to Vicksburg would have understood: the way to block integration is to take to the streets. Appear in sufficient numbers, and be sufficiently menacing, and desegregation will not happen. It is thanks to Eisenhower that integration proceeded and the Rule of Law prevails.[513]

Korda's perspective:

> Eisenhower acted with more energy—and in a more straightforward way—than either President Kennedy or President Johnson, and his choice of the 101st Airborne placed the crisis in the hands of troops whom he knew he could trust to enforce the law and maintain order. This was in accordance with his belief

> that if force was to be used at all, it must be on a scale that was irresistible; hence his preference for armed paratroopers rather than FBI agents. This was sound judgment, and it worked.[514]
>
> Aligned with Smith's and Korda's views, Nichols drew this conclusion:
>
> Eisenhower's policy in Little Rock reinforced the verdict of the Civil War—the supremacy of federal authority including federal court orders—over the states.... He adhered to his belief that "the true way" to advance civil rights was "with less oratory and more action." Although that stance damaged his reputation for civil rights leadership, he did not abandon his pledge that he would not "claim political credit for a simple matter of American justice."[515]

When Eisenhower later wrote his presidential memoir *Waging Peace,* he tied together his perspectives on the need to play hardball in the Suez Crisis of 1956 and the Little Rock Crisis of 1957, and why he believed what he'd done in both situations was necessary:

> What Little Rock was to law in the United States, Suez was to law among nations: an example of the United States government's staking its majesty and power on a principle of justice—a principle greater and higher than the particular interests of the individuals who clashed in the crisis. Both events, however tragic and unnecessary they may have been, have left to history a demonstration of a profound regard for that supreme law whose voice is the "harmony of the world," a law to which, in the words of Richard Hooker, all men owe "homage, the very least as feeling her care, and the greatest as not exempted from her powers."[516]

Eisenhower's Flaws

Regardless of his greatness as a leader in both the military and government arenas, as a mere mortal, Dwight Eisenhower had flaws.

His vice president Richard Nixon famously said in his book *Six Crises,* Eisenhower "was a far more complex and *devious* man than most people realized, and in the best sense of those words."[517] Nixon made this observation in the context that during the "Checkers" scandal of 1952, (which arose over Nixon's use of funds received from donors to reimburse him for campaign expenses), Eisenhower attempted unsuccessfully to get his running mate to resign from the ticket by using "hidden hand" methods, (meaning he got Thomas Dewey to tell Nixon he should drop out), rather than Ike simply telling Nixon he no longer wanted him as his running mate. Nixon refused to resign unless Eisenhower directly told him to drop out, which he would not do. Nixon stayed in place as vice president for the next eight years, although Eisenhower again tried unsuccessfully to get him off the ticket in 1956 by offering his vice president a Cabinet position, but Nixon saw the offer as a demotion and again refused to step down as VP.

The word "devious" is rarely thought of as a compliment. Ike was especially devious in how he used the CIA during his presidency, in the following situations:

(1) In 1953, again using his "hidden hand" sometimes devious approach, this time to gain access to more oil, Eisenhower authorized the CIA to oust Iran's legitimately elected (in a democratic election) prime minister who was believed to have communist leanings, to cause him to be replaced by the shah, a dictator, who made sure sufficient oil was made available to meet America's needs.[518]

(2) In 1954, Ike authorized the CIA to engineer a coup that overthrew the president of a democratic government in Guatemala who appeared to be headed toward communism. He was replaced by a dictator. The coup restored

favorable treatment to the dominant American company in Guatemala, the United Fruit Company, in which several people in Eisenhower's administration had an interest.[519]

(3) In 1959 to 1960, with Eisenhower's approval, the CIA began actively (though discreetly) planning to engineer the assassination of Cuba's communist leader Fidel Castro.[520]

(4) In the last half of 1960, Ike supported the CIA's efforts to overthrow Congo's Prime Minister Patrice Lumumba who had sought military assistance from the Soviet Union to defeat UN troops there to stabilize the country in the aftermath of its being extricated from Belgian colonial rule. CIA Director Allen Dulles viewed Lumumba as being of the same ilk as Castro. White House insiders later claimed that Eisenhower ordered the assassination of Lumumba, but before that order was carried out, Lumumba was killed in a coup led by Colonel Joseph Mobutu that overthrew him. Hitchcock wrote: "The CIA did everything possible to ensure Lumumba's death. In the process they formed an alliance with Mobutu, who became a loyal ally of the United States and one of history's most repellent dictators."[521]

When I interviewed Jean Edward Smith for my book *Cross-Examining History,* he drew this conclusion about Eisenhower's deviousness in the context of his being intertwined with the CIA during his presidency:

> You have mentioned probably the low point in the Eisenhower administration. Ike was not worried about a war between the United States and the Soviet Union or the possibility that the relationship between the two world powers might lead to a major military confrontation. But he was concerned about communist penetration abroad. So, he allowed himself to

> be led by the CIA and the Dulles brothers, and that became a low point in his presidency.[522]

Eisenhower had one more important flaw, although it was actually just a one-time mistake, that Ike later acknowledged, and it haunted him the rest of his life. During the 1952 presidential campaign, Red Scare villain Senator Joe McCarthy (running for reelection that year) had alleged that Ike's boss during World War II, General George Marshall, was soft on communism. When Eisenhower learned of the preposterous allegation, as he prepared to give a major speech in Milwaukee on October 3, 1952, he planned to defend Marshall's loyalty in that speech in no uncertain terms. Unfortunately, Wisconsin's Republican Party leaders wanted Ike to be elected *and* McCarthy to be reelected in a vote that would unite the party in their state, so they successfully urged Eisenhower to delete the part of his Milwaukee speech where he expressed his support for Marshall. It proved to be a colossal error in judgment for a person who almost always used good judgment, and Eisenhower never forgave himself for favoring McCarthy and Wisconsin's Republican Party leaders over one of his closest friends and greatest mentor at a critical time.[523]

Personal Application

You now know how Dwight Eisenhower would have answered the following questions about the leadership traits covered in this chapter. How do *you* answer them?

- How strong are the department heads in your firm who work under you? Do they not only fulfill their specific area of responsibility but also collaborate well with those in other departments?
- How have you set up the organizational structure of your firm to best use your people?
- What traits did you look for when choosing top lieutenants to lead the departments at your firm?

- Do you let your lieutenants do their jobs without micromanaging them such that you just "command the commanders"?
- How frequently do the most important committees in your firm meet? What is your level of engagement with those committees?
- What is the process at your firm for preparing a tight, well-considered agenda for each meeting?
- From beginning to end at the meetings you lead, do you maintain a high energy level?
- At your meetings' discussions, what is your ratio of speaking to listening? Do you actively solicit the opinions of others?
- Does everyone, including yourself, who participates in meetings prioritize civil discourse and mutual respect?
- Do you think anyone at the meetings you lead ever feels inhibited or intimidated from stating their position?
- When those attending meetings at your firm disagree on issues, do you push them to find a "Middle Way" consensus-driven solution?
- Do you believe that those below you in your firm's chain of command recognize that you are the smartest person in the room?
- When you make the most important decisions at your firm, do you believe those below you in the pecking order feel like they played a role in your decision?
- As the leader of your firm, what is your strategy for minimizing the number of unsound decisions made by those under you?
- Do you regard yourself as a patient person or an impatient person?
- Does Lincoln's approach to decision-making of "Walking slowly but never walking backward" resonate with you?

- Do you typically make your decisions late in the game after you have gathered the maximum amount of relevant information?
- When people below you at your firm make mistakes or move slower than your speed, are you typically patient with them?
- When someone at your firm manages to disrupt your efforts on a consistent basis, do you confront them head-on or do you work behind the scenes and through other people to reduce/eliminate their disruptions? Do you proactively think of ways to get ahead of your antagonist in order to block their plans?
- When eyeball-to-eyeball conflicts arise in your firm involving you and another person, do you typically win the stare down and make your adversary blink and back down?
- Are you willing to spend the time necessary to develop a close personal relationship with an antagonist to get them to think more favorably about your position?
- When someone flagrantly disobeys or double-crosses you, do you respond with overwhelming force against them? Are you able to do that even when that someone has historically been your friend?

May Dwight Eisenhower's leadership traits guide you through the answering of these questions, and may your answers result in achieving better results for your organization.

CHAPTER SEVEN

HOW TO GROW IN OFFICE, STAY CALM IN A CRISIS, AND HAVE WORDS INSPIRE PROGRESS— LIKE JOHN F. KENNEDY

The word "elusive" defines John F. Kennedy's essential core. In his fine biography of JFK, *Incomparable Grace*, Mark Updegrove explained why: "Even to intimates, he revealed different shades of a complicated, sometimes contradictory nature, never showing any of them the entirety of who he was. His wife Jackie determined, 'He really kept his life so [sic] in compartments,' and was 'so complex he would frustrate anyone trying to understand him. He didn't want to reveal himself at all.'"[524]

Outside his family, no one knew JFK better than his chief speechwriter and advisor Ted Sorensen, whom President Kennedy called his "intellectual blood bank." Sorensen's assessment of his boss: "Different parts of his life, works, and thoughts were seen by many people—but no one saw it all. He sometimes obscured his motives and almost always shielded his emotions."[525] In reflecting on the long-time relationship with his boss, Sorensen said they were "close in a peculiarly impersonal way."[526] His conclusions matched those of two other prominent Kennedy insiders, Ken O'Donnell and Dave Powers, who both spent countless hours with JFK and yet their book about him was aptly titled, *Johnny, We Hardly Knew Ye*.[527]

So, if Jacqueline Kennedy, Sorensen, O'Donnell, and Powers had trouble getting their arms around John F. Kennedy's psyche, despite having had maximum exposure to him for many years, how hard is it for a historian to analyze him? In his book, *JFK's Last Hundred Days: The Transformation of a Man and the Emergence of a Great President*, Thurston Clarke found one thing his intimates could agree on about the man: "Jackie and Bobby knew how *consumed* John Kennedy was with the verdict of history."[528]

What *is* history's verdict on JFK? Some aspects of it are easy to grasp. Of our forty-six presidents, though he served the seventh shortest stint in the White House[i], in the last two C-SPAN rankings polls (2017 and 2021), America's leading historians ranked him eighth best. In terms of his uniqueness as president, he was the first born in the twentieth century; the youngest ever elected[ii]; and the first Catholic. His impact on the American imagination in the modern era was off the charts as proven by his having the highest average approval rating (70 percent) during his presidency compared to all

i Those with shorter presidencies than Kennedy were William Henry Harrison, James Garfield, Zachary Taylor, Warren G. Harding, Gerald Ford, and Millard Fillmore.

ii Theodore Roosevelt became president at a slightly younger age than JFK, but entered the office not by election but because of McKinley's assassination.

his White House peers since 1945. James Giglio explained why in his book *The Presidency of John F. Kennedy*: "No other president in the twentieth century *combined* rhetoric, wit, charm, youth, and Hollywood appearance."[529] Using baseball parlance to describe the totality of what he brought to the White House, JFK was a five-tool player.

His high stature in the minds of most historians as well as a large segment of the American people is surely tied to his being perceived as a martyr, having been assassinated after serving slightly more than "a thousand days"[iii] as president—at a time when biographer Fredrik Logevall believes Kennedy was leading the country to "the zenith of its power."[530] With his efforts to lessen Cold War tensions, powerful civil rights advocacy, and eloquent speeches, along with the five tools identified by Giglio, these factors together produced an outpouring of grief after his death that for at least some Americans stayed in place for decades. Fifty years after JFK's assassination, civil rights leader and Congressman John Lewis said, "When he was killed, something died in those of us who knew him, and something died in America."[531]

Having covered some of the reasons for Kennedy's high ranking in the C-SPAN poll, three glaring parts of his dark side cannot be ignored and they were not known to the public until *after* his death. His first black mark: Following his father Joseph's reprehensible example, JFK was a reckless serial philanderer throughout his White House years, who cavorted at an almost frenzied pace with interns, White House staff, socialites, movie stars, prostitutes, a suspected East German spy, and a woman tied to organized crime.[532]

His second demerit: He was often medicated with mass quantities of narcotic painkillers and amphetamines supplied by quack doctors.[533] Although they allowed him to function most of the time at a high level, it is hard to believe the drugs never influenced his judgment.

The final stain on his honor: As will be addressed later in this chapter, JFK, his insiders, the media, the leaders of the Kennedy Presidential Library, and his family all aggressively collaborated to

---

iii Arthur Schlesinger Jr.'s bestselling biography of JFK's presidency that came out in 1965 was titled *A Thousand Days: John F. Kennedy in the White House.*

market fictional myths about his presidential performance in an attempt to enhance his place in history.[534] These actions resulted in the dissemination of falsehoods that were not known for years, and they constitute a major obstacle for anyone who seeks to determine what actually happened during his time in the Oval Office.[535]

With this mixed bag comprising Kennedy's lack of transparency, his appealing personality and notable achievements, the impact of his tragic death, and his egregious personal shortcomings, after removing the myth to discern the truth, the job of pulling all this together on the page makes a final assessment of the man rather difficult. Nonetheless, despite the questions and mysteries that surround his life, what is largely undisputed among those who have reached a final conclusion on his legacy is that he possessed the following three exemplary traits worthy of emulation by any aspiring leader:

- He *grew* in wisdom throughout his presidency as evidenced by his handling of foreign policy, economic policy, and the advancement of civil rights.
- His calm deft handling of the Cuban Missile Crisis in the face of conflicting advice from his closest advisors and top military and intelligence experts during the "thirteen days" from October 16–28, 1962, prevented what likely would have become World War III and a nuclear holocaust.
- He spoke to the American people with words and a sense of conviction so powerful that they inspired the nation to move *forward* with hope and a sense of purpose. To use Clarke's book's elegant conclusion, John F. Kennedy "married the poetry of his speeches to the power of the presidency."[536]

Leadership Trait # 1: Growth in Wisdom While in Office

Before becoming president of the United States, John F. Kennedy's only executive experience was serving as the commander of a seventy-eight-foot-long patrol torpedo (PT) boat in World War II, so small it held only him and twelve other seamen. When his distinguished military service ended[iv] at age twenty-nine, he embarked on an undistinguished legislative career in Washington, DC, starting as a congressman in 1946 and ending as a senator in 1960.[537] During those fourteen years, he endured serious lengthy illnesses that brought him close to death on three occasions.[538] When healthy, JFK was largely bored with what was happening in both houses. These factors caused him to have no real achievements in Congress.[539]

His eight years in the Senate as a Democrat coincided with the Republican President Eisenhower's two terms. During that time, he freely criticized Ike's performance, despite being largely unaware of the enormous challenges faced by the man on whose desk the buck stopped.[540] In fairness, as discussed in the previous chapter, Eisenhower's "hidden hand" approach to running the executive branch certainly did not make it easy for Kennedy or anyone else to grasp what Ike did in the Oval Office, though JFK certainly had access to information that would have shown him that his claims before and during the 1960 presidential campaign to the effect that during Ike's presidency, the United States had fallen behind the Soviet Union in nuclear armaments to the extent that our nation was on the short end of a "missile gap" were totally false.[541]

A. Growth in Handling Foreign Policy

Once JFK defeated Eisenhower's vice president Richard Nixon in the November 1960 election and was sworn in on January 20, 1961, it did not take long for him to realize how demanding the job was. By December 1962, when interviewed by reporters from the three major television networks, and asked about the difference between the job of president as he perceived it before his inauguration as compared to what the job really was, Kennedy acknowledged, "The problems are more difficult than I imagined them to be. The responsibilities placed

iv For his heroism during the war, JFK received the Navy and Marine Corps Medal (the highest non-combat decoration awarded for heroism by those branches of the armed services) and the Purple Heart.

on the United States are greater than I thought they'd be and there are greater limitations on our ability to bring about a favorable result than I perceived there would be. There is such a difference between those who advise, or speak, or legislate, and the man who [says], 'This must be the policy of the United States.'"[542]

JFK's Inaugural Address was initially viewed as his "Cold War manifesto," per Updegrove's description.[543] It was highly acclaimed by the media and practically everyone else, though it made some rash overreaching foreign policy promises to the effect that during his presidency, the United States would "pay any price, bear any burden, meet any hardship, support any friend, and oppose any foe to assure the survival and success of liberty" around the world.[544] Delivered at the height of the Cold War, the address sounded good and bold, but Kennedy soon realized that what he'd said on his presidency's first day did *not* constitute sound foreign policy. Would he be willing to pay any price, bear any burden, and oppose any foe to assure liberty and defeat communism in Laos? In Cuba? In Vietnam?

After less than three months in office, he moved forward with his inauguration pledge by following the advice of his top military and intelligence leaders in approving the CIA's secret plan to overthrow Fidel Castro's communist regime in Cuba.[545] The plan involved sending 1,500 guerrilla warfare troops trained in Guatemala and Nicaragua to invade the southern coast of Cuba at the Bay of Pigs.[546] The Joint Chiefs of Staff and the CIA believed that when the insurgents reached the shore, they would gain immediate support from the thousands of Cuban citizens who opposed Castro, and in an instant, they would all join together as a unified force and spontaneously prevail in a revolution to overthrow the new communist leader.[547] Unfortunately for Kennedy, when the guerrilla fighters landed, they were soon overpowered and seized by the much larger Cuban army, and they had no way out after JFK decided *not* to protect them with American air support.[548]

The Bay of Pigs fiasco lasted from April 17 to 20, 1961, and quickly became an international humiliation for the young president. To his credit, when it ended in inglorious defeat, Kennedy went on national television and accepted responsibility for the train wreck.[549] Then, miraculously, his approval ratings among the American people *increased* to 83 percent.[550] An explanation for the ratings surge was presumably that most people appreciated his having acknowledged his failure, though in the eyes of most, the dynamic new president was so personally appealing that he was readily forgiven, even when the public *knew* he had committed a horrendous error in judgment.

As Hugh Sidey pointed out in his biography of Kennedy, the Bay of Pigs was the first political defeat JFK ever suffered in his life.[551] He was so used to winning at whatever he pursued that he thought he would succeed in overthrowing Castro despite supporting a strategy that was ludicrous on its face. How ludicrous? Three weeks before the invasion, Kennedy asked Truman's esteemed Secretary of State Dean Acheson what he thought about the prospects for success of the future attack on Cuba. When Acheson learned Castro had 25,000 soldiers in place who could quickly move to the Bay of Pigs, he told the new president, "It doesn't take Price Waterhouse to figure out that fifteen hundred [invaders] aren't as good as twenty-five thousand [soldiers]."[552] Despite Acheson's response, JFK ignored the obvious fallacies in what was recommended by most of his advisors—and lived to regret it.

Rather than let the devastating loss at the Bay of Pigs weigh the young president down for any length of time, Sidey believed that the defeat activated the "chemistry of the Kennedy soul, which developed such determination after a setback that every faculty was sharpened and applied with double diligence, and in this way, ultimate success could be achieved."[553]

Plugging in his all-consuming determination, JFK learned from the Cuban fiasco, and it resulted in changes being made that impacted the rest of his presidency. In his thoughtful book *Coming to Terms with John F. Kennedy,* Stephen Knott identified some of the changes made by Kennedy following the Cuban disaster: "He became more suspect of expert advice, including from the military and the intelligence community," which caused him to remove Dulles as head of the CIA and Richard Bissell, the CIA's Director of National Reconnaissance, who drafted the ill-fated plan for the invasion;[554] he "secretly installed a tape-recording system in the White House to make sure that he, and he alone, would have important discussions 'on the record'"[v,555] after several of his advisers falsely claimed after the fact that they had opposed his decision to invade the Bay of Pigs; and he "intensified America's efforts to topple the Castro regime" in an operation called "Operation Mongoose" that included a plan to assassinate Castro.[556] The covert "Mongoose" initiative became instrumental in Khrushchev's decision to send nuclear missiles to Cuba in the fall of 1962, and its existence was not revealed to the public until twelve years after Kennedy's death.[557]

In his book, *JFK: The Presidency of John F. Kennedy*, Herbert Parmet recognized another lesson taken by Kennedy from the Bay of Pigs. The biographer quoted JFK telling his confidante Arthur Schlesinger Jr. two weeks after the loss, "If it hadn't been for Cuba, we might be about to intervene in Laos."[558] He also told Sorensen, "Thank God the Bay of Pigs prevented an even more disastrous commitment in Asia."[559]

The pertinent facts regarding the Laos decision were that shortly after being humbled by the Bay of Pigs debacle, and reluctant to engage militarily across the globe in what appeared to be a confused mess with little upside and a huge downside, Kennedy rejected his Joint Chiefs of Staffs' advice to intervene in Laos.[560] That proved to be a great decision because JFK and Soviet first secretary Khruschev ultimately negotiated a treaty at the 1962 Geneva Conference that diffused the tensions in Laos after they had agreed to a ceasefire the year before.[561] America's lead negotiator Averell Harriman described the final Laos settlement as "a good bad deal,"[562] certainly preferable to participating in another devastating defeat like the Bay of Pigs,

---

v JFK believed that the secret tapes he installed were his own personal property and thus, no one (except the few who knew about them, which included his brother Robert) would ever have access to them. After Nixon's Watergate debacle, all presidential tapes, including JFK's, became the property of the federal government, and his tapes first became available to scholars in the mid-1990s. As will be discussed later in this chapter, these tapes provided the key that unlocked the mystery of what happened eighteen months after the Bay of Pigs during the Cuban Missile Crisis. See: Stephen F. Knott, *Coming to Terms with John F. Kennedy* (University Press of Kansas 2022), 80.

except it would have been in a landlocked country halfway around the world extremely difficult to support militarily. Given how Cuba and Laos played out, it is not hard to imagine Kennedy's rereading his Inaugural Address a few months after he delivered it, and wincing about the outlandish overcommitments he had initially made in an effort to portray himself as an aggressive Cold Warrior.

Six weeks after the Bay of Pigs humiliation, doing his best to appear strong in its aftermath, Kennedy met Khruschev in Vienna for a summit that began on June 4, 1961. What had just happened in Cuba appeared to embolden Khrushchev to assert himself during their summit with an air of superiority toward his young counterpart, symbolized by his thumping JFK's chest as they covered their agenda, which mainly covered the future of West Berlin and the possibility for a nuclear test ban treaty.

When the Vienna sessions ended, JFK lamented to his colleagues that he thought Khruschev had gotten the better of him.[563] In fact, many historians believe that, at worst, Kennedy held his own.[564] Fearful of being perceived as weak in the aftermath of the Bay of Pigs, Kennedy doubled down on asserting his steadfast refusal to have West Berlin absorbed by the East Germans, and boldly advised Khruschev, "We are in Berlin *not* because of someone's sufferance. We *fought* our way there.... If we were expelled from that area and accepted the loss of our rights, *no one* would have any confidence in US commitments and pledges."[565]

Returning home after Vienna, in a televised speech on July 25, Kennedy reiterated his commitment to protect Berlin and told the world:

> We have given our word that an attack upon Berlin will be regarded as an attack upon us all. Berlin has now become—as never before—the great testing place of Western courage and will.... We cannot and will not permit the Communists to drive us out of Berlin, either gradually or by force. We will at all times be

> ready to talk, if talk will help. But we must be ready to resist with force, if force is used against us.[566]

In his book *An Unfinished Life: John F. Kennedy, 1917–1963*, Robert Dallek concluded that JFK's speech after Vienna "struck a masterful balance between the competing options of authentic negotiation or mutual annihilation."[567]

Knott determined that in Vienna, Kennedy began "developing something of a *personal relationship* with Khruschev which helped avert disaster" when the Berlin Wall went up in August 1961[568] (Kennedy's comment on the wall to O'Donnell: "A *wall* is a hell of a lot better than a *war*");[569] followed by a tank confrontation between the two nations two months later in Berlin that ended with a negotiated settlement that resulted in the mutual withdrawal of the tanks. The wall and tank stalemate served to preserve freedom in West Berlin and ultimately paved the way for JFK's becoming the city's most esteemed international hero two years later when he delivered his famous "*Ich bin ein Berliner*" speech on June 26, 1963, in front of 450,000 cheering Germans.

After dealing with the back-to-back no-win situations in Cuba, Laos, and Berlin, by September 25, 1961, realizing that the Cold Warrior bluster of his Inaugural Address was *not* workable because the United States would clearly *not* "pay any price, bear any burden, meet any hardship, support any friend, or oppose any foe" to prevail in the wide-ranging international battle between communism and democracy, the time came for John F. Kennedy to deliver a radically different message about his foreign policy to the United Nation's General Assembly shortly after the death (in a plane crash) of UN Secretary General Dag Hammarskjold. JFK's remarks that day conflicted sharply with what he had told the cheering masses eight months before, but because he had been educated and transformed by what had happened thus far in his presidency, he put on his peacemaker's hat and proclaimed a new and different foreign policy message to the UN:

> Let us invoke the blessings of peace. And as we build an international capacity to keep peace, let us join in dismantling the national capacity to wage war.... I therefore propose that disarmament negotiations resume promptly, and continue without interruption until an entire program for general and complete disarmament has not only been agreed but achieved.... I pledge that I will neither commit nor provoke aggression, that we shall neither flee nor invoke the threat of force, that we shall never negotiate out of fear, but we shall never fear to negotiate.... Surely the age will dawn in which the strong are just and the weak secure and the peace preserved.[570]

Kennedy's presenting himself as an advocate for peace at the United Nations foreshadowed his remarks almost two years later as the commencement speaker at American University on June 10, 1963, which he delivered seven and a half months after he and Khrushchev had both blinked to avoid nuclear holocaust and achieved a peaceful resolution in the high stakes Cuban Missile Crisis stare down.[571] As will be discussed later in this chapter, Khrushchev blinked by having Soviet ships turn around and go home in response to the American blockade around Cuba, and by finally removing his missiles from Cuba, while Kennedy blinked by *secretly* agreeing to remove US missiles from Turkey to reach a final settlement. As confirmed by Pulitzer-winning historian Martin Sherwin in his fine book *Gambling with Armageddon*, "In the aftermath of the crisis, a more stable US–Soviet relationship developed. As Anastas Mikoyan, Khrushchev's closest Presidium confidante, observed decades later, 'The missile crisis was the result of our adventurism.... Paradoxically, it has helped us lower the risks of war. If there had been no Cuban Missile Crisis, we should perhaps have organized it.'"[572]

By the summer of 1963, with a "more stable US–Soviet relationship" in place, and having weathered two and a half years of frequently threatening storms, without having caused the United States to participate overtly in any foreign wars, battle-tested Kennedy could tell the graduating students at American University that "the most important topic on earth is world peace—not merely peace in our time but peace for all time."[573] To achieve that goal, it was necessary for the United States to "reevaluate its attitude toward the Cold War," and no longer be in the business of "distributing blame or pointing the finger of judgment," but rather "deal with the world as it is.... No government or social system is so evil that its people must be considered as lacking in virtue."[574]

Kennedy's American University speech met with such approval by Khruschev that he had it broadcast all over the Soviet Union.[575] Within two weeks after JFK delivered it, American and Soviet representatives moved forward and successfully conducted negotiations on the first Nuclear Test Ban Treaty, consummated by an initialed agreement on July 25, 1963,[576] a fully signed agreement on August 5, 1963, a Senate ratified (by a vote of 80–14) treaty on September 24, 1963, and unanimous approval of it by the Presidium of the Supreme Soviet on September 25, 1963. This caused the treaty to go into effect October 10, 1963, and Kennedy believed it was the greatest achievement of his presidency.[577]

Three years prior to the Test Ban Treaty, while running for president on September 9, 1960, JFK told a crowd in Fresno, California, that if elected, he "had a simple wish on how he wanted to be remembered. 'All I want people to say about me is what they said about John Adams,' he allowed: 'He kept the peace.'"[578] In those remarks, JFK quoted Adams' words, in his final years, "as death drew near, he wrote to a trusted friend: 'I desire no other inscription over my gravestone than this: 'Here lies John Adams, who took upon himself *the responsibility of peace* with France.'"[579]

After learning the hazards of instigating war with Cuba in the third month of his presidency, JFK drew lessons that ultimately allowed him to follow in Adams's footsteps and fulfill the "responsibility of peace" amidst major Cold War tensions in Cuba, Laos, and Berlin. Admittedly, shortly before Kennedy's death, after an American-supported coup overthrew the Diem regime in South Vietnam on

November 1, 1963, JFK ramped up the number of American "advisors" in Vietnam to 16,000,[580] but the consensus among the impartial historians who have studied the record is that it is impossible to predict one way or another whether JFK would have escalated America's military effort there the way Lyndon B. Johnson did during his White House years.[581]

It *can* be said with a measure of certainty that during JFK's thousand-plus days in office, he transformed his country and the Soviet Union toward an attitude of less hostility, more cooperation, and an awareness that nuclear warfare would bring about the worst possible result for everyone worldwide. Jacqueline Kennedy acknowledged this achievement shortly after JFK's memorial service when she told First Deputy Premier Mikoyan, the leader of the Soviet delegation in attendance, "Tell Mr. Khrushchev from me that he and my husband would have brought peace to the world by working together. Now, Mr. Khrushchev will have to do it alone."[582]

Thus, it is *not* speculation to recognize that from April 20, 1961 (when the Bay of Pigs ended in defeat) until his death in November 1963, JFK grew in office in his handling of foreign policy to the point that he refused to abide by the Cold War rhetoric of his Inaugural Address, and slowly, surely, diplomatically, and prudently demonstrated that above all other goals, he would "bear any burden, and pay any price" to *keep the peace.*

B. Growth in Handling Economic Policy

At the end of Dwight Eisenhower's presidency, the American economy was floundering in contraction, with unemployment rising from 5.2 percent to 6.2 percent between the second and fourth quarters of 1960, and then up to 6.8 percent by the time JFK took office in January 1961. In addition, Ike's conservative fiscal policy "depressed estimated real GNP by $9.4 billion in 1960," according to Professor of Economics Ann Mari May in her study of how Eisenhower's economic policy impacted the 1960 election.[583] Facing a declining economy at the start of his presidency, as noted by Giglio, Kennedy began his White House years "with little background in economics and virtually no exposure to Keynesian economics."[584] Given those facts, early on, despite the economy's doldrums, JFK believed that the safest route toward improvement would be for him to make an Eisenhower-like commitment to maintain a balanced budget and minimize federal deficits.[585]

After a year in office, however, Kennedy had what Sidey called an "economic metamorphosis."[586] In searching for ways to bolster the economy, he reevaluated his attitude toward Keynesian economics largely through listening to his Council of Economic Advisors: Walter Heller, James Tobin, and Kermit Gordon, leading economics professors from the University of Minnesota, Yale, and Williams College, respectively.[587] Heeding their advice, Kennedy decided that the best way to stimulate the economy was by cutting taxes without decreasing federal spending.[588]

On first blush, such a strategy would surely increase the federal budget deficit, but the controlling thought was that if it succeeded in boosting the economy, a "rising tide" from the prosperity "would lift all boats." In Giglio's words, Kennedy "grasped the logic of accepting temporarily larger deficits to achieve economic well-being."[589] In a speech to the Economic Club of New York on December 14, 1962, the president explained the rationale for his new approach: "The lesson of the last decade is that budget deficits are not caused by wild-eyed spenders but by slow economic growth and periodic recessions.... The soundest way to raise revenues in the long run is to cut tax rates now."[590]

In his January 1963 State of the Union address, Kennedy advocated his new policy, saying that "one step, above all, is essential—the enactment this year of a substantial reduction and revision in Federal income taxes" because "our obsolete tax system exerts too heavy a drag on private purchasing power, profits and employment."[591] Thus, two years into his presidency, JFK reversed his initial "balanced budget" course and became a Keynesian proponent.[592]

How did this radical transformation in Kennedy's economic policy come about? Though not a student of economics before his presidency, he did not have to live in the White House long before he recognized the urgent need to do something major to stimulate the stagnant economy. In line with that objective, he took on as a personal development priority learning everything he could to fulfill his campaign commitment to "get the country moving again!" As part of his economics education, he stayed on top of the relevant statistics kept by the federal government, read all the pertinent economic analyses contained in the *New York Times* and *The Economist*, and took his extraordinary listening and information absorption skills to new heights in resetting his approach to regaining national prosperity. Heller called JFK "the best student I ever had."[593]

Sidey noted that as with his post-Bay of Pigs foreign policy decisions, Kennedy made his economic policy decisions only after analyzing conflicting opinions held by Heller, Secretary of the Treasury Douglas Dillon, and "intellectual blood bank" donor Sorensen.[594] With that approach, he made his final decisions in the context of having considered the issues from a theory, business, and political standpoint. Sidey recognized that it did not take long for JFK to understand the complex issues associated with "balance of payments, taxation, economic growth, the gold standard, and the federal budget," and he took the necessary time to "sort through the minutiae of the budget with Bureau of the Budget Director David Bell."[595]

Though Kennedy failed in getting his tax cut proposal through Congress before his death, as with his civil rights initiative, what he started Lyndon B. Johnson finished.[596] The enactment of the Revenue Act of 1964 reduced the top tax rates on individuals from 91 percent to 70 percent and on corporations from 52 percent to 48 percent. In addition, Giglio reported that the Act caused unemployment to drop from 5.5 percent in December 1963 to 4.1 percent in December 1965; and resulted in the economy's achieving an "annual growth rate rise from 2.5% in 1960 to over 6% by year end 1964, while inflation rate held at 1.3%

C. Growth in Advancing Civil Rights

Until he became president at the age of forty-three, Kennedy had had almost no meaningful contact with any African Americans.[597] Following his military service in World War II, JFK felt called to a political career that (in part to please his ambitious father) would hopefully culminate with the presidency. Since less than 7 percent of Massachusetts' residents were Black, Kennedy felt free during his congressional years to court long-serving legislators from the Jim Crow South who, in the postwar period, wielded disproportionate influence. To have any chance of succeeding as a national legislator during Kennedy's congressional days required a serious effort to do what it took to endear himself to the deeply entrenched, bigoted Southern leaders who held almost all the congressional leadership positions at the time.

In 1956, JFK started making his way into the national presidential conversation. That year, he narrowly lost his bid to become Adlai Stevenson's running mate in the election against the incumbent Eisenhower. In hopes of getting the nod, for the first time in his political career, Kennedy sought to cultivate the Black vote *and* the Southern vote simultaneously, and soon began to demonstrate a national politician's talent for speaking out of both sides of his mouth to different groups.[598]

His Pulitzer-winning book *Profiles in Courage*[vi,599] came out on January 1, 1956, and immediately became a national bestseller. It heightened JFK's name-recognition status, and thereby enhanced his chance of being selected as Stevenson's vice president. Knott pointed out that to endear himself to Southerners, in two of *Profiles*' eight chapters, "Kennedy viewed overtly racist President Andrew Johnson (from Tennessee) as the 'courageous' if 'untactful' victim of a congressional witch-hunt led by 'extremists,'...[and also] offered a glowing

---

vi It is now generally accepted that *Profiles* was actually written by Ted Sorensen and lightly edited by JFK, and the Pulitzer Prize came his way only as a result of his father Joseph Kennedy's having done some serious arm-twisting with the Pulitzer selection committee. See: Stephen F. Knott, *Coming to Terms with John F. Kennedy* (University Press of Kansas 2022), 224 n.8.

account of Lucius Q.C. Lamar of Mississippi for his alleged moderation while serving in the US Senate after the Civil War. In fact, there was nothing moderate about Lamar who believed in, as he put it, 'the supremacy of the unconquered and unconquerable Saxon race.'"[600]

In his book *Presidential Courage,* Michael Beschloss explained JFK's (ultimately unsuccessful) Southern strategy for attempting to gain Stevenson's support over his main challenger Estes Kefauver:

> His chief rival, Senator Kefauver of Tennessee, had inflamed white Southern delegates by refusing to sign the "Southern Manifesto" against integration. Hoping to win their endorsement, JFK publicly refused to embrace the Supreme Court's landmark ruling of 1954 to desegregate American public schools. Asked about *Brown v. Board of Education,* Kennedy merely replied that it was "the law" and that as a Senator, he had had "nothing to do with the decision."[601]

Though there are differences in opinion among historians regarding when JFK believed what on the subject of the need to take action toward the advancement of civil rights, Beschloss claimed that the 1958 midterm elections "shifted the Democratic Party's center of gravity toward Northern big cities." Because of that shift, Kennedy started "changing his tune on civil rights.... Dropping his Southern strategy, he wrote Martin Luther King Jr. to ask for a meeting, but the civil rights crusader had been appalled by Kennedy's courtship of the segregationists and did not respond."[602]

As the 1960 presidential race began, still courting the South, JFK recognized that in swing states, there were more votes to gain from African Americans than racist segregationists. Thus, he moved forward in his campaign by making frequent pitches as a civil rights advocate. The fact that the pitch was more of a political than a moral issue with Kennedy was revealed by Dallek in this telling incident:

> Kennedy was not happy about having to choose between the party's competing factions, but once he

> chose, he moved forward. When he saw civil rights advocate Harris Wofford in August, he said, "Now in five minutes, tick off the ten things a President ought to do to clean up this goddamn civil rights mess." Although he was uncomfortable adopting an aggressive civil rights agenda, he nevertheless followed all of Wofford's suggestions....
>
> Kennedy agreed to speak before several Black conventions, praised peaceful sit-ins at segregated public facilities across the South, criticized Eisenhower for failing to integrate public housing "with one stroke of the pen," and sponsored a national advisory conference on civil rights. In a speech, he described civil rights as a "moral question" and promised not only to support legislation but also to take executive action "on a bold and large scale." And the more he said, the more he felt. By the close of the campaign, he had warmed to the issue and spoke with indignation about American racism.[603]

After taking a reasonably strong position on civil rights during his campaign, most notably by calling and empathizing with Coretta King one week before the election while her husband had been jailed in DeKalb County, Georgia, and then being instrumental in getting him released from jail, Kennedy narrowly won the election.[604] His campaign focus toward helping African Americans, however, essentially disappeared after he was sworn in. Beginning with the first day of his presidency, his highest priority was foreign policy, as proven by the fact that his Inaugural Address made no mention at all of civil rights or any other domestic issue.[605]

Recognizing the need to have the support of Southerners in Congress (who were all Democrats), for JFK to have any chance of success with his proposed federal legislation during his White House years, he believed he should take as little action as possible on civil rights.[606] After chastising Eisenhower during the 1960 campaign over

Ike's failure to sign an executive order to integrate public housing, Kennedy proceeded to wait until after the November 1962 midterm elections before he signed the order that he had earlier acknowledged could have been effectuated "with the stroke of a pen" two years before by his predecessor.[607] Furthermore, as a stain on his early years in the Oval Office, JFK's judicial appointments to federal courts in Southern states were often staunch segregationists, as reported by Sheldon Goldman in his book *Picking Federal Judges*.[608]

Until the summer of 1963, Kennedy acted on civil rights only on a reactive basis. He dealt with the two major racial crises between January 1961 and April 1963 from the perspective of doing what it took to restore order, and *not* on the basis that confronting racism was the morally right thing to do.

The first crisis: In the spring of 1961, Black and White civil rights activists known as "Freedom Riders" rode buses from northern cities into southern states in hopes of integrating the bus terminals there. Upon arrival, they were beaten with crowbars and had their buses burned by Ku Klux Klan members whose violence was given free rein by local police officers. Kennedy's response: "Tell the Freedom Riders to call it off and go back home."[609] When they returned to the North, Kennedy refused King's request to welcome them home.[610]

The second crisis: In the summer of 1962, with the backing of the NAACP's Legal Defense and Educational Fund, African American Air Force veteran James Meredith obtained a federal court order that allowed him to register and become a student at the University of Mississippi that fall. When the first day of school arrived in Oxford, Governor Ross Barnett stood in the school's doorway and refused to let Meredith enter.

The confrontation produced rioting (in which two civilians were killed) and court orders obtained by Attorney General Robert Kennedy's Justice Department that enjoined Barnett and his lieutenant governor from blocking Meredith's registration. The skirmishing did not end until Kennedy was forced to send thirty thousand federal troops into the town to protect Meredith's entry onto the campus. In justifying his actions at Ole Miss in a nationally televised address, JFK made no mention of the moral issues in play, but said he had done what he had to do so that "orders of the court could be carried out," and Americans could not "disobey" them.[611]

During 1961 and 1962, as Kennedy responded *defensively* to civil rights confrontations, he failed and refused to initiate civil rights legislation. To his credit, he took some actions that benefited African Americans. Most notably, he hired forty Blacks to important posts in his administration, nominated Thurgood Marshall to the US Second Circuit Court of Appeals (that covered New York), and created the President's Committee on Equal Employment Opportunity. In addition, Attorney General Robert Kennedy's Justice Department pursued litigation in Southern states that sought to enjoin the Klan and the police from disrupting interstate travel and keeping bus terminals segregated. Brother Bobby also pursued over forty lawsuits in Southern states aimed at expanding African Americans' voting rights.[612]

Such actions by the Kennedy brothers were quietly applauded but nonetheless deemed insufficient by civil rights leaders who believed that the only real solution to the problem of racial injustice was the enactment of civil rights legislation with real teeth in it (unlike the 1957 Civil Rights Act) that would bring Jim Crow to an end. Kennedy chose to turn a deaf ear to their position, and missed a golden opportunity to make a strong national statement on civil rights by refusing King's request to do something special to commemorate the one-hundred-year anniversary of Lincoln's Emancipation Proclamation on January 1, 1963. King's response to JFK's non-action: "The president has the understanding and political skills to address civil rights, but the moral passion is missing."[613] Kennedy did make brief mention of Lincoln's Proclamation in his State of the Union Address on January 14, 1963, but limited his statements on civil rights in the speech to a single paragraph that only generally mentioned the need for voting rights. The following day, at a televised press conference, all JFK said about civil rights was that he was "proceeding ahead in a way which will maintain consensus and advance the cause."

In April 1963, events in Birmingham, Alabama, "the most thoroughly segregated city in the country" according to King,[614] which had a 40 percent Black population, became the watershed event that led to JFK's making a complete and genuine commitment to the advancement of civil rights. After King and over one thousand protesters were arrested for their sit-ins at segregated lunch counters and churches, Birmingham Sheriff Bull Connor directed his local policemen to shoot firehoses and unleash attack dogs on African Americans of all ages (including children) who had assembled to protest the city's segregation and refusal to allow Blacks to vote. The ugly confrontations between the police and protesters were shown on television newscasts that went around the globe and eliminated all illusions worldwide that the United States was a nation where "all men are created equal."

What happened in Birmingham, as seen by a national television audience, became a turning point for the country. Beschloss said: "Before Birmingham, only four percent of Americans considered civil rights to be the country's number-one national problem. After Bull Connor's dogs, the figure skyrocketed to fifty-two percent."[615]

As he watched Birmingham descend into chaos, JFK told his colleagues, "Bull Connor makes me sick,"[616] and recognized that there would *never* be a national consensus on what should be done politically to advance civil rights. After having to send in federal troops to quell the violence that included the bombings of King's hotel and his brother's home, and because Alabama governor George Wallace refused to deal with the situation, the lightbulb turned on inside Kennedy's heart and mind and sent the message that what he had hoped could be addressed politically and peacefully over an indefinite period of time in the future was clearly nothing but a pipe dream.

Shortly after having that epiphany, on the evening of June 11, 1963, when earlier that day Wallace had blocked the doorway to two Black students at the University of Alabama, Kennedy spoke to a national television audience (exactly one day after his landmark "peace" address on foreign policy at American University), and for the first time since Abraham Lincoln, an American president accepted the fact and assumed the responsibility that the cause of advancing civil rights for African Americans and bringing an end to Jim Crow was *not* a political issue, but rather was *a moral issue*. Knott properly called JFK's remarks to the nation that night "a seminal document in American history" and "the most important speech of his presidency."[617]

Sorensen was given only six hours to write the historic speech after the events of Birmingham finally moved Kennedy to action, and much of JFK's remarks that night turned out to be spontaneous—straight from a heart that had finally opened to African Americans who, in Martin Luther King Jr.'s immortal words, had waited "How long? *Too long*!" to be treated as people with equal rights. Some highlights from the nation-changing speech:

> We are confronted primarily with a moral issue. It is as old as the Scriptures and as clear as the Constitution.... The heart of the question is whether all Americans are to be afforded equal rights and equal opportunities, whether we are going to treat our fellow Americans as we want to be treated....
>
> One hundred years of delay have passed since President Lincoln freed the slaves, yet their heirs, their grandsons, are not fully free. They are not yet freed from the bonds of injustice. They are not yet freed from social and economic oppression. And this Nation, for all its hopes and all its boasts, will not be fully free until all its citizens are free....
>
> We preach freedom around the world, and we mean it, and we cherish our freedom here at home, but are we to say to the world, and much more importantly, to each other that this is the land of the free except for the Negroes; that we have no second-class citizens except Negroes; that we have no class or caste system, no ghettoes, no master race except with respect to Negroes?
>
> We face, therefore, a moral crisis as a country and as a people. It cannot be met by repressive police action.

> It cannot be left to increased demonstrations in the streets. It cannot be quieted by token moves or talk. It is time to act in the Congress, in your State and local legislative body and, above all, in our daily lives....
>
> A great change is at hand, and our task, our obligation, is to make that revolution, that change, peaceful and constructive for all.[618]

Kennedy's television address in response to Birmingham changed the American social landscape. Kennedy Library historian Sheldon Stern described the tectonic shift in social conscience as a "sea change."[619] For the first time since Lincoln's presidency a century before, African Americans believed they had a white political leader who not only felt their pain but was ready to take action to relieve it. Simultaneously, racists in the South and elsewhere decided Kennedy had become their enemy, and the clash between the two perspectives led to an outbreak of rioting in over thirty cities across the country and the murder of civil rights leader Medgar Evers. Soon after the speech, Kennedy's approval ratings declined nationally by 11 percent and in the South, by 20 percent.[620]

Eight days after his civil rights speech, Kennedy sent a special message to Congress urging its members to move forward with a new civil rights bill. Among the memorable words in his message:

> This is one country.... It has become one country because all of us and all the people who came here had an equal chance to develop their talents. We cannot say to 10 percent of the population that you can't have the right; that your children can't have the chance to develop whatever talents they have.
>
> To paraphrase the words of Lincoln, "In giving freedom to the Negro, we assure freedom to the free—honorable alike in what we give and what we preserve."

> In this year of the Emancipation Proclamation Centennial, justice requires us to ensure the blessings of liberty for all Americans and their posterity—not merely for reasons of economic efficiency, world diplomacy, and domestic tranquility—but, above all, because it is right.[621]

The bill submitted to Congress by Kennedy covered the waterfront of civil rights: voting rights, equal access to public accommodations, school desegregation, and employment discrimination.

Initially, Congress did not respond favorably to JFK's civil rights bill, though it could not ignore the volcanic groundswell of support it created among large blocs of the American people. This was demonstrated most vividly by the August 28, 1963 March on Washington led by Martin Luther King Jr. when in front of the Lincoln Memorial, King moved the 250,000 Black and white attendees in the overflow crowd and the national television audience to new heights of passion for civil rights with his "I Have a Dream" speech. Kennedy chose not to participate in the ceremony, believing his doing so would potentially adversely impact the chances of his civil rights bill getting passed, a decision he later regretted, though he did congratulate King afterwards at the White House, shaking his hand while looking him in the eye and saying, "I have a dream."[622]

JFK's civil rights bill was bottled up in Congress for the remaining five months of his presidency. Shortly after his death, President Lyndon Johnson pulled out his uniquely powerful lobbying skills and pushed the bill through the sausage grinder and into law on July 2, 1964, after an intense legislative battle. One of Johnson's most formidable arguments on behalf of the bill that allowed him to twist arms until minds changed was that passing the legislation was the best possible tribute Americans could make to honor and enhance their fallen leader's legacy.

Kennedy's impact on the advancement of civil rights was matched by his impact on avoiding nuclear warfare and moving nations toward a more peaceful mindset during the Cold War. Knott summed it up well:

> In a majoritarian regime, a sense of timing, prudence, and an awareness of how much change a society can bear must enter into a statesman's calculation. While that fact offers little solace to the victims of injustice, nevertheless, the injustice of it all does not negate the fact that any political order rooted in the consent of the majority requires even the noblest statesman, a Lincoln for instance, to trim at times. As historian James Giglio has observed, both Lincoln's and Kennedy's restraint made the change that ultimately did occur more acceptable to the majority.
>
> Kennedy was no Lincoln, and he did not live long enough to earn the sobriquet of "statesman," but he was on his way toward achieving that status as he entered the final months of his life. And while he had trimmed, he ultimately pointed the way for his fellow countrymen to live up to the ideal that "all men are created equal."[623]

Great leaders never stop learning and gaining wisdom. This capacity causes them to consider, and reconsider, their positions toward greater wisdom amidst constantly changing circumstances until they are satisfied they have made the best decision. Kennedy epitomized this trait during his presidency. In his foreign policy, he started his presidency as an aggressive Cold Warrior and because of his experiences, he grew into a leader who favored diplomacy as the best way to operate toward the goal of achieving peace in the world. In his economic policy, he began as a balanced budget, anti-deficit hawk, which failed to produce positive results, and then reversed his course to become a supply side Keynesian, which succeeded in revving up the economy. In his position on civil rights, he grew from originally addressing it as a law-and-order defensive political issue and turned it into his proactive passionate moral cause that ultimately led to the passage of the twentieth century's most imporegislationlation. In summary, per Knott's assessment, "He did something unusual for a president—he changed.... He continually challenged himself to think and act anew."

Because of his steady growth in these three critically important areas of presidential responsibility, the country grew with him, and American society made crucial progress during his shortened presidency. If leadership performance is best evaluated by the answer to the question "Did he make things better for those he served?" the answer to that question from John F. Kennedy's thousand days in the White House is a resounding "YES!"

Leadership Trait # 2: Calm in a Crisis

A. Separating Myth from Reality

Before discussing the particulars of John F. Kennedy's demonstration of this trait during the Cuban Missile Crisis, it is necessary to clear the air of the many falsehoods that exist concerning what took place and why during the thirteen days from October 16 to 28, 1962. Martin Sherwin said that most historians refer to these falsehoods as "counterfactual history."[624] In an effort to manipulate the verdict of history about JFK's handling of crisis, before and after his death, he and his closest compadres (which included members of the media) presented to the public all sorts of misinformation about the circumstances of how the situation arose, who said and did what while it lasted, and the terms of the deal struck with Khrushchev that finally resolved it. The dots of truth hidden by large blotches of untruths have finally been connected by diligent historians in large part because of what was revealed by the White House tapes (installed shortly after the Bay of

Pigs fiasco) of the communications that took place during the crisis, which were not made available to scholars (and later the public) until the mid-1990s.

John F. Kennedy Presidential Library historian-in-residence Sheldon Stern held that position from 1977 to 2000, and was the first non-Kennedy insider to listen to all forty-two hours of the recordings of JFK and his Executive Committee (ExComm, for short) during the crisis. What Stern learned led him to write three books on the subject, the most important being the last one, *The Cuban Missile Crisis in American Memory: Myths versus Reality*. When I interviewed Stern for my book *Cross-Examining History* in 2015, he gave this tight summary of what Americans were led to believe by JFK and his cronies about what happened during the thirteen days in October 1962, until the tapes demonstrated otherwise:

> On October 16, 1962, JFK and his advisors were shocked to learn that the Soviet Union, despite repeated denials and totally without provocation, was installing nuclear missiles in Cuba. Eight days later, Kennedy announced in a nationally televised speech that he had imposed a US naval blockade around Cuba and demanded removal of the missiles. Khrushchev blustered and threatened, but Kennedy and the best and brightest around him held fast and the two sides went eyeball-to-eyeball. Eventually, through a combination of flexibility, toughness, will, nerve, wisdom, and brilliant crisis management, Kennedy prevailed. Khrushchev agreed to remove the missiles, and nuclear war was averted.

That is a summary of the book *Thirteen Days* (written by Robert Kennedy and Ted Sorensen[625])—and *it's not true*.

What were the main falsehoods about this account of the crisis? Summarizing the conclusions of both Stern and Sherwin, there are three major areas of distortion between the Kennedy version of what happened compared to what *actually* happened:

(1) Because of America's participation in the Bay of Pigs invasion in April 1961, and then pursuing Operation Mongoose's plan to have Castro assassinated, and also having our own nuclear missiles in Turkey, in fact, there was definite "provocation" by the United States that justified Khrushchev's collaborating with Castro to get nuclear missiles into Cuba in October 1962. Dallek's assessment: "Without Kennedy's Cuban provocations, Khrushchev would have been hard-pressed to justify placing missiles on the island."[626]

(2) Regarding the American side of how the crisis was resolved, its successful conclusion on October 28, 1962 came about *only* because of JFK's calm demeanor and good judgment regarding how to strike a viable deal with the Soviet Union, and *not* because of good counsel that came from "the best and the brightest" men around him on the ExComm. For the most part, Robert Kennedy and the other ExComm insiders did *not* move the needle toward resolution; rather, they advocated the same type of aggressive retaliatory responses that was urged by the Joint Chiefs of Staff that JFK wisely rejected because to have followed their advice would have likely led to World War III.[627] Late in the crisis, JFK told Press Secretary Pierre Salinger, "Pierre, do you realize that if I make a mistake in this crisis, 200 million people are going to get killed?"[628]

(3) The deal Kennedy finally struck with Khrushchev to end the crisis, in fact, did *not* arise because the two leaders went "eyeball-to-eyeball" until JFK "prevailed" because of his "flexibility, toughness, will, nerve, wisdom, and brilliant crisis management." What happened that was *not* disclosed to the public about what brought about the settlement was

> that the two leaders made a secret trade not revealed to the public until 1989. The deal: Khrushchev "agreed to remove the missiles from Cuba" not because of JFK's "toughness" and "nerve," but only because Kennedy agreed to discreetly remove American nuclear missiles from Turkey; that is, the leaders agreed to make a like-kind exchange of missile withdrawals.[629]

What inspired these fictions of "nonfactual history" to be communicated to the American people by JFK and his accomplices? A few things. First, in October 1962 when the crisis arose, Kennedy already had his sights set on doing what it took to be reelected for a second term in 1964. For that reason, he and his closest colleagues on the ExComm wanted the Cuban Missile Crisis to be portrayed to the public as a contest between innocent American good guys vs. evil Soviet/Cuban bad guys brought about solely because of the communists' unilateral provocation. For that image of American innocence to be perpetrated, according to both Stern and Knott, "it was necessary for 'Operation Mongoose' (in which JFK had approved the effort to have Castro assassinated), to be airbrushed out of the historical record."[630]

Second, as covered previously in this chapter, Kennedy transformed himself during the first twenty months of his presidency from an aggressive Cold Warrior into a leader who recognized that the more prudent approach for directing American foreign policy was through effective diplomacy and doing what it took to avoid nuclear confrontation. Knowing that there were plenty of shoot-first-think-later Cold Warriors in the Republican Party (where super-hawk Barry Goldwater appeared to be the front runner to get the party's nomination to head the ticket in 1964) who would attempt to portray JFK as being an "appeaser" or "soft on communism" if the actual terms of the Cuban Missile Crisis settlement trade were made public, the exchange deal that was finally struck was a tightly guarded secret. In fact, only nine people in the Kennedy White House knew about it.[631]

To my amazement, Stern told me in our interview that the terms of the mutual missile withdrawal trade were not disclosed to Lyndon

B. Johnson while he was vice-president or even after he became president. This fact meant that throughout his presidency, LBJ wrongly believed that Kennedy had "prevailed" in the Cuban Missile Crisis because he was a tough guy who made Khrushchev back down.[632] In his book, *The Kennedy Assassination Tapes,* Max Holland cited specific instances found on the White House tapes where Johnson made specific references to JFK's toughness in getting the missile crisis concluded, while carryover advisors McGeorge Bundy, Dean Rusk, and Robert McNamara (who *knew* about the missile withdrawal trade) *said nothing* to correct LBJ's misunderstanding of what caused the crisis to be settled.[633]

Stern surmised that Johnson's false understanding about what caused the Cuban Missile Crisis to end may well have influenced him to believe (in error) that being a tough guy in escalating the American military effort in Vietnam (like he thought JFK had acted with Khrushchev in October 1962) would make the enemy more likely to back down and capitulate to America's terms.[634] In fact, just as no one capitulated in response to Kennedy's alleged toughness in Cuba, obviously no one capitulated to Johnson's toughness in Vietnam.

The third reason the falsehoods were perpetrated was because after Kennedy's death in November 1963, it did not take long for the family and JFK's closest colleagues to start moving toward having brother Robert position himself for a future presidential run. What better way for Bobby Kennedy to promote himself to American voters than to say that it was *he* who had been the "calming voice of reason" during the Cuban Missile Crisis? And what better way for Bobby to publicize his false claim that he was the hero than for him to write a book about it using an extreme level of "poetic license" (a.k.a., downright lies) to create a story that portrayed *him* as the guy responsible for the avoidance of a cataclysmic holocaust?[635]

Therefore, after JFK's death, in furtherance of that plan, Bobby Kennedy began writing the book that ultimately became *Thirteen Days,* believing when he wrote it (long *before* the public's right to hear presidential tapes came to the forefront during Nixon's Watergate ordeal in 1973–1974) that JFK's White House tapes would never be released to the public, and, therefore, he could get away with saying whatever he wanted about what was said and done in the ExComm and Oval Office discussions. When Bobby asked O'Donnell to give him feedback on his first draft of *Thirteen Days,* Stern reported that the day after O'Donnell read it, he said to Bobby in the presence of Dan Fenn (who later became the director of the Kennedy Library), "I thought *your brother* was the president during the missile crisis." Bobby replied, "Jack wouldn't mind. I'm now the one running. He's not."[636]

Before *Thirteen Days* was finalized, Bobby Kennedy was assassinated in June 1968, which caused the book to be completed by Sorensen. He had also been present at the ExComm meetings, knew that the way Bobby described the crisis in the book was false, and yet made no effort to correct it.[637]

D. JFK's Successful Handling of the Cuban Missile Crisis

Having now hit the high points of the Kennedy family and friends' fictionalizing of what actually happened and why during the Cuban Missile Crisis, the truth of the matter can actually be used to paint a clear picture of how John F. Kennedy stood strong, calm, and wise throughout the crisis and essentially orchestrated the successful resolution of it singlehandedly by rejecting imprudent belligerent advice from the other members of the ExComm and his Joint Chiefs of Staff.

In Rudyard Kipling's classic 1895 poem "If," he praised those of whom it could be said:

> If you can keep your head
> when all about you are losing theirs
> and blaming it on you,
> If you can trust yourself
> when all men doubt you,
> but make allowance for their doubting…
> [For them] Yours is the Earth and
> everything that's in it.

Surely, during his formative years at The Choate (boarding) School, John F. Kennedy read "If" and probably memorized it. Throughout the Cuban Missile Crisis, he epitomized these stanzas by processing a fire hose stream of information and mass quantities of conflicting advice before making the right decisions to avoid nuclear war.

He had the personality to do this, per Dallek's assessment, because in facing any struggle, JFK could "detach himself and avoid turning a dilemma into a strictly personal challenge," and then he would stand by his decisions with a "strength of will that was indispensable."[638] These traits were enhanced by other virtues identified by Sidey, who saw that JFK "did not brood," "distress did not exist long" in him, and he "never gave in to anger at his enemy."[639]

These evaluations align with those made by Pulitzer-winning historian James MacGregor Burns in his 1960 campaign biography of Kennedy, which predated the crisis by more than two years:

> One word describes him more exactly than any other—self-possession. He has never been seen—even by his mother—in raging anger or uncontrollable tears. He does not lose himself in anger. He dislikes emotional scenes, at home or at work. His driving ambition to win seems to rise from a calm evaluation of what he can do if he puts everything he has into it.... His qualities of detachment, restraint, moderation, and self-protection come from a fear of making too much of a commitment, of going off the intellectual deep end. To be emotionally or ideologically committed is to be captive.[640]

Consistent with all these descriptions, Knott recognized that a big part of why JFK was so good in confronting crises came from the fact that he "was a president who always pushed the envelope in terms of weighing all the angles."[641] When Kennedy learned from Bundy on the morning of October 16, 1962, that American U-2 reconnaissance planes had photographed the Soviets' starting to install nuclear missiles in Cuba, he quickly called a meeting of the ExComm in the White House Cabinet Room.[vii,642] The first thing JFK had them do was identify and explore potential options regarding possible ways the United States could respond to the threat.[643]

Among the options considered were an immediate US military air attack on Cuba to bomb the missiles; an invasion of Cuba by American troops; and having the US Navy implement a blockade in the waters around Cuba to prevent Soviet ships from transporting any more missiles there.[644] Above all, Kennedy and his ExComm knew that allowing the missiles to stay and become operational in Cuba was *not* an option. His brother Bobby advised JFK that for him to do nothing to remove the missiles "would be an impeachable offense."[645]

To add to the tension, something had to be done on an expedited basis to quell the threat before the missile installation was completed, and President Kennedy knew he had to take immediate action *before* commencing any diplomatic overtures to Khrushchev. Such discussions would likely result in stalemate, and any material delay in diplomatic talks might well give the Russians and Cubans the time they needed to make the missiles operational.[646]

Initially, on day one of the crisis, per Sherwin, JFK was "determined to bomb the missile sites in Cuba."[647] Within the next two days, however, he reflected, recalibrated, and then decided that he preferred the blockade option. Shortly before disclosing his plan to

---

vii ExComm was made up of National Security Advisor McGeorge Bundy, Secretary of State Dean Rusk, Secretary of Defense Robert McNamara, Attorney General Robert Kennedy, Vice President Lyndon B. Johnson, CIA director John McCone, Secretary of the Treasury Douglas Dillon, chief counsel Ted Sorensen, Undersecretary of State George Gall, Deputy Undersecretary of State Alexis Johnson, chairman of the Joint Chiefs of Staff Maxwell Taylor, Assistant Secretary of State for Latin America Edwin Martin, former ambassador to Russia Llewellyn Thompson, Deputy Secretary of Defense Roswell Gilpatric, and Assistant Secretary of Defense Paul Nitze. A few others—UN ambassador Adlai Stevenson, White House appointments secretary Kenneth O'Donnell, and former Secretary of State Dean Acheson—attended one ExComm meeting. See: James N. Giglio, *The Presidency of John F. Kennedy, Second Edition, Revised* (University Press of Kansas 2006), 207.

the American people, he chose to soften the effect of the maneuver by calling it a naval "quarantine"—to distinguish the public's perception of it from the Soviets' Berlin blockade. Sherwin explained why the blockade option was the most appealing to Kennedy: "It was an action that invited negotiation and avoided the certainty of Soviet bloodletting."[648]

Sidey explained how it would work:

> We could poise our forces for an invasion, throw a cordon of ships into the Caribbean to halt any new shipments of offensive weapons, and demand the dismantling of the missiles and their removal along with the bombers. Our Navy was the mightiest afloat, and the Caribbean was our water. If the Russians chose to challenge us on the seas, victory in a limited battle was assured. No one who talked to Kennedy in these hours thought the Russians wanted to go beyond [naval confrontation] and risk nuclear war.[649]

Kennedy gave his perspective on the blockade's logistics:

> The consensus was that we should go ahead with the blockade beginning on Sunday night. Originally, we should begin by blockading Soviets against the shipment of additional offensive capacity, [and] that we could tighten the blockade as the situation requires. I was most anxious that we not have to announce a state of war existing, because it would obviously be bad to have the word go out that we were having a war rather than that it was a limited blockade for a limited purpose.[650]

Unlike his inept approach of rubber-stamping the advice of military and intelligence experts prior to the Bay of Pigs invasion, in the Cuban Missile Crisis, per Giglio's assessment, Kennedy "revealed a more perceptive, discerning, and questioning approach, in which he kept his own counsel."[651]

Sidey reached the same conclusion: "The failure to coordinate, the lack of inner communication that transpired during the Bay of Pigs would be prevented. An aide said, 'On that very first morning, the president gathered all the threads together in his hands and he *held* them….' The president became like a defense attorney. Every witness who came before him was questioned exhaustively to see if there was a weakness in his testimony. This would *not* be another Bay of Pigs if the president could prevent it."[652]

During the crisis, Kennedy attended almost all the ExComm meetings but also worked privately in the Oval Office and had separate caucuses with some of the committee's members as well as other advisors. When listening to those who favored invading and/or bombing Cuba, he reminded them of what he had learned during the Bay of Pigs as well as during his years as a naval officer in World War II: "We all know how quickly everybody's courage goes when blood starts to flow."[653]

On October 22, day seven of the crisis, Kennedy decided the time had come for him to tell the leaders of Congress in private and the American public in a nationally televised speech what was going on in Cuba and why he was implementing the blockade/quarantine. Sherwin believed:

> It was the most consequential speech Ted Sorensen ever drafted…. The goal was to persuade both Americans and the global audience that the Soviet Union was guilty as charged, and to convince Khrushchev that a diplomatic resolution was his best alternative. Its lawyerly, academic tone suggested that everything had been carefully considered, and that the president was in firm control…. The president spoke for seventeen minutes and forty-three seconds, but what most listeners heard can be summarized in ten words; *Nuclear war with the Soviet Union was a real possibility.*[654]

As the crisis went on and the American blockade/quarantine succeeded in causing Soviet ships carrying missiles bound for Cuba to turn around, negotiations between Khrushchev and Kennedy commenced, made up entirely of ten letters and no phone conversations. Finally recognizing that Kennedy would *never* agree to allow the nukes to stay in Cuba, the Soviet leader ultimately proposed the withdrawal-of-missiles-for-missiles trade in a message he sent to Kennedy and over the radio in Moscow. Sherwin: "Khrushchev knew that he didn't want war, and that he would negotiate his missiles out of Cuba. But he would trade *only* if he believed an American invasion of Cuba was imminent."[655] JFK definitely communicated that intention.

Except for UN Ambassador Adlai Stevenson (who actually proposed the missile withdrawal trade to Kennedy on the first day of the crisis),[656] the rest of the president's advisors opposed the trade, but JFK rejected their advice. Stern heard JFK say in essence to his colleagues in the White House recordings (as confirmed by the tape transcript):

> Any rational person who looks at the situation is going to say that this trade makes a lot of sense and is reasonable. How are we going to explain going to war over a bunch of useless missiles in Turkey? Who cares about those missiles particularly when we're soon going to replace them with Polaris missiles which are even more effective and far less vulnerable to attack? Are the Jupiter missiles in Turkey reason enough to risk a nuclear war?[657]

From his analysis of the tapes, Stern determined that during the thirteen days, "there were approximately a dozen times where Kennedy received—in my judgment—terrible, provocative, dangerous advice and in every case but one he rejected it."[658] The single instance where JFK heeded bad advice involved how to track and intimidate Soviet submarines off the coast of Cuba. The approved confrontational tactics *almost* caused a Soviet captain to fire off nuclear-tipped torpedoes, but then "cooler heads" in the Soviet chain of command dissuaded him.[659]

When an American U-2 plane was shot down over Cuba near the end of the crisis and its pilot killed, Kennedy's hawkish advisors wanted to retaliate immediately by bombing and invading Cuba. The president's response, per Giglio:

> Once again, Kennedy exercised considerable restraint in arguing that the shooting might have been accidental. He favored waiting a day or two until the completion of other U-2 flights. Ball remembered that the president was "by far the most calm and analytical" in the room as JFK explained, "It isn't the first step that concerns me, but both sides escalating to the fourth and fifth step—and we don't get to the sixth because there's no one around to do so." Kennedy quickly ordered the missiles in Turkey defused to prevent any accidental firing, which shocked some military leaders, who believed he "had cracked and folded."[660]

Later it was determined that the Soviet general in Cuba who ordered the firing of the shots at the U-2 had done so in violation of Khrushchev's orders.[661]

When the Cuban Missile Crisis ended with the secret trade of American missiles being secretly withdrawn from Turkey in exchange for Soviet missiles being publicly withdrawn from Cuba (Sherwin reported that the secrecy part of the proposal was first suggested by Sorensen, and then JFK and Rusk agreed to accept the suggestion on the evening of October 27, day twelve of the crisis),[662] as described earlier in this chapter, aspects of the deal and how it came to be were intentionally misrepresented to enhance the legacies of the Kennedy brothers. Having acknowledged that, given the fact that JFK's actions *did* serve to prevent a likely nuclear confrontation that could have destroyed much of the world as we know it, historian Alan Brinkley's biography of JFK provided this tight summary of why Kennedy's actions in bringing the crisis to an end make him a worthy role model on how best to handle a crisis:

> As time has passed and the archives of the former Soviet Union became available, Kennedy's efforts have become more understandable, and in many ways more impressive. Unknown for some time, Kennedy and Khrushchev *together* worked diligently through the crisis to avoid a catastrophic confrontation. They communicated with each other almost every day, not only during the crisis but well beyond.
>
> They *quietly* agreed that Kennedy would remove the missiles in Turkey shortly after Khrushchev removed the missiles in Cuba. Kennedy did *not* make the deal public, fearing it would damage him politically. And while almost any course Kennedy might have chosen would have been risky, he avoided the most dangerous ones. He rejected the strong preference of the military to "take out" the Cuban missiles with air strikes and chose instead a relatively passive alternative: a naval blockade, during which the United States never fired a shot. Nor did Kennedy take action when the Soviet air force shot down the U-2 plane during the crisis.... In the end, Kennedy and Khrushchev dealt with this difficult crisis cautiously, deftly, and safely.[663]

In line with Brinkley's conclusion, Updegrove gave his explanation of why Kennedy's exemplary handling of the Cuban Missile Crisis became the capstone event of his presidency: "His triumph over the crisis owed to his own restraint, dispassion, and cool head. Khrushchev acknowledged as much in his memoirs: 'In the final analysis, Kennedy showed himself to be sober-minded and determined to avoid war. He didn't let himself be frightened, nor did he become reckless. He didn't overestimate America's might, and he left himself a way out of the crisis.' At that most perilous hour, his equanimity made all the difference."[664]

Leadership Trait #3: Use and Deliver Words That Inspire Progress

A. What Makes for Great Rhetoric

In his biography of John F. Kennedy, Updegrove reached back into history to find words that apply to JFK's third and final defining leadership trait: "British Prime Minister Clement Atlee said in 1945 of his predecessor Winston Churchill's oratorical splendor during World War II, 'Words at great moments of history *are* deeds.'"[665]

In a president's use of his exalted position as a bully pulpit, word power delivered with a compelling voice can expand the nation's horizons. Knott explained why in his book's final paragraphs:

> Kennedy understood that the presidency is the keeper of the nation's tablets and can play a vital role as a unifying head of state. Critics who claim that he emphasized rhetoric over legislative legwork are guilty of denigrating the power of ideas, particularly those enunciated to an audience of millions through the medium of television and radio. As the nation's head of state, the president possesses an extraordinary platform to educate and ennoble his fellow citizens....
>
> He appealed to our 'better angels,' and urged us to devote ourselves to something higher.... His aspirations for the nation point the way for all of us. And for that reason alone, his place in the American mind should be secured.[666]

Yes, the words used in many of JFK's most important speeches largely came from the brilliant mind of Sorensen, although JFK always actively edited his speechwriter's drafts down to the final product before he delivered it. The two men worked together in synchronicity because Sorensen *knew* what JFK wanted to say and could take his thoughts and turn them into golden words, some of which are now chiseled in stone.

It is one thing to have eloquent words written into a speech, it is something else to deliver them in a way that resonates, reverberates, and penetrates. Presentation power to enhance word choice excellence (per the examples of Abraham Lincoln and Winston Churchill, well-known to Kennedy the history lover) is what turns good speeches into great speeches and inspires listeners to stand up and *take action* in response to what they have heard. JFK explained the key to his presentation power from the podium: "You have to be able to communicate a sense of conviction, intelligence, and…some integrity. Those three qualities are really it."[667]

No one ever accused JFK of being unintelligent. He *knew* he was smart, and as the youngest elected president in history, he *knew* he had to demonstrate that fact to the masses to gain credibility. Certainly, it being widely believed that he had authored the celebrated bestselling Pulitzer-winning history book *Profiles in Courage* suggested that JFK was a bright guy, but even bestselling books never reach most people.

Kennedy hungered to show the country how intelligent he was *on television*, knowing that in that medium, tens of millions could see him in action, and he could demonstrate his brilliance in uncanned spontaneity in response to unscreened questions. He did this not only during his debates with Richard Nixon during the 1960 campaign, but also in his frequent televised press conferences once he entered the White House. Dallek noted:

> He knew news conferences allowed him to put his wit and intelligence on display. Arthur Schlesinger, Jr. remembered the conferences as "a superb show, always fun, often exciting, relished by the reporters and the television audiences…. They offered a showcase for a number of Kennedy's most characteristic qualities—

> the intellectual speed and vivacity, the remarkable mastery of government data, the terse self-mocking wit, the exhilarating personal command."
>
> His quick mastery of the press interviews before TV cameras and microphones persuaded Kennedy that "we couldn't survive without TV." It allowed him not only to charm the public, but also to reach people directly without the editorializing of the news media through interpretation or omission. Perhaps most important, whether on television or in person, Kennedy came across to the public as *believable*. Unlike Nixon, who never overcame a reputation for deceitfulness, Kennedy's manner—his whole way of speaking, choice of words, inflection, and steady gaze—persuaded listeners to *take him at his word*. And the public loved it. By April 1962, a Gallup poll showed that nearly three out of every four adults in the country had seen or heard one or more of the president's news conferences. Ninety-one percent of them had a favorable impression of his performance, and only 4 percent were negative. In addition, by a 61 to 32 percent margin, Americans favored the spontaneous TV format.[668]

JFK's frequent use of Sorensen's written word eloquence was taken to the next level by his dynamic performances at press conferences. And it was those unscripted bravura displays of intelligence, conviction, and integrity that laid the foundation for the ultimate power of his speeches. JFK had ten press conferences in his first three months in office and they led the American people to accept the fact early on that he had genuine *substance* to go along with his Hollywood good looks. This took Sorensen's elegant wordsmithing to the highest possible level.

B. Leading Examples of JFK's Words Inspiring Progress

Although Kennedy's Inaugural Address was previously discussed in this chapter in the context of its overstated message about how the United States should move forward in addressing the Cold War, its most quoted lines are: "And so, my fellow Americans, ask *not* what your country can do for you—ask what *you* can do for your country."

It did not take long for those words to inspire action. A little over a month later, on March 1, 1961, he signed an executive order that created the Peace Corps, "to help foreign countries meet their urgent needs for skilled manpower," and which would "allow our people to exercise more fully their responsibilities in the great common cause of world development.... Men and women will be expected to work and live alongside the nationals of the country in which they are stationed—doing the same work, eating the same food, talking the same language...in hopes that their service will be a source of satisfaction and a contribution to world peace."[669]

Soon thereafter, young people began volunteering and were sent to third world countries to teach English, construct needed homes and buildings, and deliver food to the hungry. Although *officially* the Peace Corps was *not* to be "an instrument of diplomacy, propaganda, or ideological conflict,"[670] it was certainly hoped that the Corps' good works would advance the causes of democracy and liberty in emerging countries to combat the Soviet Union's efforts to promote communism around the world.

During its first year of operation under the skilled leadership of JFK's brother-in-law Sargent Shriver, the Corps attracted nine hundred volunteers who served in sixteen countries, and within five years, those numbers grew to over sixteen thousand young people working in fifty-two countries. Dallek summed up the success of the program:

> The Peace Corps proved to be one of the enduring legacies of Kennedy's presidency. As with some American domestic institutions like Social Security and Medicare, it became a fixture that Democratic and Republican administrations alike would continue to

> finance for over forty years. It made far more friends than enemies and, as Kennedy had hoped, convinced millions of people abroad that the United States was eager to help developing nations raise their standards of living.[671]

In addition to the Inaugural Address's call to action, another example of Kennedy's words inspiring deeds and real progress came with his endorsement of America's active participation in the space race against the Soviets, capped off with his pledge that the United States would land a man on the moon by the end of the 1960s decade. Four months into his presidency (thus, a month after the Bay of Pigs fiasco), in what he called his second State of the Union Address, Kennedy told Congress and the American people that winning the space race was a Cold War necessity: "If we are to win the battle that is now going on around the world between freedom and tyranny," winning the space race "may hold the key to our future on Earth."[672]

As Charles Fishman pointed out in his book *One Giant Leap: The Impossible Mission That Flew Us to the Moon*, by seeking to get Congress to make the budgeting commitment to accomplish the moonshot on such a fast track, Kennedy was "committing the nation to do something we couldn't do" at the time because "we didn't even know what we would need" to put a man on the moon.[673]

Knott pointed out how Kennedy's words ultimately became transformed into Congress's budgetary deeds: "When Kennedy set the moon landing goal in 1961, NASA's space budget that year was one million dollars. A measure of his success in altering the nation's priorities can be seen in the fact that five years later, NASA would be spending on space one million dollars every three hours, all day, every day."[674]

Amid his inspiring Congress to keep increasing the space budget, on September 12, 1962, shortly after touring NASA's new Manned Spacecraft Center, President Kennedy delivered a speech in Houston at Rice University's football stadium. Updegrove wrote: "This speech written by Ted Sorensen was an eloquent expression of the race to the moon as a distinctly American proposition, a fulfillment of our destiny as a nation."[675]

JFK's most memorable words that day in Houston:

> The exploration of space will go on whether we join in it or not. And it is one of the great adventures of all time. No nation which expects to be the leader of other nations can expect to stay behind in this race for space….
>
> We mean to be a part of it. We mean to lead it…. But why, some say, the moon? Why choose this as our goal? And they may ask why climb the highest mountain? Why, 35 years ago, fly the Atlantic? Why does Rice play Texas?
>
> We choose to go to the moon in this decade and do other things, not because they are easy, but because they are hard, because that goal will serve to organize and measure the best of our energies and skills, because that challenge is one that we are willing to accept, one we are unwilling to postpone, and one which we intend to win.
>
> We ask God's blessing on the most hazardous, dangerous, and greatest adventure on which man has ever embarked.[676]

In addition to his inspiration for the success of the Peace Corps and the advancement of the space program, previously covered in this chapter (in connection with Kennedy's first leadership trait of growing in wisdom while in office as proven by his decreasing of Cold War tension) was his speech at American University on June 10, 1963, which inspired Khrushchev and the Soviets to move forward, negotiate, and ultimately sign the first Nuclear Test Ban Treaty.

Also mentioned in that part of the chapter was Kennedy's *"Ich bin ein Berliner"* speech on June 26, 1963 in Berlin (only sixteen days after his American University speech). Former Kennedy Presidential Library Director Thomas Putnam concluded that JFK's words that day strengthened the Germans in West Berlin and renewed their commitment to hold fast and stay strong while they lived in such a highly stressful environment, such that the speech provided "a defiant defense of democracy and self-government," and gave them the power to proceed with a steadfast mindset toward withstanding their circumstances.[677]

In addition to the American University and Berlin speeches, also covered previously in this chapter was the discussion of JFK's transforming America's consciousness toward the advancement of civil rights until it became the nation's top priority. It was Kennedy's televised speech on June 11, 1963, in response to the Birmingham chaos, that prompted him and many members of Congress to move forward with new civil rights legislation that would be strong enough to bring an end to Jim Crow.

So, these are five nation-changing examples of JFK's political rhetoric, written mainly by Sorensen and edited and delivered by Kennedy. They were so moving that they inspired major positive changes in world order and American society—all because when the people heard Kennedy speak in Washington, DC, Houston, and Berlin, and on television, they *knew and believed in* his intelligence, conviction, and integrity regarding those issues, and then had their hearts and minds changed by the eloquence of his words and the power of his presentation.

Kennedy's Flaws

To tell the truth (which is now recognized as such) and *not* the fictional myths of how John F. Kennedy used his three top leadership traits to produce the success he had as president, it was necessary at the beginning of this chapter to put them into context and acknowledge his glaring flaws. His sexual promiscuity, extensive drug use, and his (and his cronies' and family's) misrepresentations and material omissions, which for a time significantly distorted the historical record of his presidency, all combine to make a fair assessment of JFK's performance something that requires a delicate balancing of very good vs. very bad conduct. The challenge of performing this balancing act is reflected in the title to Knott's book, *Coming to Terms with John F. Kennedy*.

More than with our other great presidents, any person attempting to evaluate JFK's legacy as a leader must "come to terms" with his dark side. Yes, O'Donnell and Powers, like you, in many respects, the American people can honestly say, "Johnny, we hardly knew" about your egregious misconduct, yet when the facts are all revealed—thanks to the diligent work of the many historians quoted in this chapter—there are at least the three traits described herein that should allow John F. Kennedy's good side to prevail in this challenging assessment, with his "verdict in history" being recognized as a great (though deeply flawed) leader.

Personal Application

You now know how John F. Kennedy would have answered the following questions about his most important leadership strengths. How do *you* answer them?

- Do you present yourself to your family and closest colleagues as being whole-souled and internally consistent or is a more accurate assessment of your actions that you are contradictory because your internal wiring is compartmentalized?
- Are you *consumed* by what others will conclude about your ultimate legacy?
- Is the record of your leadership performance distorted because of misrepresentations and material omissions in the narrative that you have perpetrated?
- While you have held a leadership position, have you learned new things that caused you to discern, reconsider, and change your original position on issues?

- Now that you better understand the challenges of your current leadership position, have you been fair in your assessment of your predecessor?
- When you make serious mistakes in directing your firm, do you afterward dwell on them and cause them to hamper your present and future performance?
- When you make big decisions for your firm, do you question and reflect upon conflicting advice that you've received from your top colleagues?
- What is your level of due diligence in evaluating the data and advice you receive from your colleagues?
- Have the mistakes you recognized from your past performance provided you with lessons learned that guide your present and future decisions?
- When dealing with a competitor or adversary, do you state your position on disputed issues with conviction and clarity so there will be no misunderstandings about where you stand?
- When dealing with a competitor or adversary, do you attempt to develop some level of personal relationship and rapport with him?
- When your competitor or adversary does something that appears to change the entire dynamic of the situation or dialogue, do you drill down to make sure you've read his actions and words correctly?
- When your original words/plans turn out to be wrong and need to be adjusted, are you willing to make the change necessary to improve your position, even though it's embarrassing to have to acknowledge your earlier error?
- Are you truly willing to take in new thoughts and data that may well establish that your original position was flawed?

- When situations arise at your firm that involve moral issues, do you address them with your colleagues as such?
- When addressing a crucial moral issue that arises at your firm, do you commit to take strong action to deal with it and then do what it takes to fulfill that commitment?
- Are you sometimes guilty of talking out of both sides of your mouth to different constituencies at your firm? If so, do you recognize the trouble that it is likely to cause?
- When a major crisis arises at your firm,
    - Do you keep your head while your colleagues are losing their composure?'
    - Do you have a high confidence level in your decision-making such that you have the *will* necessary to follow through and effectuate your decisions?
    - Do you warm to the challenge of addressing it?
    - Do you often brood and/or get angry about it?
    - Do you immediately prioritize identifying multiple options that may help solve the problem?
    - Do you demonstrate patience and resist the temptation to hurry into making an important decision?
    - When your colleagues are adamant about wanting to pursue what you believe to be an ineffective option, do you have the inner strength to stand alone and reject their flawed advice?
- As a leader in charge of directing your firm, have you taken the steps necessary to establish with your colleagues that you have the intelligence, conviction, and intellectual integrity to deal with the issue at hand?

- When addressing your firm in a presentation, have you done everything possible to use the most effective words to make your points, and rehearsed your remarks repeatedly to make sure your delivery is as good as it can be?
- Have you established a track record that the words you communicate to your firm, in fact, turn into the desired progress you intended?

May the explanation of John F. Kennedy's three leadership traits covered in this chapter guide you through answering these questions, and result in achieving better results for your organization.

CHAPTER EIGHT

HOW TO INSPIRE OPTIMISM AND MAINTAIN PRINCIPLED VISION—LIKE RONALD REAGAN

Two-time Pulitzer finalist H. W. Brands has written acclaimed biographies of Franklin D. Roosevelt and Ronald Reagan. Here's his nutshell on their places in history: "What FDR was to the first half of the twentieth century, Reagan was to the second.... Both restored Americans' faith in their country."[678] Along the same glowing lines, in his Reagan biography, Richard Reeves gave this assessment of the two giants' impact: "What Roosevelt was for liberals, Reagan was for conservatives. Larger than life. Indispensable."[679]

The direct connection between the two titans was brief but important. Voting for the first time in 1932, Reagan cast his ballot for FDR at age twenty-one. Impressed by Roosevelt's charisma and gaining inspiration from his Fireside Chats throughout the Great Depression and World War II, Reagan stayed on FDR's bandwagon in the 1936, 1940, and 1944 elections. He then continued to support Democratic candidates after Roosevelt's death until having an epiphany about the problems caused by big government and higher taxes that caused Reagan to switch to the Republican Party in 1962. For the rest of his life, he gave this stock answer to explain his decision: "I didn't leave the Democratic Party. The party left me."[680]

FDR was such a hero to Reagan that even after joining the GOP, Reagan kept quoting FDR in his speeches, presumably hoping to attract Democratic votes.[681] It worked. His victories in the 1980 and 1984 presidential elections became landslides due to crossover voting by mass quantities of "Reagan Democrats."[682]

The life stories of the two men align on many fronts. Among their similarities:

- In terms of their upbringing, both were reared by dominant mothers and less involved fathers. Hands-on moms Sara Delano Roosevelt and Nelle Wilson Reagan made their sons believe the world was their oyster. Reagan's daughter Maureen said of her grandmother, "She had a gift for making you think you could change the world."[683] To explain the future presidents' disconnect with their dads, James Roosevelt was old enough to be his son's grandfather, became an invalid in his later years due to heart problems, and died when FDR was eighteen. Jack Reagan was an undependable alcoholic.
- Both had a positive and important relationship with Dwight Eisenhower who, therefore, served as a bridge figure between

them. Ike, of course, was chosen by FDR to serve as the Supreme Allied Commander in Europe during World War II, where he devised and then executed the plan that brought on Germany's surrender on May 7, 1945. After Reagan's October 1964 "A Time for Choosing" speech in support of Republican presidential nominee Barry Goldwater, Eisenhower became Reagan's biggest fan and mentor among the top Republican leaders at the time, and their relationship stayed strong until Ike's death on March 28, 1969.[684]

- As noted by Jacob Weisberg in his Reagan biography, upon their entry into the political fray, both men were judged by their peers to have "second class intellects" but "first class temperaments."[i,685] It could also be said that they were "a mosaic of strengths and weaknesses."[ii,686]
- Once they reached the White House, both maximized the power of the presidency's bully pulpit by delivering compelling speeches as well as giving effective conversational radio presentations (and, in Reagan's case, also television presentations). In his book *President Reagan: The Role of a Lifetime,* Lou Cannon concluded that Reagan's "cadences echoed the optimism of his old hero Franklin Roosevelt" which allowed both men to "transcend partisan barriers."[687]
- As president, they both pursued their era's challenges in a mode of steadfast optimism that became contagious as they elevated morale and pride nationwide, starting with their first inaugurations. Cannon could see that "Rexford Tugwell's description of Franklin Roosevelt as 'a man with fewer doubts than anyone I had ever known' was also a perfect description

---

i Supreme Court Justice Oliver Wendell Holmes Jr. first said this of Roosevelt. See: Jacob Weisberg, *Ronald Reagan* (Times Books 2016), 4.

ii Derek Leebaert described FDR this way in his book *Unlikely Heroes: Franklin Roosevelt, His Four Lieutenants, and the World They Made.* Reagan's glaring weaknesses will be covered later in this chapter. See: Scott Borchert, "'Unlikely Heroes' Review: FDR's Key Quartet," *Wall Street Journal,* February 24, 2023.

of Reagan. His optimism was unquenchable."[688] The two leaders maintained their good cheer while overcoming major obstacles in life (for FDR, polio; for Reagan, an itinerant childhood marked by the challenge of dealing with a frequently intoxicated father, and later the steady decline of his acting career).

- Although they each had electric interpersonal charm, for reasons known only to themselves (though speculated upon by their biographers), both presidents had a "heavily forested interior,"[iii,689],[690] making them emotionally distant, essentially unknowable to family members (Nancy Reagan once said, "You can get just so far with Ronnie and then something happens"[691]), and devoid of close friendships. This trait has caused historians to describe the two men with adjectives like "enigmatic," "opaque," and "sphinx-like." Weisberg gave this tight perspective on what Reagan was like to those he encountered: "Sunny at a distance; murky up close."[692]
- Both entered the Oval Office by trouncing dour, unsuccessful, one-term incumbents (Herbert Hoover for FDR, Jimmy Carter for Reagan); restored Americans' confidence in the presidency; transformed and grew their political parties to the detriment of those in the other tent; changed the national conversation about the role of government; won all their elections decisively; held the office as long as they could; vanquished totalitarian regimes abroad; dominated American life for at least a decade; and had high approval ratings when their years in the White House ended.
- Despite their many political victories, both also suffered serious disappointments. FDR's New Deal failed to lift the nation out of the Great Depression, and it took his buildup

---

iii This was how Roosevelt's speechwriter Robert Sherwood famously described FDR's inner thoughts, and it certainly aligns with the evaluation of Reagan's inner life shared by everyone who knew him. See: Arthur Schlesinger Jr., "The Man of the Century," *American Heritage* 45, no. 3, May/June 1994.

of World War II's war machine to bring about the return of economic prosperity. Though Reaganomics invigorated the economy, it also produced massive deficits. Both FDR and Reagan also had embarrassing setbacks: Roosevelt's egregious (and thankfully failed) overreach of authority by attempting to expand and pack the Supreme Court with favorable justices; and Reagan's humiliating Iran-Contra scandal[iv] where he failed to supervise his National Security Council's leaders when they went rogue on him and supplied arms to Nicaraguan rebels in violation of federal law.

- Despite their coming from wholly different backgrounds, both men grasped the essence of the American character and then spoke to it. Brands said: "What Roosevelt demonstrated, and Reagan later discovered and also demonstrated, was that a president with the ability to channel the power of the American people into his voice can accomplish a great deal."[693] Having this hold on and being the mouthpiece for the nation's psyche made them the right people at the right time to lead the United States out of dark periods toward brighter days, with both men elevating hopes in major speeches with the promise that their generation had "a rendezvous with destiny."

---

iv To refresh memories about the details of the Iran-Contra scandal: The US sold missiles to Israel to replace the missiles the Israelis sold to Iran, in hopes of causing seven American hostages to be released who were being held by an Iranian Islamic paramilitary group (called Hezbollah) tied to the regime of Ayatollah Khomeini; National Security Council representative Colonel Oliver North then took the proceeds from the arms sale and sent the funds to support rebel insurgents in Nicaragua (called "contras") who were attempting to overthrow the socialist Sandinista government there. Doing so violated the Boland Amendment to the Defense Appropriations Act of 1983, signed into law by Reagan on December 21, 1982, which prohibited US assistance to the contras in Nicaragua. When the facts became known, Reagan appointed former Senator John Tower to lead a commission to investigate the facts. The Tower Commission determined that Reagan had approved of the arms-for-hostages trade but not the illegal funding of the contras in Nicaragua. The Commission's findings about the nature and extent of Reagan's involvement matched those of Independent Counsel Lawrence Walsh in his investigation of the Iran-Contra affair. Walsh ultimately obtained the indictment of Secretary of Defense Caspar Weinberger, and also indictments and convictions against representatives of the National Security Council, State Department, and CIA.

Bound together in so many ways with our third greatest president Franklin D. Roosevelt, and despite never having led the country through a war (which, except for Lyndon Johnson, typically elevates a president's ranking), Reagan has been ranked America's ninth best president by historians in the last two C-SPAN polls in 2017 and 2021. In addition to restoring national hope and pride, he is also credited with bringing an end to the Cold War through his "peace through strength" diplomacy, eliminating an entire class of nuclear armaments through the INF Treaty consummated in 1987, strengthening America's military forces and its international alliances, and igniting the American economy (albeit with rising deficits) out of Jimmy Carter's stagflation "malaise."

In summary, using Will Inboden's words in his acclaimed book *The Peacemaker: Ronald Reagan, the Cold War, and the World on the Brink*, Reagan "transformed the art of the possible," by "not just restoring the country's faith in itself, but also restoring the world's belief in America—not as a perfect nation, but as a strong and good nation."[694] Cannon made a similar assessment: "Reagan dreamt big dreams and gave back to the world the America he had inside of him."[695]

Regardless of the murkiness of Ronald Reagan's inner thoughts, his historic words and deeds stand out with crystal clarity, making his extraordinary leadership traits easily recognizable and worthy of emulation by anyone who aspires to move mountains for the betterment of his enterprise.

Leadership Trait #1:
Inspire Optimism Among Constituents

As a starting point for having this trait, to inspire optimism among those he leads, a person in charge must *be* a sincere optimist himself who can maintain positive thoughts even in depressing circumstances. Ronald Reagan met this test.

In his 1965 memoir *Where's the Rest of Me,*[v,696] coauthored with Richard Hubler, which came out a year before his first successful run for governor of California (i.e., written with the hope of enhancing his political future), Reagan described his childhood as "one of those rare Huck Finn–Tom Sawyer idylls."[697] In fact, his formative years were often dreadful, in large part due to his often intoxicated father, a salesman who searched for greener pastures but could never quite find them. In his book *Reagan's America: Innocents at Home,* Garry Wills recognized the tension that must have existed in the family since wife and mother Nelle "hated liquor" so much that she "wrote a temperance play for her church in which a young girl whose dad was a drunkard said, 'I love you, Daddy, except when you have that old bottle.'"[698]

In support of his conclusion that the future president's childhood was *not* Huck/Tom "idyllic," Wills revealed that between the ages of six and ten, Reagan "attended a different school every year for four years in a row (in [the Illinois towns of] Galesburg, Monmouth, Tampico, and Dixon);" and "lived in five different places in Dixon, four different ones in Tampico, and two in Galesburg—all rented, always living in suitcases," such that Ronald Reagan "had no boyhood home."[699]

Despite the vagabond upbringing and his dad's binges, spurred on by his nurturing mom who, come what may, maintained high hopes for her golden boy son, Reagan flourished in high school—he played football, acted in plays, and got elected student body president. In the caption beneath his picture in the yearbook of his senior year, Reagan chose these words: "Life is just one grand, sweet song, so start the music!"[700]

---

v * In the 1942 movie *King's Row,* one of Reagan's most famous roles was the character Drake McHugh who injured his legs in an accident. He came out of surgery and saw that while he was anesthetized, his legs had been amputated by an evil doctor who didn't like him. As he awakened and was justifiably horrified, seeing that his lower limbs were no longer there, Reagan (as McHugh) screamed, "Where's the rest of me???!!!" In time, Drake McHugh accepted his fate and developed an optimistic spirit toward leading a productive life as an amputee. See: Lou Cannon, *President Reagan: The Role of a Lifetime* (Public Affairs 1991), 147.

Yes, beginning at a young age, Reagan went through life as an optimist, humming a grand sweet song regardless of his itinerant poverty, dysfunctional family, and major hurdles throughout his adult years, which he invariably surmounted. Weisberg wrote: "He *willed himself* to be an autonomous, self-reliant person."[701] Edmund Morris, in his book *Dutch: A Memoir of Ronald Reagan,* wrote: "He struggled against circumstance and *bent it to his will*.... From the time he was president of his high school, Ronald Reagan smilingly, honestly, affably, got what he wanted."

Cannon recounted President Reagan's favorite story about the nature of optimistic living. Those who worked around him heard it so many times it became a joke, to the point that his budget director David Stockman parodied it in his book *The Triumph of Politics*.[702] For Reagan, the story never got old and he deemed it so important that he felt called to share it in hopes of inspiring others to see the world as he saw it: with the proverbial glass half full. Imagine a fully energized Ronald Reagan, eyes twinkling, attempting to inspire a colleague to act like the boss and push through the day with a smile on his face no matter what. Here's Cannon's version of the story Reagan would often tell:

> There were two little boys, one a dour pessimist and the other an extreme optimist, who were taken to a psychiatrist by their parents. The parents wanted to provide encouragement to the pessimistic son and make the optimistic boy more conscious of life's obstacles. To accomplish this, the psychiatrist put the pessimist in a room filled with shiny toys and the optimist in a room with mounds of horse manure. After a while, the parents went to the room where the pessimist child had been placed and found him crying in frustration. He couldn't bring himself to play with the toys for fear he'd break them. Then the parents went to the optimistic son's room and found him happily shoveling manure. The boy beamed at them and

> exclaimed, "With this much manure around, I know there's a pony in here someplace!"[703]

Cannon determined that "Reagan was *always* the boy who sought the pony, the child who believed success was there for the finding, and surely it would come his way."[704]

Driven by a can-do spirit from childhood on, Reagan moved through life on the days when the fates surrounded him with shiny toys and also when he was encircled by manure. Like most people, he had plenty of both days. Unlike most people, he radiated authentic optimism *every single day*. Cannon noted: "Nothing got him down for long. When his films went out of fashion, he secured a new career in television. When that career faded, he emerged as a spokesman for Barry Goldwater, one of the most badly beaten presidential candidates in U.S. history, and Reagan used the platform and lost cause of that campaign to become a two-term governor of California and two-term president of the United States."[705]

Because Reagan never sat down with anyone and explained exactly *why* he always managed to maintain his optimism, to answer the question requires connecting dots based on what is known. His most important motivator appears to be that he kept believing and repeating mantras, many of which were surely drilled into his head by his mother Nelle. Among the most notable:

- "Everything will always work out for the best in the end."[706]
- "We're here to do whatever it takes."[707]
- "Nothing is impossible."[708]
- "God has a plan for each of us."[709]
- "If it's to be, it will be."[710]
- America had what it took to fulfill pilgrim leader John Winthrop's vision of the Massachusetts Bay Colony: "a shining city on a hill."[711] Winthrop's words came from Jesus Christ's Sermon on the Mount, found at Matthew 5:14: "You are the light of the world. A town built on a hill cannot be hidden."

- His strategy for the nation's ultimate objective in the Cold War: "We win. They lose."[712]
- A favorite quote from Thomas Paine: "We have it in our power to begin the world all over again."[713]
- On his Oval Office desk, "It CAN be done."[714]
- Another favorite quote, this one from Pope Pius XII: "Into the hands of America, God has placed the destinies of an afflicted mankind."[715]
- In his farewell address: "I know that for America there will always be a bright dawn ahead."[716]
- On the opening of his presidential library, words later engraved on his casket: "I know in my heart that man is good, that what is right will eventually triumph, and there's a purpose and worth to each and every life."[717]

If a leader approaches each day with thoughts like these pulsating through his soul and repeats them to himself often enough with a sense of conviction, he soon comes to believe that he and his constituents can prevail over anything. Reagan's steadfast level of high optimism about himself and the potential for greater American exceptionalism became multiplied far beyond what it had been before when he survived an assassin's bullet on March 30, 1981, two months after his inauguration. Bouncing back miraculously at age seventy, his positive spirit shifted into a higher gear fueled by his belief that God had spared his life so he could fulfill a greater purpose for himself, his nation, and the world. In his book *The Age of Reagan: The Conservative Counterrevolution 1980–1989*, Steven Hayward described Reagan's transformation in the aftermath of the shooting as reflected in two important conversations:

> On Good Friday, less than three weeks after the shooting, out of the blue, Reagan told Mike Deaver he wanted to talk to a clergyman. Deaver, an ex-seminarian, arranged for Terence Cardinal Cooke to come

> down from New York on short notice to visit with Reagan in the family residence at the White House. Reagan told the cardinal: "I have decided that whatever time I have left is for Him." Separately, Mother Teresa told Reagan that God had spared him for a purpose.[718]

After recovering, his providential mission going forward would be to attack every day from the perspective that he had been *chosen* by God to bring an end to the Cold War, defeat communism, reduce the possibility of nuclear warfare, and "change America, and the world," as he later acknowledged in his Farewell Address. In other words, per Morris, after he left the hospital, Reagan's purpose in life would be "coming to terms with evil…and particularly attempting to bring an end to that institutional murderer of all liberties known as Soviet communism" for the remainder of his presidency.[719]

It is one thing for a leader to be optimistic that he has what it takes to accomplish great things. It is something else when a leader can inspire *others* to adopt his positive mindset. Reagan showed he could do it beginning on Day One of his political career.

His foray into politics started with his being an advocate for Barry Goldwater's ill-fated presidential campaign in 1964. This gave Reagan the opportunity to deliver his first nationally televised political speech on October 27, 1964, a week before the election Lyndon B. Johnson won in a landslide. Using the patriotic themes he had honed in his hundreds of presentations to the people who worked at General Electric's facilities from 1954 to 1962 as part of his personal services contract in the years he hosted *GE Theater* on television (an experience Hayward described as his "political apprenticeship"[720]), Reagan spoke to the nation purportedly on behalf of Goldwater (he rarely mentioned the Republican nominee's name in the speech), on the theme "A Time for Choosing." Some of the highlights from the speech written entirely by Reagan:

> I have been permitted to choose my own words and discuss my own ideas regarding the choice that we face next week....
>
> This is the issue of this election: whether we believe in the capacity for self-government or whether we abandon the American revolution and confess that a little intellectual elite in a far-distant capital can plan for our lives better than we can plan them ourselves....
>
> You and I are told increasingly we have to choose between a left or a right. Well I'd like to suggest there is no such thing as a left or right. There's only an up or down: Up, man's aged old dream, the ultimate in individual freedom consistent with law and order, or down to the ash heap of totalitarianism....
>
> You and I have the courage to say to our enemies, "There is a price *we will not pay*." "There is a point beyond which *they must not advance*...."
>
> You and I have a rendezvous with destiny [quoting FDR].
>
> We'll preserve for our children this, the last best hope of man on earth [quoting Lincoln], or we'll sentence them to take the last step into a thousand years of darkness.

The national response to the speech was off the charts. Top Republicans from Dwight Eisenhower on down saw and wanted to start riding a new political thoroughbred capable of breaking the tapes in future national elections, and after Goldwater's blowout defeat, the party sure needed to find a winner. To tweak the Paine quote, beginning with his "A Time for Choosing" speech, Reagan was showing the world that he "had it in his power" to begin his life and career "all over again."

Stuart Spencer, the political consultant who became Reagan's campaign manager when he entered the 1966 governor's race in California, explained how the actor-turned-politician compared to Goldwater: "He believed basically what Barry believed. He said a lot of things Barry said, but he said them *differently*. Style was the difference. Barry was a hard-nosed up front Arizonian cowboy, and that's what scared people. Reagan said things in a soft more forgiving way and soon became the best communicator I've seen in my political life."[721]

Fast forward two years after the "Time for Choosing" speech, and matching 1966 Kentucky Derby-winning thoroughbred Kauai King stride for stride in leading the race from start to finish, Reagan, the new political thoroughbred from the West, won the Republican Party's race to be its nominee for governor of California that year, running away from the competition by getting almost two-thirds of the vote.

When he moved on from his primary victory to start his campaign against California's formidable Democratic incumbent governor Pat Brown (who had gained his second term by beating Richard Nixon in the 1962 governor's race), the national media could see a "star is born" script coming to life before their very eyes. The former actor who had not been in a hit movie in more than two decades was transforming himself into a political juggernaut in his first political race. *TIME* magazine put Reagan on its October 7, 1966 cover and its article on the new political phenomenon declared, "the candidate from Warner Bros. has turned out to be the most magnetic crowd puller California has seen since John F. Kennedy first stumped the state in 1960. A polished orator with an unerring sense of timing and his listener's mood, Reagan can hold an audience entranced for 30 or 40 minutes while he plows through statistics, gags, and homilies."[722]

Using his dulcet voice to speak from the bottom of his pure heart, the man who had slogged his way through a steadily declining career in the entertainment business since World War II suddenly had "started the music" and was singing a "grand, sweet song" with full voice in his new calling: politics.

The switch from his old line of work to the new one made perfect sense. Politics has been called "show business for ugly people," though just like the recently befallen president John F. Kennedy, Reagan was not ugly. Furthermore, like JFK, he had a package of traits that readily translated into political success: a genuine smile, eloquence in his speeches, the ability to tell tasteful jokes and use self-deprecation to make crowds chuckle, a confident walk that wasn't a swagger, the capacity to interact with strangers in a spirit of friendly informality, the communication smarts to tell memorable stories that packed a purpose (like Lincoln did), and, most important of all, using an actor's flair, the power to inspire others with his sincere optimistic beliefs about the present as well as what the future could hold with him as the elected leader, which meshed with what most Americans of his era believed.

Proving that his optimism was contagious and his political strengths readily translated into power at the polls, Reagan beat Brown with 57.5 percent of the vote, winning fifty-five of California's fifty-eight counties with a total victory margin of almost one million votes. He then won a second term in 1970 by decisively defeating esteemed California Assembly leader Jesse Unruh, and the nation could now see that the man who had been on the verge of fading into television oblivion as the host of *Death Valley Days* all of a sudden had become the electrifying Republican reincarnation of Franklin D. Roosevelt.

As governor of California, Reagan had success in imposing law and order on protesters, reducing the state's deficit, and promoting welfare reform. He so thoroughly enjoyed political life that he soon set his sights on the grand prize: the White House, though given his age, his "race against the clock" timing was tricky. At fifty-seven, less than two years into his first term as governor, he made a half-hearted run at the presidency in 1968 entering the race as a California favorite son candidate for the Republican nomination. The effort went nowhere since it was clearly too early in his nascent political career for him to compete with the likes of longstanding party leader Richard Nixon who won the party's nomination that year and then beat LBJ's vice president Hubert Humphrey in the election determined by Johnson's disastrous handling of the Vietnam War.

After Nixon had a successful first term while the Democratic Party continued to implode after its nationally televised humiliation at the 1968 convention in Chicago, he won a lopsided reelection victory over George McGovern in 1972. Dealt that hand, during his second term as governor of California, Reagan knew that the first time he could be a viable candidate to become the Republican Party's presidential nominee would be in 1976 when he would be sixty-five.

Then, unexpected circumstances (a.k.a., "good luck") arose that changed Reagan's timetable for reaching the Oval Office. Through all of 1973 and until August 9, 1974, the Watergate scandal steadily brought Nixon down until he was forced to resign. He was replaced by Gerald Ford who had taken over the vice presidency after Spiro Agnew resigned in December 1973 upon the discovery that he had taken kickbacks during his years in Maryland state government. This unprecedented chain of events meant that even though Ford had never been nominated to serve on a national ticket, all of a sudden, he was the president of the United States. Not surprisingly, Ford decided he liked being the most powerful person in the world so he decided to pursue the Republican Party's presidential nomination in 1976.

Ronald Reagan, always the optimist ("Nothing is impossible!" "It CAN be done!") believed that the 1976 election might well be his last chance to run for president before American voters would deem him too old to run the country. So, conventional wisdom be damned! Regardless of any unwritten rules, he boldly announced that he would oppose his own party's sitting president in the Republican primaries, believing that 1976 might well be his last chance before the Republican Party decided it was timed for this political thoroughbred to be put out to pasture.

To the amazement of everyone, Reagan almost won. Ford *barely* secured the necessary majority of Republican delegates (getting 1,187 votes to Reagan's 1,070), finally winning the race on the convention floor in Kansas City. After the sincere but ineloquent president gave an underwhelming acceptance address, at Ford's invitation, Reagan stepped up to the podium and delivered a powerhouse concession speech that ignited the crowd all the way up to the rafters at Kemper

Arena. It caused many (if not most) Republicans around the country to realize—just as they had done in 1964—that they had chosen the *wrong candidate.*[723] And they were right. Ford lost to Democratic nominee Jimmy Carter in the November election by a margin of 240–297 electoral votes.

Then good luck again came Reagan's way. Things again "worked out for the best in the end" for the relentless optimist. Carter proved to be a weak president, ineffective in dealing with double digit inflation, high unemployment, slow economic growth, and an energy crisis that produced long gas lines. His final setback came when he was unable to secure the release of the fifty-two American hostages who had been seized by Iranian revolutionaries loyal to the Ayatollah Khomeini at the US embassy in Tehran on November 4, 1979, and were held prisoner throughout the 1980 election year.

Still frisky at sixty-nine, eager to mount his ride as the long-awaited pony came into view after years of patiently digging his way through the mess of presidential politics, and knowing he had the wits, energy, and political skills necessary to remove all doubts about his age and ability to handle the job, Ronald Reagan met the other aspiring Republican presidential challengers head on in early 1980 and quickly emerged as the frontrunner. None of the other candidates could compete with Reagan at delivering a winning message to the effect that Carter should be defeated by a Republican committed to winning the Cold War, restoring vitality to the economy, and, above all else, restoring America's self-confidence at home and abroad.

Only George H. W. Bush briefly gained a semblance of traction in the 1980 primaries after winning January's Iowa caucus, but then Reagan defeated Bush in the New Hampshire primary a month later by more than a two-to-one margin. Thereafter, the race went Reagan's way as he maintained his two-to-one lead through the rest of the primary season until Bush withdrew in May in hopes (later fulfilled) of being chosen vice-president on the Republican ticket.

As he had done with his "A Time for Choosing" speech in 1964, Reagan made his 1980 campaign theme against Carter about the fact that once again, the time had come for Americans to make a choice:

Did they want to vote for a beaming optimist who truly believed (and made others believe) that he could get the country out of the ditch it was in, or did they want four more years of being led by a poor performing pessimist who seemed unaware that there were still plenty of shiny toys and even a pony available to those with the good fortune to live and believe in America's present and future? Yes, the toys and horse would be there for all to enjoy once the country "chose" to elect a leader who could inspire people to turn away from Carter's "misery" and "malaise," and turn the nation toward the liberating bliss of inhabiting "a shining city on a hill."

Reagan loathed pessimists with the same animosity he had toward communists. Wills explained how that fact came in to play in the 1980 presidential race:

> In Reagan's campaign and presidency, the principal accusation he made against his Democratic predecessors and rivals was that they were guilty of pessimism. Reagan, speaking at a Notre Dame graduation as Jimmy Carter had before him, lamented that "little men[vi] with loud voices cry doom." The alternative Reagan offered was a discipline of cheer. As he said in the 1980 campaign, "Our optimism has once again been turned loose. And all of us recognize that these people who keep talking about the age of limits [i.e., Carter] are really talking about their own limitations, not America's."[724]

Knowing how most Americans felt about Carter's dismal performance in the White House, in his closing statement at the end of their single televised debate in Cleveland on October 28, 1980, Reagan locked his eyes into the camera with an actor's poise and a look that former California governor Brown had once described as "cool inten-

---

vi * Carter was 5'10, Reagan was 6'1. Ironically, after Reagan's death in 2004, among his other words of praise for the man who beat him, Carter said of his successor in the White House that he was "one of our greatest optimists. President Reagan's belief in America was infectious."

sity." He then delivered the punch that knocked Carter off his feet and onto the mat where he stayed flattened through Election Day:

> Ask yourself, "Are you better off than you were four years ago? Is it easier for you to buy things in the stores than it was four years ago? Is America as respected throughout the world as it was four years ago? Do you feel our security is as safe and we're as strong as we were four years ago?"
>
> If you answer these questions, "Yes," well then, I think your choice is obvious as to who you'll vote for. If you *don't* agree and think this course we've been on for the last four years is *not* what you'd like to see us follow for the next four years, then I suggest there's another choice you have....
>
> I would like to have a crusade today and I would like to lead that crusade with your help. And it would be one to take government off the backs of the great people of this country and turn you loose again to do those things that I know you can do so well, because you did them and made this country great.[725]

Reagan proceeded to crush Carter, winning the electoral votes of forty-four states and receiving 50.8 percent of the popular vote, ten percentage points higher than Carter who got only 41 percent while third-party candidate John B. Anderson came in with 6.67 percent. The music for one grand, sweet song again started playing for the eternal optimist from Dixon, Illinois, and his legions of followers. By January 20, 1981, Reagan had grown from a boy shuffling along with his suitcase between small-town rental houses into a man with complete access to all the rooms in the White House and there found not just a pony, but lots of shiny toys. Morris explained why Reagan thoroughly enjoyed the presidency starting with Day One: "The job suited him better than any he had ever had, with its flawless scheduling, variety of interests, frequent opportunities to perform, and sense of huge purpose."[726]

Upon entering the Oval Office, though turning seventy three weeks after being sworn in (and keep in mind that "old man" Eisenhower had left the presidency at age seventy in 1961), Reagan already planned to be a two-term president. Cannon's biography confirmed it:

> He had felt destined to be president. Once he reached the White House, he felt destined to be president again. Two days after Reagan's inauguration in 1981, George Will called on him and asked if he would be a two-term president. Reagan laughed and said, "Well, you know I never could have achieved welfare reform in California without a second term." Will decided then and there Reagan planned to spend eight years in the White House.[727]

Receiving a compelling mandate from the voters and holding a job in which he and the nation flourished most of the time, Reagan became the darling of not only his party, but also of the many "Reagan Democrats" who were moved to support him. When I interviewed him for my book *Cross-Examining History*, Brands explained Reagan's popularity, throughout his era and all the way to the present:

> The reason Reagan remains an icon for Republicans and conservatives is because he was that rare, almost unique example of a cheerful conservative. Conservatives generally grumble about how the world is going to hell in a handbasket. The essence of conservatism is: hold what we have because change is usually for the worse. Reagan, on the other hand, firmly believed America's brightest days were ahead of it.[728]

Reagan's success in his first term made the nation share his optimism. Biographer Lee Edwards noted: "Reagan's tax cuts enacted by the Economic Recovery Tax Act of 1981 ignited an unparalleled period of economic growth in the 1980s that continued into the 1990s."[729] In addition to growing GDP in large part by cutting taxes, President Reagan had the good fortune to have inherited Paul Volcker as Federal Reserve Chairman who steadfastly kept interest rates high, which succeeded in bringing an end to runaway inflation by 1983.

Presidential historian Fred Greenstein summarized Reagan's triumphant handling of the economy that started early in his first term:

> In his first eight months in the White House, Reagan presided over a display of political effectiveness that will be studied for years to come. By the summer of 1981, Reagan and his associates had persuaded Congress to institute the greatest change in government priorities since the New Deal.... Reagan himself was crucial for his program's success. He was a masterful public enunciator of his administration's policies.... The upshot of his efforts was the passage of a pair of measures that reduced the next year's domestic spending by $35.2 billion, while slashing taxes by 25 percent over the next three years. Whatever their substantive merits, Reagan's 1981 economic enactments were a political accomplishment of the highest order.[730]

In addition to turning the economy around, Reagan also won enthusiastic praise in his first term for his response to the air traffic controllers union's strike in August 1981, when they threatened to shut down air travel until their compensation demands were met. After giving them two days' notice to return to work, a warning they ignored, Reagan fired them and replaced them with US military controllers. In explaining the rationale for his decision, he quoted one of his favorite presidents Calvin Coolidge: "There is no right to strike against the public safety of anybody, anywhere, at any time."[731]

Message delivered to his constituents' delight: We know how to handle people who try to jeopardize the good life in America.[vii,732,733]

To set the tone of strength in his foreign policy, at year end 1983, the commander-in-chief protected the lives of six hundred American medical students studying in Grenada by deploying over eight thousand troops to the island in the midst of political violence in what became known as Operation Urgent Fury. In three days, US military forces removed the communist regime that had seized power in a coup and ruled Grenada for the prior four years. Message delivered, again with the resounding approval of most Americans: In the aftermath of the Vietnam War that had caused many political leaders to resist any future US military interventions abroad, what was done in Grenada made the bold statement to the world, "Our days of weakness *are over*. Our military forces are back on their feet and standing tall."

The American people recognized that the economic turnaround, the appropriate toughness in dealing with the air traffic controllers, and the show of military strength in Grenada were all actions that neither Carter nor any other Democratic presidential wannabe would have *ever* accomplished. Unlike their response at the end of Carter's single term, Americans *knew* in 1984 that they were better off after Reagan's four years in the White House than they had been before he took office, and, therefore, had every reason to be optimistic about the nation's future as long as the man in the White House got to stay there for four more years.

---

vii Reagan's handling of the traffic controllers' strike established a precedent soon followed by business leaders who decided they should deal with unions just like Reagan did. In a 2019 segment on the subject, National Public Radio reporter Julia Simon said: "[with his handling of the air traffic controllers strike], Reagan flipped the script on strikebreaking. Strikers were no longer the sympathetic ones. Now they were lawbreakers screwing over regular Americans."[55] NPR reporter Kenny Malone noted: "Suddenly, around America, strikebreaking became the thing to do. Striking copper miners in Arizona—fired. Striking paper workers in Maine—fired. Meat packers, bus drivers—so many strikes in the 1980s were broken to the point where unions realized that employers wanted them to strike so they could fire them and replace them with non-union workers." See: Julia Simon and Kenny Malone, "Looking Back on When President Reagan Fired the Air Traffic Controllers," NPR Network, August 5, 2021.

When the time came to run for reelection, Reagan fully embraced his campaign slogan that matched the nation's revived hopeful spirit: "It's Morning Again in America." His Democratic opponent Walter Mondale (Carter's vice president) never had a chance. Reagan won forty-nine states (losing only Mondale's home state of Minnesota) and 58.8 percent of the popular vote compared to Mondale's 40.6 percent, as contagious optimism for the future backed by a successful first-term performance produced an unbeatable combination.

The Iran-Contra scandal (described in a footnote earlier in this chapter) certainly tarnished Reagan's second term from the time it became known to the American public in November 1986 until he publicly accepted responsibility for it in a televised address on March 4, 1987 (reminiscent of JFK's taking responsibility for the Bay of Pigs fiasco in April 1961). Despite the setback, Mikhail Gorbachev proved to be the greatest good luck blessing of Reagan's presidency when he became the Soviet Union's leader on March 11, 1985 (two months after Reagan's second inauguration), as he and President Reagan soon moved forward with serious diplomacy and world-changing dialogue at their summits in Geneva, Reykjavik, Washington, DC, and Moscow. The successful negotiations caused the president's "We win; they lose" optimism to become a fulfilled prophecy before Reagan left the White House in January 1989.

The second section of this chapter explores Reagan's critically important leadership trait of maintaining steadfast principled convictions to support prudent long-term vision regardless of constant criticism, as exemplified by his foreign policy. Before starting that analysis, however, it is important to recognize that an essential element of this second virtue was Reagan's having optimism so strong that it made others accept it and believe that their shared convictions were *right* and ultimate policy goals would come true.

A closing quote on Reagan's steadfast optimism from the man himself, which came at the dedication of his presidential library in 1991:

> I have been described as an undying optimist, always seeing a glass half full when some see it half empty.

> It's true, I *always* see the sunny side of life. And that's not just from my strong faith in God, but also from my strong and enduring faith in man.[734]

Not only did Reagan believe those statements about himself, he made most Americans believe it about themselves.

Leadership Trait #2:
Maintain Principled Convictions that Support a Clear Long-Term Vision, While Having Sufficient Flexibility to Make Minor Compromises When Necessary to Get Deals Done

On February 6, 2023, Henry Kissinger spoke at the Reagan Presidential Library on what would have been Ronald Reagan's 112th birthday. With the benefit of over three decades worth of reflection, here were some of Kissinger's most important thoughts that day:

> Reagan's *abiding vision* had both a moral and strategic clarity, and he refused to believe that leaders had to choose between the two. He was convinced, as Churchill put it, that there is nothing which adversaries "admire so much as strength, and there is nothing for which they have less respect than military weakness." But he also knew that a country that demands moral perfection in its foreign policy will achieve neither perfection nor security.
>
> He came to the Presidency powered by his anti-Communist *convictions*. While in office, these did not waver—he saw the fundamental moral failures of the Soviet system—but they were tempered by the responsibility he felt for avoiding catastrophic war.
>
> Great leaders take their societies from where they have been to where they have never imagined going. Ronald Reagan did that.[735]

Maintaining a strong commitment to one's principled convictions as the foundation for a clear vision of what the future can hold while staying sufficiently flexible to get deals done without having to abandon one's beliefs is an essential trait for great leadership. As with his optimism, no one can say for sure where Ronald Reagan got this second trait, but everyone recognized that he had it.

How did he get it? As with his optimism, no one knows for sure. Conservative columnist George Will spent considerable time with President Reagan, wrote dozens of op-ed pieces about him, and frequently commented on his policies and performance for national television networks. Because Reagan said so little at White House briefings, held few press conferences, and *never* shared his inner thoughts with anyone except his wife, Will had to do some heavy lifting in his quest to explain to readers and viewers exactly what made the president of the United States so committed to doing what he did and saying what he said. Cannon's description of Will's assessment of Reagan's intellectual uniqueness:

> The president once turned to Will and asked, "What makes the Blue Ridge Mountains blue?" Will didn't have the foggiest notion of the answer, but he never forgot the question. He was struck by Reagan's lack of concern about displaying ignorance and became convinced over time that the president possessed an "eclectic curiosity" about matters outside the boundaries of his settled views. "On the first nine levels, Reagan is the least interesting of men," Will said, "But if you postulate a tenth level, then he's suddenly fascinating."[736]

Cannon then went on to say that he himself had "interviewed Reagan at least forty times over two decades and been with him in informal or social settings on many occasions, watched him give hundreds of speeches and perform at scores of question-and-answer sessions.... [and despite all that exposure to his subject], it was difficult to understand how Reagan's mind worked."[737]

Thus, to grasp *why* Ronald Reagan was so steadfast in holding on to his principles and equally strong vision about what he believed should happen in the future while still finding ways to make a deal, requires a search to find his unique and undefinable "tenth level of personality," while recognizing that he held onto his beliefs and visions with such tenacity that a 1970 *Newsweek* magazine article said they were as "fixed and unyielding as Scripture."[738] In his "memoir" of the Reagan presidency filled with the author's conclusions after being beside him for years as his hand-picked presidential biographer, Morris determined that Reagan's convictions were as "unerasable as the grooves of an L.P."[739]

Herein lies one of Reagan's great gifts: On the one hand, he was "fixed and unyielding" and "unerasable" in his principles and visions, while on the other hand, he could compromise off of them, at least a little bit, to be able to make deals with Democratic congressional luminaries like Tip O'Neill and Dan Rostenkowski in getting Social Security and tax reform bills passed (in 1983 and 1986 respectively), as well as with Gorbachev in their summit negotiations.

In my interview with Reagan's first term White House Chief of Staff and second term Treasury Secretary James Baker in *Cross-Examining History*, he said of his former boss, "he was not hung up on idealism at all costs. He understood the importance of getting things done."[740] In his autobiography, Baker said:

> Reagan was willing to compromise to get the best deal he could. "Jim," he often told me as we discussed strategy, "I'd rather get 80% of what I want than to go over the cliff with my flag flying...." To turn ideas into policies, a leader must be prepared to fight hard—yes—but also to accept victory on the terms that can be won, even when they are short of perfection. He understood that we judge our presidents not just on their beliefs, but more importantly on the basis of

> what they get accomplished—meaning how much of their programs and policies they can get through Congress.[741]

Brands expounded upon Baker's assessment: "Reagan understood that he didn't have to get to his goal all at once. He knew that if he could get 80% today, then he could come back the next day and shoot for the last 20%."[742]

As demonstrated by too many of the people who followed Reagan into the White House in January 1989, for a president to maintain his principled convictions while being shaken by unforeseen events and/or by receiving a constant stream of criticism from leading media figures, members of the opposing party, and even from the ranks of his own political party and administration, is truly a herculean task. Throughout his years in the Oval Office, come what may, Reagan proved he could hold fast to his beliefs and hopeful vision for the future with the same level of inner strength and willpower as he did with his optimism. Of special significance in recognizing the importance of this leadership trait, Beschloss concluded in his book *Presidential Courage,* "Like the most effective American Presidents, Reagan ultimately proved that he was *not the captive* of his political base *but its leader.*"[743]

In his book on Reagan's foreign policy, Inboden identified his subject's eight fundamental principles from which he never wavered during his presidency and around which his White House agenda revolved in resetting America's place in the world after Carter's unsuccessful presidency:

(1) To be a force for good in the world, American morale and its economy, which are necessarily tied together, had to be strong;

(2) Soviet communism as a system of government was essentially evil, and, therefore, needed to be "delegitimized;"

(3) To be the dominant force whenever America's interests abroad needed to be advanced or were threatened, US military forces had to grow and be the most technologically advanced in the world since peace would only come if America was perceived as having stronger firepower and a stronger defense than its foes;

(4) Anti-communist insurgents around the world who operated in countries controlled by communists needed to overthrow their oppressors;

(5) The ever-present possibility of "mutual assured destruction" between countries armed with nuclear weapons needed to end;

(6) To transform the hearts and minds of people around the world into becoming more favorably inclined toward democracy, America needed to be in the business of promoting human rights and freedom;

(7) Through its military and trade policies aimed at bringing down the Soviet economy, the US needed to undermine the Soviets enough that they would select a new, more conciliatory leader open to negotiating an end to the Cold War and shifting Russia away from its totalitarian government; and

(8) The number of nuclear weapons in the world needed to be reduced, and, if everything fell into place, ultimately abolished.[744]

To transform these beliefs into reality, Reagan knew he had to move forward with specific policies on several fronts. First, at home, he had to reduce inflation through the Federal Reserve's maintaining high interest rates as long as necessary, and increase America's GDP and thereby reduce unemployment by getting Congress (despite the fact that Democrats held the House every year and the Senate the last two years of Reagan's presidency) to agree to cut taxes. To rebuild our national defense system, he also had to have Congress increase America's defense budget.

On the international front, to move forward with his goal of "winning" the Cold War, Reagan had to persuade the world that the communist government of the Soviet Union was an "evil empire," and motivate America's allies to join the United States in the "moral war" effort to bring down the Soviet regime. This could be achieved by making every decision involving the Soviet Union calculated to require them to spend more money on defense, decrease the market for their oil (the product that propped up their economy), and thereby have less money available to support the rest of their ailing economy. Accelerating the decline of their financial condition would hopefully make it necessary for the Soviets to choose a new leader who recognized that the only way to get their economy off the ropes would be by accepting America's terms in their diplomatic negotiations. Furthermore, in his summit negotiations with the Soviets after Gorbachev was chosen General Secretary early in Reagan's second term, it was imperative to maintain his non-negotiable commitments to the Strategic Defense Initiative (SDI), human rights advancements, and nuclear armament reductions.

Finally, in accordance with the policy that became known as "the Reagan Doctrine," to stop the expansion of communism in third world nations, he aspired to get Congress to fund the supplying of arms (but not soldiers) to insurgents in those countries to help them defeat existing communist regimes.

These eight principles and the accompanying policies that effectuated them were all aligned with a foreign policy vision for a brighter future *that only Reagan saw*. As Kissinger said in his assessment of Reagan found in Adelman's book, on the one hand the president "was *sui generis*. I cannot explain him;"[745] but on the other hand, per his 2023 Reagan Library remarks, Kissinger acknowledged that, "Ronald Reagan laid the groundwork for the peaceful resolution of the Cold War."[746]

In sync with Kissinger's sui generis assessment of Reagan's unique capacity for bringing to fruition his big picture vision, in his book *The*

Reagan I Knew, William F. Buckley agreed with Kissinger's assessment: "The *intuition* of Ronald Reagan was superior to that of the sophisticates, in both the conservative and liberal worlds."[747] Adding color to this word picture, Morris believed Reagan had "a Daliesque ability to bend reality to his purpose."[748]

After his extensive coverage of Reagan during his California governorship and through his presidency, Cannon reached the same conclusion as Kissinger, Buckley, and Morris, in explaining Reagan's unrivaled talent at seeing the future and knowing how to bend circumstances to match his vision: "He had a sense of the world *as it would be* and *as it might be,* not merely as it was. He wanted [and then saw and moved toward achieving] a world without nuclear weapons, walls, and iron curtains. He was, in this respect, a man for the age."[749]

How did his profound insights and intuitions about the future come out of Reagan's crystal ball and produce the big picture vision that inspired his uniquely successful foreign policy strategy? Might it have come from the "tenth level" of intelligence recognized by Will, the "intuition" that impressed Buckley, or the "Daliesque ability" Morris witnessed? Here was Hayward's answer to those challenging questions:

> The philosopher Bernard Lonergan studied the subject [of what leads to insight about what the future may hold] in depth. He determined that "insight [i.e., vision] is reached not by learning rules, not by following precepts, not by studying methodology.... It's a function not of outer circumstances but of inner condition, pivots between the concrete and the abstract, and passes into the habitual texture of one's mind.... Were there rules for discovery, then discovery would be mere conclusions. Were there precepts for genius, then men of genius would be hacks." Insight IS discovery, not deduction; it shares the same element of genius that creates great new art.[750]

In Reagan's clear vision that inspired Americans to believe in a brighter future, the eternal optimist offered this to support his thoughts: "The difference between an American and any other kind of person is that an American lives in anticipation of the future because he *knows* it will be a great place."[751] Cannon concluded that Reagan's gift of effectuating what needed to happen prospectively to make the world a better place was "the central purpose of the presidency."[752] In his 1980 campaign, Reagan emphasized his view of the nation's prospects for better days: "*They* (Carter and the Democrats) say the United States has had its day in the sun; that our nation has passed its zenith. They expect you to tell your children that the future will be one of sacrifice and few opportunities. My fellow Americans, I *reject* that view."[753]

Among Reagan's most notable big-picture visions that arose out of his eight previously described principled convictions (outlined by Inboden) were the following:

(1) The Cold War *needed to end* (or *not* continue indefinitely) on the basis of an American victory and Soviet Union defeat; and with the right moves, it *would end* by his doing what it took to accelerate the Soviet economy's decline and then be in a position to successfully impose America's most important terms in his summit negotiations with Gorbachev;[754]

(2) For there to be some possibility of achieving world peace in the future, the nuclear arms race and the threat of nuclear attack also *had to end,* which *could be achieved* on a faster track by the implementation of the advanced technological SDI shield capable of stopping nukes before they hit their target. Although the SDI never materialized technologically, the *mere idea* behind it brought sufficient fear into Soviet leaders' minds that it served its purpose. Arms Control Director Ken Adelman (who was with the president at his summits with Gorbachev) believed that it was Reagan's

non-negotiable commitment to push forward with the SDI that became "the straw that broke the Communist camel's back"[755] and caused the Soviet Union to collapse. George Shultz reached the same conclusion.[756]

(3) People living in the Soviet Union and the Eastern European countries controlled by it needed to have the same "Bill of Rights" freedoms that Americans have had, especially religious freedom. Only with these rights in place could human beings flourish and have any chance of achieving their full potential. Reagan explained how he thought the future would materialize in a conversation he had with his aide James Rosebush shortly before the Geneva Summit with Gorbachev:

> These [communist] systems will crumble by the sheer fact that a growing majority of people living under their rule have a pent-up desire to be free to worship more than the state; and this demand to know and worship God, and to have a free and open relationship with Him, is what will bring totalitarianism and communism down. Of this I am sure. The people will do it themselves. We need to do everything we can to help them accomplish this.[757]

Knowing the ultimate success Reagan had in his second term by relying on his principled convictions in furtherance of fulfilling his long-term visions, and knowing how well he communicated those convictions and visions to crowds and in his one-on-one negotiating sessions with Gorbachev, just as JFK had done during his presidency (as described in this book's previous chapter), Reagan transformed ideas into words, and then words into the deeds that achieved his goals. Looking back with the benefit of twenty-twenty hindsight, what Reagan did in devising and then implementing his foreign policy appears to have been highly sensible and profoundly wise. At the time he advocated his beliefs as the basis for policies, however, critics on many fronts scoffed, presumably hoping to persuade him to change his course.

As a first example of Reagan's immunity to criticism, George H. W. Bush, his principal opponent in the 1980 Republican primaries, labeled Reagan's "supply side" approach to revitalizing the nation's financial state of affairs as "voodoo economics";[758] Democrats called it "trickle-down economics," claiming it would benefit rich people more than it would help the middle and lower classes.[759] Bush and the Democrats were wrong; Reagan was right in implementing a policy that elevated the economy to new heights during his presidency, although its overuse and abuse by subsequent presidents who cut taxes while increasing spending has led to the massive escalation of the federal deficit.

For another example, when Reagan called the Soviet communist regime "evil" and said it needed to be defeated in his speeches starting with the 1980 campaign and later in his first term, Beschloss noted how Carter responded by "declaring that Reagan's 'radical' intentions would escalate the arms race and violate the foreign policy of every president since Truman."[760] Carter then passed the failed-Democratic-presidential-campaign-against-Reagan baton to Mondale in 1984, and Beschloss noted that the former vice-president followed Carter's fearmongering tactics and "ran commercials warning that Reagan's 'Star Wars scheme' (SDI) would extend the Cold War 'into the heavens.'"[761] Again, his Democratic presidential opponents were wrong and Reagan was right.

Reagan also found himself on the receiving end of critics from his own party when he argued that America's Cold War strategy should have as its objective causing the Soviet Union to surrender in negotiations after yielding to America's "peace through strength" tactics, instead of continuing to pursue the policy of "peaceful coexistence" détente, which Reagan called "a one way street that gives the Soviets what they want."[762] Later in his presidency, when he pressed hard in his diplomatic summits with Gorbachev seeking nuclear arms reduction and the SDI's defensive shield, those same critics blasted him.

In widely circulated editorials, Nixon and Kissinger, his Secretary of State and National Security Advisor, argued in Reagan's first term that Reagan's "surrender" vs. detente approach was misguided, and in his second term, that the intimate-bonding-with-Gorbachev method of summit negotiations was also misguided and not likely to achieve the desired result.[763] In both instances, those from his own party who had guided America's foreign policy in the past were wrong and Reagan was right.

When Reagan spoke in his June 1982 speech at Westminster Palace in London of the Soviet economic system's being in a state of serious decline, and the free world's needing to do what it took to drive the Soviets' financial state of affairs further downward as a means of opening the door for the Russian people to start a groundswell toward bringing freedom and democracy to their government, Reeves noted in his Reagan biography that ABC's Sam Donaldson and Frank Reynolds, NBC's Marvin Kalb and Tom Brokaw, and CBS's Tom Fenton all responded to that message with a yawn, saying his thoughts were "naïve" and, thus, "vintage Reagan."[764] In this instance, the mainstream media was wrong and Reagan was right.

Criticism even came from his administration's inner circle. Before Reagan emphatically told Gorbachev in Berlin at his June 1987 Brandenburg Gate speech to "tear down this wall!", his secretary of state George Shultz and national security advisor Colin Powell had done everything they could to remove from the text those most impactful words of his presidency. Hayward gave these specifics about the nature of their dire warnings to the president:

> You'll embarrass your host, West German chancellor Helmut Kohl. You'll anger and provoke Mikhail Gorbachev, with whom you've just started making progress on arms control. You'll whip up false hope among the East Germans—for surely the Berlin Wall isn't coming down any time soon. Besides, Germans have grown used to the wall. The ultimate reason: You'll look naïve and foolish, Mr. President.[765]

On this historic occasion, his most trusted foreign policy advisors Shultz and Powell were wrong; their boss was right.

Finally, as President Reagan moved forward aggressively with his objective of winning the Cold War by achieving a negotiated surrender with the Soviet Union in his second term, James Mann reported in his book *The Rebellion of Ronald Reagan* that "media [typically favorable to Reagan] such as *National Review* and columnists such as George Will despised his unfolding diplomacy with Gorbachev."[766] In this unending pattern of having harsh unmeritorious criticism leveled at him, the conservative media was wrong and Reagan was right.

In all these instances, Ronald Reagan ignored his critics—Republicans, Democrats, his own Cabinet, mainstream media, and the conservative media—and *never* wavered from his convictions about the best course of action for his administration to take toward achieving what he considered his God-ordained mission to bring an end to Soviet communism and win the Cold War. Beschloss: "Reagan's strong beliefs and optimism moved him to do things from which others might have flinched."[767]

Yes, it's a virtue to hold fast to one's principled convictions and vision for the future. It's even more of a virtue when after withstanding attacks from several fronts, those steadfast beliefs are proved to be true and produce the desired result. Mann's assessment of Reagan's success in finding a middle way that worked between the conflicting foreign policy views of conservatives and liberals:

> The judgment on which Reagan based his policy toward the Soviet Union during this period usually turned out to be correct—even when, in retrospect, other prominent American political leaders and foreign-policy experts were wrong. Reagan guessed that Gorbachev represented significant change—that he was not just another in a line of leaders eager to reassert Soviet power around the globe, despite what both conservatives and old hands like Richard Nixon and Henry Kissinger were arguing. He sensed that the

> Soviet economy was in desperate shape. He figured, rightly, that the Soviet Union would eventually be willing to enter into arms-control deals without the series of conditions it had previously set. He decided that Gorbachev would not react strongly to his speech at the Berlin Wall. Above all, Reagan recognized that the Cold War was not a permanent state of affairs; that it could, one day or another, draw to a close….
>
> If Reagan had been merely a puppet of the American right, there would have been no embrace of Gorbachev, no drive to reduce America's supplies of nuclear weapons and missiles, and no treaty to ban intermediate-range missiles in Europe….
>
> At home, Reagan gradually brought the American public toward an awareness that the Soviet Union was changing and the Cold War subsiding. Gorbachev and his aides recognized Reagan's political significance. "His big plus was his authority inside the country," said Anatoly Adamishin, the Soviet deputy foreign minister. "Other leaders, like [Vice President and 1988 presidential candidate George H. W.] Bush, had to cater to political forces. But Ronald Reagan could overcome the resistance of the hawks."[768]

Mann's assessment aligns with the *Wall Street Journal*'s lead editorial on March 16, 2023, which addressed why America's foreign policy toward the Ukraine should model Reagan's foreign policy:

> The modern GOP model is Ronald Reagan, who combined principle with practicality and sold his policy to the public through persuasion. He paired a rapid expansion of U.S. military power with diplomatic efforts to end the Cold War. He saw the struggle against the Soviets as moral, but he didn't hesitate to arm enemies of communism, even impalatable

> ones. Aiding Ukraine now is in that Reagan Doctrine tradition....
>
> Reagan also didn't indulge a false choice between influencing world affairs and managing economic and social programs at home. He saw a roaring economy and cultural cohesion as essential elements of national power. Reagan hated nuclear weapons and wanted to protect against their use. But he didn't let Soviet threats dictate U.S. actions, as the populist U.S. right is doing now with Mr. Putin....
>
> The Gipper's "peace through strength" approach remains the benchmark for Republican success in world affairs.[769]

As mentioned previously, in his recovery from the March 1981 assassination attempt, and the epiphany that followed after his conversations with Cardinal Cooke and Mother Teresa, Reagan believed God had spared his life so he could lead the nation toward the realization of his foreign policy goals. Inboden explained how this epiphany strengthened his convictions about what he needed to do moving forward to fulfill his destiny:

> For Reagan, the Cold War was a religious war. His personal convictions and the policies of his administration cannot be understood apart from the role of religious faith and religious freedom. Faith provided personal inspiration to Reagan, who believed God had called him to defeat Soviet communism and abolish nuclear weapons. This divine mandate gave Reagan the resolve to pursue his policies in the face of overwhelming criticism and opposition, and also a serenity and equipoise even as the world teetered on the brink of nuclear apocalypse.[770]

After successful relationship-building and negotiating with Gorbachev at the Geneva, Reykjavik, and Washington, DC summits produced the Intermediate-Range Nuclear Forces (INF) Treaty in the last half of 1987 (which banned the US and the Soviet Union from using land-based ballistic missiles, cruise missiles, and missile launchers), President Reagan traveled to Moscow in May 1988 for a final summit in which he achieved a triumphant culmination of seeing his principled convictions and visions become reality. In his fine biography of George Shultz titled *In the Nation's Service*, Philip Taubman tightly summarized the significance of the Moscow summit: It "reflected the arc of Reagan's Soviet odyssey from anti-Communist crusader to Kremlin friend."[771]

During the four days in Moscow, in his time with Gorbachev, Reagan advocated the need for religious freedom in the Soviet Union; rejected the issuance of a joint statement that said their mutual goal was "peaceful coexistence" (a term from the prior détente era, which Reagan abhorred); heard Gorbachev tell him and others at the dinner table that he expected democracy to come to the Soviet Union with genuine elections and term limits for leaders; and when they walked around the Red Square together, Reagan confirmed the geopolitical transformation he had engineered when he responded to the question from ABC News' Sam Donaldson: "Do you still believe the Soviet Union is an 'evil empire?'" The president's answer: "No, I was talking about another time and another era."[772]

The most magical dream-come-true moments of the trip to Moscow came when Reagan got to do what *all* his critics had believed was impossible: Tell the Russian people in person, and on their television network, with the full knowledge and implied consent of their leaders, about the liberating benefits of democracy and freedom. Here are edited highlights from what he told 600 students and faculty members at Moscow State University and a national television audience on May 31, 1988, standing beneath a bust of Lenin, in a performance that Lou Cannon called Reagan's "role of a lifetime:"

First I want to talk to you as I would to any group of university students in the United States, not just of the realities of today but the possibilities of tomorrow...

Progress is not foreordained. The key is freedom—freedom of thought, freedom of information, freedom of communication. The founding father of this university, Mikhail Lomonosov, knew that, "It is common knowledge that the achievements of science are considerable once the yoke of slavery is cast off and replaced by the freedom of philosophy."...

Freedom is the right to question and change the established way of doing things. It is the continuing revolution of the marketplace. It is the understanding that allows us to recognize shortcomings and seek solutions. It is the right to put forth an idea, scoffed at by the experts, and watch it catch fire among the people. It is the right to dream—to follow your dream or stick to your conscience, even if you're the only one in a sea of doubters. Freedom is the recognition that no single person, no single authority or government has a monopoly on the truth, and every life is infinitely precious, that every one of us has been put here for a reason and has something to offer....

Americans always seek to make friends of old antagonists. After a colonial revolution with Britain, we cemented the ties of kinship between our nations. After a Civil War between North and South, we healed our wounds and found unity as a nation. We fought two world wars against Germany and one with Japan, but now the Federal Republic of Germany and Japan are two of our closest allies....

We do not know what the conclusion will be of this journey, but we're hopeful that the promise of reform

> will be fulfilled. In this Moscow spring, may freedom blossom forth in the rich fertile soil of your people. May we be allowed to hope that the marvelous sound of a new openness will keep ringing through, leading to a new world of reconciliation, friendship, and peace....[773]

When he finished the speech, the students and faculty of Moscow State University gave the President of the United States a standing ovation.

Two days later, speaking at the Moscow airport before Air Force One's departure, in a scene described by Taubman in which "the anti-Communist warrior of yesteryear had vanished, supplanted by a peacemaker,"[774] Reagan delivered these closing remarks to Gorbachev that ended the trip on a diplomatic mountaintop:

> Mr. General Secretary, I think you understand that we're not just grateful to you and Mrs. Gorbachev, but we want you to know we think of you as friends. And in that spirit, we would ask one further favor of you. Tell the people of the Soviet Union of the deep feelings of friendship felt by us and by the people of our country toward them. Tell them, too, Nancy and I are grateful for their waves and smiles, and tell them we will remember all of our days their faces—the faces of hope—hope for a new era in human history, an era of peace between our nations and our peoples.[775]

After leaving Moscow, Ronald Reagan put a wrap on the final months of his presidency, concluding with his Farewell Address on January 11, 1989. In that speech, he reminded Americans that over the course of the last eight years in the White House, the success of his presidency had come because of his commitment to his principled convictions and visions. Here were some of the high points from Reagan's final address:

Well, back in 1980, when I was running for President, it was all so different. Some pundits said our programs would result in catastrophe. Our views on foreign affairs would cause war. Our plans for the economy would cause inflation to soar and bring about economic collapse. I even remember one highly respected economist saying, back in 1982, that "The engines of economic growth have shut down here, and they're likely to stay that way for years to come." Well, he and the other opinion leaders were wrong. The fact is, what they called "radical" was really "right." What they called "dangerous" was just "desperately needed....

As long as we remember our first principles and believe in ourselves, the future will always be ours. And something else we learned: Once you begin a great movement, there's no telling where it will end. We meant to change a nation, and instead, we changed a world....

I've spoken of the shining city all my political life, but I don't know if I ever quite communicated what I saw when I said it. But in my mind it was a tall, proud city built on rocks stronger than oceans, wind-swept, God-blessed, and teeming with people of all kinds living in harmony and peace; a city with free ports that hummed with commerce and creativity. And if there had to be city walls, the walls had doors and the doors were open to anyone with the will and the heart to get here. That's how I saw it, and see it still....

My friends: We did it. We weren't just marking time. We made a difference. We made the city stronger, we made the city freer, and we left her in good hands.[776]

This segment of the chapter will end by returning to Henry Kissinger's February 2023 remarks at the Reagan Library. He closed his speech with these statements about the ultimate impact of President Reagan's optimism and commitment to his principled convictions and visions:

> Dealing with pressing developments around the world requires *a combination of strength and conciliation.* The "Peacemaker," as a recent formidable biography [meaning Inboden's book] describes the President, understood perhaps better than any prior or subsequent leader how to integrate these elements.
>
> Today we need Ronald Reagan's *courage* [his commitment to do the right things no matter what]. As he said, "The future doesn't belong to the fainthearted; it belongs to the brave." We need his *civic faith* [his optimism]: "We are too great a nation," he reminded us, "to limit ourselves to small dreams." And we need his *vision.* In his farewell address, he described the "City on the Hill," as he had always seen our country: "a beacon, a magnet for all who must have freedom, for all the pilgrims from all the lost places, who are hurtling through the darkness, toward home."
>
> What we need most is another Ronald Reagan.[777]

Ronald Reagan's Flaws

Though Reagan was great at generating contagious optimism, staying committed to his beliefs, and fulfilling his visionary prophecies, by all accounts he was weak as an administrator. Inboden described Reagan's approach to managing a staff as "dreadful" with the strife among his key players being "plagued by acrimony and infighting" and "bedeviled by constant leaks, fierce policy differences, and occasional criminality."[778]

Cannon determined that the nonstop strife between Reagan's Cabinet officers and other key lieutenants resulted from the fact that the boss refused to address conflict because "he abhorred personal quarrels of any sort and would go to extreme lengths to avoid them. He detested confrontation. It caused him to be resolutely indecisive."[779] In his biography, Reeves reported that when inter-office conflict arose, and was brought to the president's attention, Reagan's standard response was, "Fellas, you work that out and get back to me."[780] The unceasing in-fighting throughout Reagan's presidency produced, in Morris's words, "a White House power struggle of Lebanese intricacy."[781]

In addition to avoiding conflicts with his key personnel, Reagan also avoided taking the time necessary to know the details that laid the predicate for fully understanding his major policy positions. This flaw produced disastrous results in the Iran-Contra scandal. After reviewing the historical record, Inboden determined:

> Reagan seems genuinely to have been surprised and baffled to learn of the Contra diversion.... He had made clear for years his fervent commitment to the contras and his disinterest in many details of governing. Scheming zealots such as Oliver North exploited these conditions.
>
> What at Reykjavik had been a virtue for Reagan, his resolve, self-confidence and belief in his vision despite naysayers on all sides—now turned into a vice of self-deception. He willed himself to believe he had not traded arms for hostages...despite overwhelming evidence including his own previous diary confessions, that he had in fact done just that.[782]

By all accounts, Reagan chose to ignore the details behind his major policy positions because he believed his focus as president should be only on "the big issues." He was fine with leaving the task of absorbing the details that supported his big issue positions to others. Cannon wrote: "Reagan focused on a few high visibility issues of great importance to him....[though he] lacked a technical grasp of any issue and was usually bored by briefings."[783] This unfortunate trait led to his "limitations on issues [such as whether the MX intercontinental ballistic should be deployed] where he needed *not* an "actor's understanding of the public presidency but a command of strategic knowledge and technical detail."[784]

Reagan's focus on "big issues" and inattention to details caused big problems in his handling of the economy. Yes, as Edwards and Greenstein pointed out, he started his first term with tax cuts and spending cuts that jumpstarted Carter's depressed economy and kept it rising. In addition to his commitment to those two measures, however, Reagan had also campaigned on the promise that he would balance the budget. Not only did he never balance the budget during his presidency, in fact, as Weisberg pointed out, beginning in the second year of his presidency, Reagan discreetly began *raising* taxes and *increasing* federal spending.

Just as JFK compartmentalized the chronic infidelities in his personal life, Ronald Reagan compartmentalized his conflicted handling of the economy. Weisberg gave this explanation of how the process worked inside the president's mind:

> His diaries suggest he thought about economic issues in the same segmented way he talked about them. Taxes triggered one set of views, defense another, deficits a third. This compartmentalization allowed him to deal with the reality of the economy without having to reconcile his ideology and practical necessity.... He consistently made a default choice of increasing the deficit over tax increases or limiting military spending, which he regarded as "not a budget issue...."
>
> Once the economy bounced back, government expanded with it. Over Reagan's two terms, domestic spending went from $303 billion to $565 billion. Overall

> federal spending rose from $671 billion in 1981 to $1.144 trillion in 1989.... The federal workforce grew by 5% during the Reagan years.
>
> [While Reagan increased other taxes], he did legitimately reduce income taxes from a top rate of 70% when he took office to 28% when he left.... The decline in federal revenue [from the income tax cut] caused the national debt to balloon from $998 billion in 1981 to $2.857 trillion in 1989. Despite these numbers, Reagan believed he was making government smaller.
>
> What he did change was the nation's *attitude* toward government. Reagan took citizens who a generation before had turned to Washington for solutions [during FDR's presidency] and told them to look elsewhere to voluntarism, to the free market, to themselves.[785]

On the personal side, Reagan's previously described desire to maintain emotional distance from others caused him to have a distant relationship with all four of his children (Maureen and Michael with his first marriage to Jane Wyman and Patti and Ron with Nancy) and essentially no close friendships. Maureen and Michael basically accepted their fate and never caused problems, but Patti and Ron rebelled, and became squeaky wheels during their dad's presidency whom he chose not to grease.

Brands gave this description of Reagan's keeping his distance from others: "He got cooler the closer a person got to him. Nancy Reagan was really her husband's only friend. I would say, with a little hyperbole, that if Reagan hadn't been famous and attracted the attention he did, no one would have come to his funeral except Nancy. He never gave of himself the way you have to do in order to form true friendships."[786]

PERSONAL APPLICATION

You now know how Ronald Reagan would have answered the following questions. How do *you* answer them?

- Do you think of yourself as an optimist or a pessimist? Is the glass half full or half empty? Do you regard yourself as an upbeat, cheerful person or not? If you are not upbeat, are you satisfied by living in that state of mind, or are you taking steps to become more optimistic?
- Are you generally optimistic about your business? Your family? Your city? Your state? Your nation? The future of the world?
- If you think of yourself as an optimist, do you believe that you *radiate* optimism in such a way that your optimism inspires others who work in your organization to be optimistic? What are some examples that support your belief that you have inspired others to be optimistic?
- When times get tough, or something happens that disappoints you, does your optimism fade?
- Is your optimism so strong that you believe you can *will* good things to happen? If so, do others believe you have that power?
- To maintain and be able to share your optimism, do you have mantras that you repeat to yourself and to others? Do you keep optimistic statements around your work space or on the walls of your office?
- Do you believe that God or some higher power has a plan for you to have a successful career and life or has *called* you to do something great? If so, have you ever communicated that to others?
- When you speak with passion either one-on-one or to a group, is it usually a positive energy passion or a negative angry passion?

- When facing your colleagues, do you mainly smile or mainly frown?
- When you interact with strangers, are you informally positive and friendly, or not?
- Does your optimism inspire you to take bold risks in pursuing potentially impactful opportunities?
- Do you believe that the future opportunities in your life are limited or unlimited?
- Do you thoroughly enjoy your work and the people with whom you work? If not, how is that impacting your mental state? What are you doing to make things more positive in your workplace?
- When you have competed for jobs or some type of recognition, do you usually get what you want or not? If not, how do you typically respond to disappointment?
- When things go wrong, and it is at least partially your fault, do you acknowledge your part in the setback, and then move on to the next challenge?
- How committed are you to your beliefs concerning what your organization needs to do?
- Have you made your beliefs well known throughout your organization? Have you explained to others the guiding principles that support your beliefs? Do you reiterate them often? Have you made a speech or written a memorandum about them to formalize them to your firm?
- Have your beliefs led you to have a vision about today's strategy as well as the long-term future of your enterprise? If so, have you made that vision well known to your people?
- Do you feel like your convictions and vision for the future came as a result of substantial reflection from a place deep inside you? At least on occasion, are you an abstract thinker?

- Have your convictions and vision been criticized by people whom you respect? If so, did the criticism cause you to change your perspective?
- Is your vision for your organization's future in the process of being fulfilled? If not, why not?
- Have you ever found your convictions and vision to conflict with those of others in your organization? If so, how did you respond to that conflict? Did the conflict cause you to modify your positions?
- Do you recognize the need for compromise on some issues to get a deal done that gets you almost everything you want in the final deal?
- Do you consider yourself to be intuitive? If so, what are some examples of where you had an insight or intuition about the future that proved to be true?

May the explanation of Ronald Reagan's two key leadership traits covered in this chapter guide you through answering these questions, and result in achieving better results for your organization.

CLOSING THOUGHTS

I have now lived with these eight presidents in my house for almost two years after having had them come and go in my intel lectual neighborhood for decades. Something about the process of knowing their lives on an up-close-and-personal basis, and then distilling my research and reflections into the stories behind their most important leadership traits, has made me enjoy them much more after the completion of each chapter than I ever did before. Closeness made my heart grow fonder.

As this book has hopefully established, these men were not only the reigning giants of their eras, they are all on the short list of the greatest giants in American history. Their lives show how the twenty-four leadership traits covered in these pages carried them to achieve extraordinary success in steering our ship of state to new and better places.

But for the assassins' bullets that killed Abraham Lincoln and John F. Kennedy and Theodore Roosevelt's regretted decision not to run for reelection in 1908, all of them would have surely served two full terms. The six elected to second terms (and for Franklin D. Roosevelt, third and fourth terms) won their reelection races by huge margins, demonstrating that after observing four years of high performance by these men as the nation's chief executives, most Americans wanted them to continue working at the desk where the buck stopped.

As I reread the chapters to put together these "closing thoughts," here are my final impressions of these presidents' legacies, recognizing how much they have meant to our nation and now, after finishing this book, how much they mean to me as an American beneficiary:

> **George Washington:** He got the American experiment off to a great start by consistently exercising sound judgment regarding how the new nation and its president should con-

duct business, while always operating in a mode of unimpeachable integrity and a trust-inspiring manner, with all such traits having been acquired through the hard knocks of experience.

Thomas Jefferson: His being a visionary genius, eloquent wordsmith, endearing relationship-builder, and shrewd dealmaker made him uniquely capable of moving the nation forward during the make-or-break second decade of its existence.

Abraham Lincoln: Through the word power that flowed from his steel-trap mind, and his never wavering magnanimity, equanimity, and promise-keeping shown to all Americans, he won the Civil War, reconnected the nation, and abolished slavery, which allowed the United States to survive its darkest hours.

Theodore Roosevelt: Just as Thomas Jefferson jumpstarted the nineteenth century's first decade, TR did the same in the early twentieth century, using his electric energy and brilliant mind to seize new presidential leadership opportunities, keep the peace through his "speak softly but carry a big stick" diplomacy at home and abroad, and act as a powerful advocate to aid the multitudes who found themselves below the top quadrant in the American pecking order.

Franklin D. Roosevelt: His refusal to be defeated by polio is the most inspirational story in this book, and beyond that, he provided hope to an economically depressed people, moved our nation's foreign policy away from isolationism, and stoked American industry into becoming a powerful war machine strong enough to defeat the Axis powers in World War II, thereby allowing the United States to establish its position as the dominant nation in the world.

Dwight Eisenhower: Like George Washington, Ike was both a superior military *and* political leader who made the organization of the Allied forces *and* the federal government run like a well-oiled machine, and made it all operate so smoothly that his presidency was marked by eight years of peace and prosperity—all because he knew when to be patient and when to play hardball as complex issues arose.

John F. Kennedy: Growing in wisdom throughout his shortened presidency, he prevented the Cuban Missile Crisis from becoming World War III by rejecting the hawkish advice of his military leaders and Executive Committee, and also inspired the nation with words and a style of delivery that produced positive concrete results.

Ronald Reagan: His White House years proved the power of an optimistic leader to inspire his constituents, especially when the purveyor of positivism stayed the course with his principled convictions and the capacity to not only foresee the future but also bring it to fruition as he wound down the Cold War with his "peace through strength" diplomacy.

I chose John Avlon to write my foreword because in his books on Washington and Lincoln, he impressed me as today's master of "applied history," which he defines as "not simply the study of what happened but *why* it happened, and how the answers to those questions can guide us *now*. *Useful* wisdom is the goal."

In the spirit of John's commitment to making sure a knowledge of history can help guide us in making decisions regarding today's most important issues, I will now use the information contained in the prior chapters as the basis for providing my best guess at what each of these presidents would say *now*, if given a one sentence limit, to tell Americans *today* what would be on their hearts if they looked at our present circumstances.

George Washington: "Because we Americans had the wisdom, integrity, perseverance, and strength to declare our independence from England, then win that independence in the Revolutionary War, then create the new government model finalized in the Constitution, and finally move forward with a checks-and-balances system that has now lasted more than two centuries, the challenges presented today clearly pale in comparison to those we prevailed over in my era and, therefore, they *can be met*."

Thomas Jefferson: "For those who believe today's political polarization presents an insurmountable problem to effective governance, don't just stand there and complain about it; instead make it *your job* to build positive relationships with those who hold opposing views—just as I did repeatedly throughout my presidency in the aftermath of the Sedition Act to bring down the walls that divided and threatened to destroy America's house."

Abraham Lincoln: "Anyone can go low and do harsh things when major conflicts arise over deciding what is best for the future; but what separates Americans from the rest of the world is our longstanding commitment to take the high road whenever problems arise, and then make good decisions about how to solve them guided by the 'better angels' of our conscience."

Theodore Roosevelt: "Even though I always savored the short time I spent with the Rough Riders in the Cuban battlefield, I also learned the hard way about the devastating loss and anguish of war by knowing what it did to two of my sons in World War I, which has resulted in my sincere belief that prudent people must always fully explore every available diplomatic option before making the decision to declare war on an enemy."

Franklin D. Roosevelt: "Never underestimate the power of the human spirit in a person *and* a great nation to triumph over adversity, and evolve one-step-at-a-time toward making sound decisions through the process of reflection and heeding the advice of sage counsel."

Dwight Eisenhower: "Human endeavors of any size have the best chance of succeeding if the person at the top puts into place a support team of competent people who can give the leader what he needs to allow him to make the best decisions; which means that a person in charge who opts to make decisions and pursue challenges by himself or in a mode of disorganization is surely traveling on the road to disaster."

John F. Kennedy: "To be in the best position to lead people forward to new and better heights requires the courage to learn what you don't know, listen with discernment to advice that may or may not be correct, and recognize that final decisions about how best to deal with crucial issues often involve moral imperatives and not just political considerations."

Ronald Reagan: "There will always be plenty of pessimists and naysayers who do their best to block progress, and history largely forgets or ignores them; but if a leader has beliefs and a vision that what will produce a brighter future for his people, no critic should have the power to block him from achieving his goals."

Just as Lou Cannon determined that the presidency was the "role of a lifetime" for Ronald Reagan, outside of my commitments to faith, family, and friends, I believe that putting the facts and thoughts together in this book has been the most important role of my lifetime. Here's hoping you have enjoyed and learned from reading the final product as much as I enjoyed and learned from researching and writing it.

ACKNOWLEDGMENTS

Anyone who embarks on the writing of a presidential history book knows that it better be accurate and complete in its analysis. To make sure this book satisfied those objectives, on the front end, I committed to having major biographers of the eight presidents featured in my chapters review and assess my work to make sure I hadn't misstated any facts or failed to cover something important about their subject's leadership traits.

The following biographers performed that function for me:

For the George Washington chapter—David O. Stewart and David and Jeanne Heidler.

For the Thomas Jefferson chapter—Annette Gordon-Reed and Peter Onuf.

For the Abraham Lincoln chapter—Ronald White and John Avlon.

For the Theodore Roosevelt chapter—Douglas Brinkley and Clay Risen.

For the Franklin D. Roosevelt chapter—Doris Kearns Goodwin, Geoffrey Ward, James Tobin, and David Michaelis (who wrote a wonderful biography of Eleanor Roosevelt).

For the Dwight D. Eisenhower chapter—Evan Thomas, David Eisenhower, and Susan Eisenhower.

For the John F. Kennedy chapter—Sheldon Stern, Mark Updegrove, and Stephen F. Knott.

For the Ronald Reagan chapter—H. W. Brands, Will Inboden, and Philip Taubman (who wrote a fine biography of Reagan's Secretary of State George Shultz).

To these eminent historians, I offer my most heartfelt appreciation. In addition to them, I also received helpful feedback from my special history-loving friends: Sandy Kress, Marvin Blum, David Harrison, Bill Parrish, David Randolph Smith, Tim Beeton, Dale Petroskey, John Grisham, Tom Leppert, and Bob Townsend.

This book turned into reality thanks to my agent Austin Miller's connecting me with Alex Novak at Post Hill Press, and Alex has been a pleasure to work with every step of the way.

I dedicate this book to David O. Stewart, who has been not just a friend but a guiding hand for my writing life over the last decade. As a high-quality professional, first as a lawyer and then a historian, he has proven that such a dual calling can be achieved. As a devoted family man with the highest integrity, David goes through life as a stabilizing factor for all who cross his path. He is also a man of letters who cares deeply about the present and future of books, as proven by his having started and then expanded the *Washington Independent Review of Books*, which has now been doing great things for authors, reviewers, and readers since 2011.

David's biography of George Washington came out in February 2021, and it provided the spark for my wanting to write this book. It explained how George "did it" as a successful political leader, and made me want to research and tell the stories of how Thomas, Abraham, Theodore, Franklin, Dwight, John, and Ronald "did it" to achieve the success they had in their presidential years. David not only provided the foundation for my Washington chapter, he also carefully critiqued all my chapters and delivered affirmation and constructive criticism that surely enhanced the final product.

To give me confidence about the potential viability of the book, when I first considered writing it three years ago, I bounced my proposed theme off my friend Evan Thomas. Evan said I was the only guy he knew who had my "feet fully planted in both camps: the history world and the business world," which would be necessary to execute a history project aimed at inspiring non-political leaders. His final words in our phone conversation that day stayed with me: "Talmage, if anyone can do it, you're the guy!" Evan's faith in my capabilities at the outset gave me a much-needed boost to believe in this book's worthiness and marketability.

As I mentioned in the "Closing Thoughts" mini-chapter, John Avlon's vision for the necessity of "applied history" in today's world, as he demonstrated so vividly in his masterpiece *Lincoln and the Fight for Peace,* struck a major chord with me when we met in early 2022. John's willingness to write my foreword, and then say what he said in it are acts of generosity that have certainly elevated my confidence in this project.

I wrote this book in the early mornings and evenings while practicing law during business hours at the firm Shackelford, Bowen, McKinley & Norton, LLP. My managing partner John Shackelford has been fully supportive of my history endeavors through the years we have worked together and his friendship and appreciation of my avocation is a great blessing in my life. My assistant Jennifer Neyland has been a steady, diligent, warm-hearted presence in typing each chapter's many revisions which was necessary for me to believe that the wordsmithing in the final version was as good as I could make it.

On the home front, my wife Claire put up with having dozens of presidential biographies piled up on various tables around our house over the last three years while also providing me with the gift of silence whenever I was researching and writing, which allowed me to focus more clearly on the task at hand.

What keeps me grounded in my daily living and allows me to be productive in dealing with the challenges of essentially holding two jobs (full-time lawyer and full-time historian) are (1) the members of our family circle: Claire, son Scott, daughter Lindsey, son-in-law Mitchell, and grandsons Nolan and Miles; (2) the Fellowship Sunday School Class at Highland Park United Methodist Church in Dallas sponsored by Don and Fran Jackson (which has been a vital part of my life for the last thirty-eight years); and (3) my nineteen University of Texas Law School buddies known as "the Canoe Brothers" (Messrs. Blum, Smith, Wilson, Beeton, Parrish, Gibson, Geren, Elmquist, Payne, Peper, Fleming, Askamit, Windham, Watler, Ernst, Waldron, Luzzato, Hart, and Fitzpatrick) with whom I'm joined at the hip after being friends with these guys for almost a half century.

Last and most important in the overall scheme of things, I praise God from whom all blessings flow.

THE TWENTY-FOUR LEADERSHIP TRAITS OF OUR TOP PRESIDENTS

George Washington

- Learn from your mistakes.
- Use the power of nonverbal communication: "Less is More" and the Gift of Silence.
- Be humble in order to embrace collaborative decision-making.
- Act as Conscience-in-Chief.
- Advance unity among constituents.
- Avoid the image of being a self-promoter.

Thomas Jefferson

- Be proactive in building harmony among friends and foes to maintain progress in the midst of conflict.
- Use the sequence of: knowledge base, imagination, and peer feedback to formulate long-term vision.
- Once the vision is set for moving forward, turn it into reality through principled pragmatism.

Abraham Lincoln

- Maintain magnanimity coupled with equanimity.
- Keep your promises.

Theodore Roosevelt

- Never stop learning.

- Boldly expand in new directions, not limited by conventional wisdom or others' practices.
- Use every tool in the diplomat's tool kit to avoid war.

Franklin D. Roosevelt

- Fearlessly stare down adversity to inspire others to do the same.
- Keep one's finger on the pulse of constituents, and never get more than one step ahead of them when it's time to change their opinion.

Dwight Eisenhower

- Stay actively engaged with a well-oiled-machine organization.
- Exercise patience to reap big dividends.
- Play hardball when necessary.

John F. Kennedy

- Grow in wisdom while in office.
- Stay calm in a crisis.
- Use and deliver words that inspire progress.

Ronald Reagan

- Project optimism to inspire constituents.
- Maintain principled convictions that support long-term vision, while making minor compromises when necessary to get deals done.

ENDNOTES

CHAPTER ONE: GEORGE WASHINGTON

1 David O. Stewart, *George Washington: The Political Rise of America's Founding Father* (Dutton 2021).
2 Ibid., 212.
3 Ibid., 10.
4 Lee's eulogy at George Washington's funeral, December 26, 1799.
5 Stewart, *George Washington,* 65–66.
6 Ibid., 102–103.
7 Ibid.
8 Ron Chernow, *Washington: A Life* (Penguin Press 2020), 91–93.
9 Stewart, *George Washington,* 22–23.
10 Washington's letter to James Anderson, December 21, 1797.
11 Stewart, *George Washington,* 392–393.
12 Ibid., 393.
13 David S. Heidler and Jeanne T. Heidler, *Washington's Circle: The Creation of the President* (Random House 2015), 6.
14 Mark K. Updegrove, *Baptism by Fire: Eight Presidents Who Took Office in Times of Crisis* (Thomas Dunne Books 2008), 31, 46.
15 Adams's letter to Benjamin Rush, November 11, 1807.
16 Chernow, *Washington,* 789.
17 Stewart, *George Washington,* 147–148.
18 Chernow, *Washington,* 785–786.
19 Stewart, *George Washington,* 298.
20 Ibid., 332–334.
21 Ibid., 314.
22 Ibid., 389–390.
23 Ibid., 649.
24 Chernow, *Washington,* 306.
25 Jefferson's letter to Walter Jones, January 2, 1814.
26 Heidlers, *Washington's Circle,* 404.
27 Stewart, *George Washington,* 6.
28 Ibid., 212.
29 Chernow, *Washington,* 559, 595.
30 Washington's letter to Bushrod Washington, July 27, 1789.

31 Washington's letter to Henry Lee, July 21, 1793.
32 Stewart, *George Washington*, 78.
33 Jefferson's letter to Walter Jones, January 2, 1814.
34 Stewart, *George Washington*, 379.
35 Michael Beschloss, *Presidential Courage: Brave Leaders and How They Changed America 1789–1989* (Simon & Schuster 2007), 32.
36 Matthew 12:25 (King James Version); Lincoln's acceptance speech, receiving Illinois Republican Party's nomination for US Senator, June 16, 1858.
37 Nathaniel Philbrick, *Travels with George: In Search of Washington and His Legacy* (Viking 2021), xvi.
38 Ibid.
39 Heidlers, *Washington's Circle*, 414.
40 Stewart, *George Washington*, 192.
41 Chernow, *Washington*, 457.
42 Philbrick, *Travels with George*, 310–311.
43 Ibid., 340–341.
44 Stewart, *George Washington*, 342–343.
45 Ibid., 346.
46 Ibid., 401.
47 Ibid., 118.
48 Washington's letter to his stepson John Parke Custis, February 28, 1781.
49 Stewart, *George Washington*, 133–134.
50 Ibid., 201–202.
51 Philbrick, *Travels with George*, xii.
52 King George II's statement made to the portrait artist Benjamin Rush, though date of statement is uncertain.
53 Stewart, *George Washington*, 293.
54 Chernow, *Washington*, 547.
55 Ibid., 548.
56 Jefferson's letter to Walter Jones, January 2, 1814.
57 Stewart, *George Washington*, 401.

CHAPTER TWO: THOMAS JEFFERSON

58 Walter Isaacson, *The Code Breaker: Jennifer Doudna, Gene Editing, and the Future of the Human Race* (Simon & Schuster 2021), 390.
59 Jon Meacham, *In the Hands of the People: Thomas Jefferson on Equality, Faith, Freedom, Compromise, and the Art of Citizenship* (Random House 2020), xvi.

60 Merrill D. Peterson, *Thomas Jefferson and the New Nation* (Oxford University Press 1970), viii.

61 Peter S. Onuf, *The Mind of Thomas Jefferson* (University of Virginia Press 2007), 58.

62 Peterson, Jefferson and the New Nation, ix.

63 Jon Meacham, *Thomas Jefferson: The Art of Power* (Random House 2012), 316.

64 Annette Gordon-Reed and Peter S. Onuf, "Most Blessed of the Patriarchs": Thomas Jefferson and the Empire of the Imagination (Norton 2016), 199.

65 Joseph J. Ellis, *American Sphinx: The Character of Thomas Jefferson* (Knopf 1997), 182.

66 Jefferson's First Inaugural Address, March 4, 1801.

67 John Quincy Adams' Diary [Nov. 23, 1804] in Hayes, ed. *Jefferson in His Own Time* (University of Iowa Press 2012), 38.

68 Jefferson's letter to David R. Williams, January 31, 1806, Thomas Jefferson Papers, Library of Congress.

69 Meacham, *Jefferson: Art of Power*, 362.

70 Onuf, *Mind of Jefferson*, 37.

71 Meacham, *Jefferson: Art of Power*, 398.

72 Gordon-Reed and Onuf, *Patriarchs*, 256.

73 Ibid., 255.

74 Ibid., 197.

75 Meacham, *Jefferson: Art of Power*, 395–396.

76 Ibid., 93.

77 Ibid., 396.

78 Ibid., 319.

79 Ibid., 434.

80 Ibid., xxiv.

81 Gordon-Reed and Onuf, *Patriarchs*, 13.

82 Ibid., xvi.

83 Ibid., 268.

84 Ellis, *Sphinx*, 192–193.

85 Meacham, *Jefferson: Art of Power*, 35.

86 David O. Stewart, *Madison's Gift: Five Partnerships That Built America* (Simon & Schuster 2015), 131.

87 Ellis, *Sphinx*, 188.

88 Peterson, *Jefferson and the New Nation*, 614.

89 Meacham, *Jefferson: Art of Power*, 226.
90 Ellis, *Sphinx*, xi.
91 Peter Baker and Susan Glasser, *The Man Who Ran Washington: The Life and Times of James A. Baker III* (Doubleday 2020).
92 Meacham, *Jefferson: Art of Power*, xx.
93 Joyce Appleby, *Thomas Jefferson* (Times Books 2003), 5.
94 Ellis, *Sphinx*, 212.
95 Ibid., 199.
96 Henry Adams, *History of the United States of America*, Vol. 1 (Scribner's Sons 1889), 445.
97 Appleby, *Jefferson*, 71.
98 Jefferson's letter to Gideon Granger, August 13, 1800.
99 Onuf, *Mind of Jefferson*, 65.
100 Jefferson's letter to James Madison, September 6, 1789.
101 Gordon-Reed and Onuf, *Patriarchs*, 280.
102 Ellis, *Sphinx*, 191.
103 Gordon-Reed and Onuf, *Patriarchs*, 162.
104 Ellis, *Sphinx*, 13.
105 Meacham, *Jefferson: Art of Power*, 364.
106 Ibid., 132.
107 Ellis, *Sphinx*, xii, 38, 130.
108 Ibid., 123.
109 Onuf, *Mind of Jefferson*, 39.
110 Gordon-Reed and Onuf, *Patriarchs*, 257.
111 Ellis, *Sphinx*, 183,186.
112 Meacham, *Jefferson: Art of Power*, xxiii.
113 Jefferson's letter to John Randolph, December 1, 1803.
114 Ron Chernow, *Alexander Hamilton* (Penguin Press 2004), 323, 326.
115 Ibid., 328.
116 Ellis, *Sphinx*, 205.
117 Jefferson's letter to Robert Livingston, April 18, 1802.
118 Jefferson's letter to Albert Gallatin, August 23, 1803.
119 Jefferson's letter to John C. Breckenridge, August 12, 1803.
120 Jefferson's letter to Levi Lincoln, August 30, 1803.
121 Jefferson's letter to Wilson Cary Nicholas, September 7, 1803.
122 Ellis, *Sphinx*, 210.
123 Ibid., 205, 208–212.

124 Meacham, *Jefferson: Art of Power*, 384.
125 Onuf, *Mind of Jefferson*, 25.
126 Gordon-Reed's comment to this author after she read this chapter.
127 Ellis, *Sphinx*, 123.
128 Ibid., 123–124.
129 Ibid., 228, 237, 238.
130 Ibid., 238.
131 Meacham, *Jefferson: Art of Power*, 406.

CHAPTER THREE: ABRAHAM LINCOLN

132 Reinhold Niebuhr, "The Religion of Abraham Lincoln," in *Lincoln and the Gettysburg Address: Commemorative Papers*, ed. Allan Nevins (University of Illinois Press 1964), 72–73.
133 Hans J. Morgenthau, "The Mind of Abraham Lincoln," in Kenneth W. Thompson, ed., *Essays on Lincoln's Faith and Politics* (University Press of America 1983), 59.
134 Doris Kearns Goodwin, *Team of Rivals: The Political Genius of Abraham Lincoln* (Simon & Schuster 2005), 747.
135 Douglas L. Wilson, *Honor's Voice: The Transformation of Abraham Lincoln* (Knopf 1998), 303.
136 Goodwin, *Team of Rivals*, 319.
137 Ibid., 364.
138 Ibid.
139 David Herbert Donald, *Lincoln* (Simon & Schuster 1995), 599.
140 Goodwin, *Team of Rivals*, 679–680.
141 Ibid., 680.
142 Ibid., 681.
143 Ibid., 665.
144 Swett's letter to William Herndon, January 17, 1866; William Lee Miller, *Lincoln's Virtues: An Ethical Biography* (Knopf 2007), 407.
145 David S. Reynolds, *Abe: Abraham Lincoln in His Times* (Penguin Press 2020), xvi.
146 Donald, *Lincoln*, 319.
147 James M. McPherson, *Battle Cry of Freedom: The Civil War Era* (Oxford University Press 2003), 364.
148 Goodwin, *Team of Rivals*, 373.
149 William Lee Miller, *President Lincoln: The Duty of a Statesman* (Knopf 2008), 173.

150 Lincoln's letter to Cuthbert Bullitt, July 28, 1862.
151 Ronald C. White Jr., *Lincoln's Greatest Speech: The Second Inaugural* (Simon & Schuster 2002), 170.
152 Lincoln's "Response to a Serenade," November 10, 1864; Miller, *President Lincoln*, 369.
153 James M. McPherson, *Tried by War: Abraham Lincoln as Commander in Chief* (Penguin Press 2008), 177.
154 Miller, *President Lincoln*, 236.
155 Goodwin, *Team of Rivals*, 539.
156 Henry J. Raymond, *The Life of Abraham Lincoln, Volume II* (National Union Executive Committee 1864), 741.
157 Miller, *President Lincoln*, 309.
158 Lincoln's first debate with Stephen A. Douglas at Ottawa, Illinois, August 21, 1858.
159 Lincoln's First Inaugural Address, March 4, 1861.
160 Ibid.
161 Ibid.
162 Miller, *President Lincoln*, 365.
163 Ronald C. White Jr., *A. Lincoln: A Biography* (Random House 2009), 663.
164 Ibid., 666.
165 Lincoln's Second Inaugural Address, March 4, 1865.
166 White, *A. Lincoln*, 666.
167 Ron Chernow, *Grant* (Penguin Press 2017), 485.
168 White, *A. Lincoln*, 670.
169 Donald, *Lincoln*, 374.
170 John Avlon, *Lincoln and the Fight for Peace* (Simon & Schuster 2022), 5.
171 Ibid., 157.
172 White, *A. Lincoln*, 110.
173 Ibid., 108.
174 Michael Burlingame, *An American Marriage: The Untold Story of Abraham Lincoln and Mary Todd* (Pegasus Books 2021), 7.
175 Ibid., 81–82; Wilson, *Honor's Voice*, 216.
176 Ibid., throughout entire book.
177 Donald, *Lincoln*, 106.
178 Avlon, *Fight for Peace*, 142–143.
179 Burlingame, *American Marriage*, 262.
180 Ibid., 262–263.

181 Wilson, *Honor's Voice,* 233–265.
182 Ibid., 236.
183 Ibid., 309.
184 Ibid., 249.
185 Ibid., 255.
186 Ibid., 256.
187 Stephen R. Covey, *The 7 Habits of Highly Effective Families* (Golden Books 1997), 56.
188 Nancy Koehn, *Forged in Crisis: The Power of Courageous Leadership in Turbulent Times* (Scribner 2017), 186.
189 Letter of Joshua Speed to William Herndon, December 6, 1866.
190 William H. Herndon, *Herndon's Lincoln: The True Story of a Great Life* (Belford, Clarke & Company 1889), 273; Donald, *Lincoln,* 102.
191 Donald, *Lincoln,* 42.
192 Ibid., 81.
193 Miller, *Lincoln's Virtues,* 408.
194 Wilson, *Honor's Voice,* 309.
195 Miller, *Lincoln's Virtues,* 63–64.
196 Koehn, *Forged in Crisis,* 106–107.
197 Ibid., 132–133.
198 Lincoln's first debate with Stephen A. Douglas in Ottawa, Illinois, August 31, 1858.
199 Harold Holzer, *Lincoln and the Power of the Press* (Simon & Schuster 2014), xv–xvi.
200 Reynolds, *Abe,* 321.
201 Ibid., 99–100, 346.
202 Ibid., 358.
203 Lincoln's Copper Union speech, February 27, 1860.
204 McPherson, *Tried by War,* xxii.
205 Lincoln's Second Annual Message to Congress, December 1, 1862.
206 Greg Weiner, *Old Whigs: Burke, Lincoln & the Politics of Prudence* (Encounter Books 2019), 46.
207 Lincoln's letter to Albert Hodges, April 4, 1864.
208 Lincoln's letter to Eliza P. Gurney, October 26, 1862; White, *A. Lincoln,* 524.
209 Noah Feldman, *The Broken Constitution: Lincoln, Slavery, and the Refounding of America* (Farrar Straus and Giroux 2021), 4.

210 White, *A. Lincoln,* 517.
211 McPherson, *Tried by War,* 149–150.
212 Goodwin, *Team of Rivals,* 501.
213 Miller, *President Lincoln,* 312.
214 Reynolds, *Abe,* 812.
215 Goodwin, *Team of Rivals,* 687–690.
216 Ibid., 687.
217 Ibid., 690.
218 Chernow, *Grant,* 459.
219 Ibid., 468.
220 Weiner, *Old Whigs,* 9.
221 Miller, *Lincoln's Virtues,* 438.
222 White, *A. Lincoln,* 115–116.

CHAPTER FOUR: THEODORE ROOSEVELT

223 Douglas Brinkley, *The Wilderness Warrior: Theodore Roosevelt and the Crusade for America* (HarperCollins 2009), 13.
224 Edmund Morris, *The Rise of Theodore Roosevelt* (Coward, McCann & Geoghegan, Inc 1979), 27–28, 331.
225 Ibid., 302.
226 Edmund Morris, *Colonel Roosevelt* (Random House 2010), 242.
227 Edmund Morris, *Theodore Rex* (Random House 2001), 246.
228 Talmage Boston, *Cross-Examining History: A Lawyer Gets Answers from the Experts About Our Presidents* (Bright Sky Press 2016), 179.
229 Doris Kearns Goodwin, *Leadership in Turbulent Times* (Simon & Schuster 2018), 264.
230 Morris, *Rise of TR,* 496.
231 Ibid., 26.
232 Geoffrey C. Ward and Ken Burns, *The Roosevelts: An Intimate History* (Knopf 2014), 20.
233 Ibid., 43.
234 Morris, *Rise of TR,* 453.
235 Morris, *Theodore Rex,* 126.
236 Ibid., 445–446.
237 Morris, *Rise of TR,* 23.
238 Boston, *Cross-Examining History,* 180.
239 John Milton Cooper Jr., *The Warrior and the Priest: Woodrow Wilson and Theodore Roosevelt* (Belknap Press of Harvard University press, 1983), 73.

240 Kathleen Dalton, *Theodore Roosevelt: A Strenuous Life* (Knopf 2002), 9–10.
241 Ibid., 285–286.
242 Goodwin, *Leadership*, 245.
243 Ibid., 258.
244 Ibid., 246–247, 260.
245 Louis Auchincloss, *Theodore Roosevelt* (Times Books 2001), 46.
246 Ibid.
247 Goodwin, *Leadership*, 267.
248 Ibid., 247.
249 Ibid., 247–248.
250 Ibid., 248.
251 Theodore Roosevelt's Address to representatives of miners and operators, Washington, October 3, 1902.
252 Dalton, *Theodore Roosevelt*, 235.
253 Boston, *Cross-Examining History*, 181.
254 Allen Guelzo, *Fateful Lightning: A New History of the Civil War and Reconstruction* (Oxford University Press 2012), 439.
255 McPherson, *Tried by War*, xxii.
256 Morris, *Colonel Roosevelt*, 494.
257 Dalton, *Theodore Roosevelt*, 202.
258 Ibid.
259 Ibid.
260 Doris Kearns Goodwin, *The Bully Pulpit: Theodore Roosevelt, William Howard Taft, and the Golden Age of Journalism* (Simon & Schuster 2013), 37.
261 Morris, *Theodore Rex*, 351.
262 Carlos Castaneda, *Journey to Ixtlan: The Lessons of Don Juan* (Simon & Schuster 1972), carlos-castenada.com.
263 Morris, *Theodore Rex*, 422.
264 Dalton, *Theodore Roosevelt*, 289.
265 Morris, *Rise of TR*, 421.
266 Brinkley, *Wilderness Warrior*, 14.
267 Auchincloss, *Theodore Roosevelt*, 53.
268 Ibid.
269 Goodwin, *Bully Pulpit*, 2.
270 Brinkley, *Wilderness Warrior*, 123–124.
271 Kay Redfield Jamison, *Exuberance: The Passion for Life* (Knopf 2006), 297–299.

272 Ibid.
273 Brinkley, *Wilderness Warrior,* 123–124.
274 Morris, *Rise of TR,* 18.
275 Morris, *Theodore Rex,* 452.
276 Morris, *Colonel Roosevelt,* 247.
277 Ibid., 469, 471–472.
278 Auchincloss, *Theodore Roosevelt,* 132.
279 Ibid., 129–132.
280 Morris, *Colonel Roosevelt,* 549.
281 Ibid., 553.

CHAPTER FIVE: FRANKLIN D. ROOSEVELT

282 Jill Lepore, *These Truths: A History of the United States* (W.W. Norton 2019), 430.
283 1940 GDP figure from Louis Johnston and Samuel H. Williamson, "The Annual Real and Nominal GDP for the United States, 1789–Present," Economic History Services, March 2004. 1945 GDP figure calculated using Bureau of Labor Statistics, "CPI Inflation Calculator," available at http://data.bls.gov/cgi-bin/cpicalc.pl. Defense spending figures from Government Printing Office, "Budget of the United States Government: Historical Tables Fiscal Year 2005."
284 Geoffrey C. Ward, *A First-Class Temperament: The Emergence of Franklin Roosevelt 1905–1928* (Harper & Row 1989), 591.
285 James Tobin, *The Man He Became: How FDR Defied Polio to Win the Presidency* (Simon & Schuster 2013), 93–94.
286 Doris Kearns Goodwin, *No Ordinary Time: Franklin and Eleanor Roosevelt: The Home Front in World War II* (Simon & Schuster 1994), 10.
287 Ibid., 107.
288 Amy Berish, "FDR and Polio," FDR Library & Museum, 8; Ward and Burns, *The Roosevelts,* 332.
289 Geoffrey Ward, statement to the author after reviewing this chapter.
290 Berish, Ibid.
291 Tobin, *The Man He Became,* 190.
292 Goodwin, *No Ordinary Time,* 532.
293 Geoffrey Ward, statement to the author after reviewing this chapter.
294 Goodwin, *Leadership,* 163; Robert Dallek, *Franklin D. Roosevelt: A Political Life* (Penguin Books 2018), 84.
295 Jean Edward Smith, *FDR* (Random House 2007), 279, 369.

296 Dallek, *Roosevelt*, 236.
297 Goodwin, *No Ordinary Time*, 510.
298 Smith, *FDR*, 250.
299 Ward and Burns, *The Roosevelts*, 267.
300 Boston, *Cross-Examining History*, Ward interview, 238.
301 James MacGregor Burns, *Roosevelt: The Lion and the Fox* (Konecky & Konecky 1984), 88–89.
302 Dallek, *Roosevelt* 168, 243.
303 Smith, *FDR*, 301.
304 Dallek, *Roosevelt*, 46.
305 Boston, *Cross-Examining History*, Tobin interview, 231.
306 Ibid., Ward interview, 244.
307 Goodwin, *No Ordinary Time*, 16–17.
308 Dallek, *Roosevelt*, 87.
309 Lepore, *These Truths*, 428.
310 Nelson Mandela, quote appears in multiple sources.
311 Eleanor Roosevelt, *You Learn by Living: Eleven Keys for a More Fulfilling Life* (Harper & Brothers Publishers 1960), 29–30.
312 Boston, *Cross-Examining History*, Tobin interview, 235.
313 Burns, *Lion and Fox*, 144.
314 Ibid.
315 Lincoln, first debate with Stephen Douglas, Ottawa, Illinois, August 21, 1858.
316 Dallek, *Roosevelt*, 4.
317 Smith, *FDR*, 250; Goodwin, *Leadership*, 179.
318 Dallek, *Roosevelt*, 8.
319 FDR, First Inaugural Address, March 4, 1933.
320 Ibid.
321 Lincoln's letter to Albert Hodges, April 4, 1864.
322 FDR, First Inaugural Address, March 4, 1933; Lepore, *These Truths*, 430.
323 Smith, *FDR*, 312–313.
324 FDR, First Fireside Chat, March 12, 1933.
325 Burns, *Lion and Fox*, 186.
326 Goodwin, *Leadership*, 302.
327 FDR, Second Fireside Chat, May 7, 1933.
328 FDR, Oglethorpe University Address, May 22, 1932.
329 Dallek, *Roosevelt*, 143.

330 Lepore, *These Truths*, 437.
331 Smith, *FDR*, 306.
332 Burns, *Lion and Fox*, 223.
333 FDR, Second Inaugural Address, January 20, 1937.
334 Smith, *FDR*, 383.
335 Ward and Burns, *The Roosevelts*, 345.
336 Lepore, *These Truths*, 465.
337 Burns, *Lion and Fox*, 331–332.
338 Smith, *FDR*, 395–396.
339 Ward and Burns, *The Roosevelts*, 298.
340 Burns, *Lion and Fox*, 203–205.
341 Dallek, *Roosevelt*, 170.
342 David Michaelis, *Eleanor* (Simon & Schuster 2020), 313.
343 Goodwin, *Leadership*, 300–301.
344 Ibid., 300.
345 Goodwin, *No Ordinary Time*, 236, 255; Dallek, *Roosevelt*, 487.
346 Dallek, *Roosevelt*, 297.
347 Ibid., 143.
348 Beschloss, *Presidential Courage*, 158.
349 Lepore, *These Truths*, 475.
350 Ward and Burns, *The Roosevelts*, 364.
351 National WWII Museum, "Research Starters: US Military by the Numbers, nationalww2museum.org; "Ship Force Levels 1917–Present," history.navy.mil.
352 FDR, Radio Address, April 7, 1932; Smith, *FDR*, 263.
353 FDR, Speech at Democratic National Convention, July 19, 1940.
354 FDR, First Inaugural Address, March 4, 1933.
355 Smith, *FDR*, 286.
356 Dallek, *Roosevelt*, 144.
357 Ibid., 349.
358 Burns, *Lion and Fox*, 448–449.
359 Goodwin, *No Ordinary Time*, 240.
360 Dallek, *Roosevelt*, 437.
361 Burns, *Lion and Fox*, 200.
362 Goodwin, *No Ordinary Time*, 608.
363 Goodwin, *Leadership*, 363.
364 Burns, *Lion and Fox*, 371–372.

365 Dallek, *Roosevelt*, 621.
366 Smith, *FDR*, 487.
367 Beschloss, *Presidential Courage*, 190.
368 Statement by David Michaelis to author after reviewing this chapter.
369 Dallek, *Roosevelt*, 293; Michaelis, *Eleanor*, 178.
370 Goodwin, *No Ordinary Time*, 517–521.
371 Ward and Burns, *The Roosevelts*, 449–457.
372 Smith, *FDR*, 403–408.
373 Ibid.
374 Ibid.
375 Dallek, *Roosevelt*, 196.
376 James MacGregor Burns, *Roosevelt: The Soldier of Freedom* (1940–1945) (History Book Club 2006), 247.
377 Burns, *Lion and Fox*, 142, 156, 198.
378 Dallek, *Roosevelt*, 271–276.
379 Ibid., 454.
380 Ibid., 498.
381 Ibid., 520.
382 Smith, *FDR*, 401.
383 Smith, *FDR*, 398–401, 549–553, 609–612; Goodwin, *No Ordinary Time*, 163, 252, 321, 454.
384 Burns, *Lion and Fox*, 423.

CHAPTER SIX: DWIGHT EISENHOWER

385 Fred I. Greenstein, *The Hidden-Hand Presidency: Eisenhower as Leader* (Johns Hopkins University Press 1982), 5–6; Chester J. Pach Jr. and Elmo Richardson, *The Presidency of Dwight D. Eisenhower, Revised Edition* (University Press of Kansas 1991), 213–214; Evan Thomas, *Ike's Bluff: President Eisenhower's Secret Battle to Save the World* (Little, Brown and Company 2012), 255, 308–316; William I. Hitchcock, *The Age of Eisenhower: America and the World in the 1950s* (Simon & Schuster 2018), 396–398, 461, 471–472, 480, 489.
386 Thomas, *Ike's Bluff*, 386; Susan Eisenhower, *How Ike Led: The Principles Behind Eisenhower's Biggest Decisions* (Thomas Dunne Books 2020), 301.
387 Thomas, *Ike's Bluff*, 369–374; Hitchcock, *Age of Eisenhower*, 461–463.
388 Ibid., Thomas, *Ike's Bluff*, 374–377; Hitchcock, *Age of Eisenhower*, 463–465.
389 Ibid., Thomas, *Ike's Bluff*, 381–382; Hitchcock, *Age of Eisenhower*, 468.
390 Hitchcock, *Age of Eisenhower*, 516–517.

391 Arthur Larson, *Eisenhower: The President Nobody Knew* (Scribner's Sons 1968), 193.
392 Jean Edward Smith, *Eisenhower in War and Peace* (Random House 2021), xiii.
393 Greenstein, *Hidden-Hand*, 31.
394 Ibid.
395 Dwight D. Eisenhower, *The White House Years: Mandate for Change, 1953–1956* (Doubleday 1963), 87.
396 Eisenhower, *How Ike Led*, 150.
397 Greenstein, *Hidden-Hand*, xii.
398 Hitchcock, *Age of Eisenhower*, 89.
399 Smith, *War and Peace*, 551.
400 Ibid.
401 Ibid., 557.
402 Greenstein, *Hidden-Hand*, 113.
403 Ibid., 566–567.
404 Eisenhower, *How Ike Led*, 121, 147, 149.
405 Greenstein, *Hidden-Hand*, 114–116.
406 Smith, *War and Peace*, 567.
407 Thomas, *Ike's Bluff*, 45.
408 Eisenhower, *How Ike Led*, 147.
409 Ibid.
410 Ibid., 149
411 Greenstein, *Hidden-Hand*, 26–27.
412 Eisenhower, *How Ike Led*, 171.
413 Greenstein, *Hidden-Hand*, 116.
414 Ibid., 115.
415 David Eisenhower's comments to author after reviewing this chapter.
416 Ibid., 116–117.
417 Smith, *War and Peace*, 568.
418 Ibid., 569.
419 Eisenhower, *How Ike Led*, 150.
420 Hitchcock, *Age of Eisenhower*, 107–108.
421 Ibid., 108.
422 Ibid.
423 Ibid.
424 Ibid., 109.

425 Greenstein, *Hidden-Hand,* 126–127.
426 Ibid., 126.
427 Ibid., 129.
428 Smith, *War and Peace,* 613–614.
429 Michael J. Birkner, "More to Induce Than Demand: Eisenhower and Congress," *Congress & the Presidency* 40, no. 2 (May 2013), 183.
430 Ibid., 174; Greenstein, *Hidden-Hand,* 107.
431 Stephen Hess, "What Congress Looked Like From Inside the Eisenhower White House," (Brookings Institute 2012).
432 Smith, *War and Peace,* 581.
433 Eisenhower, *How Ike Led,* 152.
434 Ibid., 151–152.
435 Birkner, *Congress & the Presidency,* 174.
436 Pach and Richardson, *Presidency,* 50.
437 Birkner, *Congress & the Presidency,* 174.
438 Hitchcock, *Age of Eisenhower,* 281.
439 Hess, "What Congress Looked Like."
440 Birkner, *Congress & the Presidency,* 166–167.
441 Ibid., 166.; Smith, *War and Peace,* 597.
442 Ibid., 650–654.
443 Eisenhower, *How Ike Led,* 153; Birkner, *Congress & the Presidency,* 167.
444 Ibid., 182; Greenstein, *Hidden-Hand,* 42.
445 Smith, *War and Peace,* 654.
446 Eisenhower, *How Ike Led,* 153–154.
447 Greenstein, *Hidden-Hand,* 117.
448 Ibid., 133.
449 Larson, *Eisenhower,* 171.
450 Thomas, *Ike's Bluff,* 331–332.
451 Ibid., 89, 415.
452 Ibid.
453 Jon Meacham, *And There Was Light: Abraham Lincoln and the American Struggle* (Random House 2022), xx.
454 David A. Nichols, *Ike and McCarthy: Dwight Eisenhower's Secret Campaign Against Joseph McCarthy* (Simon & Schuster 2017), xiii.
455 David Eisenhower's statements to the author after reviewing this chapter.
456 Ibid.
457 Nichols, *Ike and McCarthy,* 10.

458 Pach and Richardson, *Presidency*, 67.
459 Nichols, *Ike and McCarthy*, 29–30.
460 Ibid., 30.
461 Michael Korda, *Ike: An American Hero* (Harper Collins 2007), 680.
462 Hitchcock, *Age of Eisenhower*, 145.
463 Smith, *War and Peace*, 659.
464 Hitchcock, *Age of Eisenhower*, 209.
465 Ibid., 403.
466 Eisenhower, *How Ike Led*, 253.
467 Ibid., 247.
468 Hitchcock, *Age of Eisenhower*, 416.
469 Thomas, *Ike's Bluff*, 281.
470 Ibid., 247.
471 Eisenhower, *How Ike Led*, 60–62.
472 Ibid., 64.
473 Thomas, *Ike's Bluff*, 47.
474 Henry Kissinger, *Leadership: Six Studies in World Strategy* (Penguin Press 2022), 92.
475 Korda, *Ike*, 691.
476 Kissinger, *Leadership*, 92.
477 Smith, *War and Peace*, 697.
478 Hitchcock, *Age of Eisenhower*, 323.
479 Smith, *War and Peace*, 704.
480 David A. Nichols, *Eisenhower 1956: The President's Year of Crisis: Suez and the Brink of War* (Simon & Schuster 2011), 284, 286.
481 Smith, *War and Peace*, 727.
482 Eisenhower, *How Ike Led*, 245.
483 David A. Nichols, *A Matter of Justice: Eisenhower and the Beginning of the Civil Rights Revolution* (Simon & Schuster 2007).
484 Ibid., 2.
485 Ibid., 4.
486 Ibid., 152.
487 Ibid., 158–159.
488 Ibid., 167–168.
489 Ibid., 170–171.
490 Ibid., 169.
491 Ibid., 172.

492 Ibid.
493 Ibid.
494 Ibid., 173.
495 Ibid.
496 Ibid., 174.
497 Ibid., 168.
498 Ibid., 174.
499 Ibid., 174–175.
500 Ibid., 182.
501 Ibid., 186.
502 Ibid., 187.
503 Ibid., 189.
504 Ibid., 191.
505 Ibid., 192.
506 Ibid.
507 Ibid., 194.
508 Ibid., 196.
509 Ibid., 198–199.
510 Ibid., 199.
511 Smith, *War and Peace*, 726.
512 Nichols, *A Matter of Justice*, 200.
513 Smith, *War and Peace*, 729.
514 Korda, *Ike*, 699.
515 Nichols, *A Matter of Justice*, 281.
516 Larson, *Eisenhower*, 123.
517 Hitchcock, *Age of Eisenhower*, 292.
518 Smith, *War and Peace*, 617–627.
519 Ibid., 627–633.
520 Hitchcock, *Age of Eisenhower*, 451–453.
521 Ibid., 484.
522 Boston, *Cross-Examining History*, Smith interview, 268.
523 Nichols, *Ike and McCarthy*, 2–5; Eisenhower, *How Ike Led*, 189.

CHAPTER SEVEN: JOHN F. KENNEDY

524 Mark K. Updegrove, *Incomparable Grace: JFK in the Presidency* (Dutton 2022), 121.
525 Thurston Clarke, *JFK's Last Hundred Days: The Transformation of a Man and the Emergence of a Great President* (Penguin Press 2013), xi.

526 Robert Dallek, *An Unfinished Life: John F. Kennedy, 1917–1963* (Little, Brown and Company 2003), 471.

527 Kenneth P. O'Donnell and David F. Powers with Joe McCarthy, *"Johnny, We Hardly Knew Ye": Memories of John Fitzgerald Kennedy* (Little, Brown and Company 1970).

528 Clarke, *Last Hundred Days*, 362.

529 James N. Giglio, *The Presidency of John F. Kennedy, Second Edition, Revised* (University Press of Kansas 2006), 1.

530 Fredrik Logevall, *JFK: Coming of Age in the American Century, 1917–1956* (Random House 2020), xiv.

531 Stephen F. Knott, *Coming to Terms with John F. Kennedy* (University Press of Kansas 2022), 70.

532 Updegrove, *Incomparable Grace*, 112.

533 Dallek, *Unfinished Life*, 398–399, 704–706.

534 Knott, *Coming to Terms*, 84–86, 178–179, 195–196, 203.

535 Ibid.

536 Clarke, *Last Hundred Days*, 362.

537 James MacGregor Burns, *John Kennedy: A Political Profile* (Harcourt, Brace & World 1959), 99–224; Giglio, *Presidency*, 40.

538 Burns, *Kennedy*, 131, 148, 156–157, 159; Giglio, *Presidency*, 6–7.

539 Burns, *Kennedy*, 99, 224; Giglio, *Presidency*, 40.

540 Burns, *Kennedy*, 197–200.

541 Dallek, *Unfinished Life*, 228–229, 337–338.

542 Updegrove, *Incomparable Grace*, 204.

543 Ibid., 21.

544 Kennedy's Inaugural Address, January 20, 1961.

545 Dallek, *Unfinished Life*, 363.

546 Ibid., 361.

547 Ibid., 359, 364.

548 Ibid., 364–365.

549 Ibid., 367–368.

550 Ibid., 370.

551 Hugh Sidey, *John F. Kennedy, President* (Atheneum 1963), 104.

552 Dallek, *Unfinished Life*, 361.

553 Sidey, *Kennedy*, 112–113.

554 Knott, *Coming to Terms*, 80.

555 Ibid.

556 Ibid., 80–82.
557 Ibid., 81–82.
558 Herbert S. Parmet, *JFK: The Presidency of John F. Kennedy* (The Dial Press 1983), 136.
559 Ibid.
560 Ibid.; Dallek, *Unfinished Life*, 353.
561 Giglio, *Presidency*, 70.
562 Ibid., 97.
563 Updegrove, *Incomparable Grace*, 101–102.
564 Knott, *Coming to Terms*, 105–106; Alan Brinkley, *John F. Kennedy* (Times Books 2012), 80; Dallek, *Unfinished Life*, 411.
565 Ibid., Brinkley, *John F. Kennedy*, 80.
566 Ibid., 82.
567 Dallek, *Unfinished Life*, 423.
568 Knott, *Coming to Terms*, 105–106.
569 Updegrove, *Incomparable Grace*, 118.
570 Kennedy's speech to United Nations General Assembly, September 25, 1961.
571 Knott, *Coming to Terms*, 116.
572 Martin J. Sherwin, *Gambling with Armageddon: Nuclear Roulette from Hiroshima to the Cuban Missile Crisis* (Knopf 2020), 37.
573 Kennedy's speech at American University, June 10, 1963.
574 Ibid.
575 Dallek, *Unfinished Life*, 621.
576 Ibid., 627.
577 Updegrove, *Incomparable Grace*, 246.
578 Ibid., 139.
579 JFK's speech to California Democratic Council Convention, Fresno, California, February 12, 1960.
580 Ibid., 144.
581 Ibid., 271; Giglio, *Presidency*, 268–269.
582 Clarke, *Last Hundred Days*, 357.
583 Ann Mari May, "President Eisenhower, Economic Policy, and the 1960 Presidential Election," *Journal of Economic History* 2, no. 2 (June 1990): 419; Copyright: The Economic History Association.
584 Giglio, *Presidency*, 125.
585 Ibid., 126.
586 Sidey, *Kennedy*, 303.

587 Ibid., 306.
588 Ibid., 313.
589 Giglio, *Presidency*, 137.
590 Ibid., 139.
591 Kennedy's State of the Union Address, January 14, 1963.
592 Giglio, *Presidency*, 137.
593 Sidey, *Kennedy*, 307.
594 Ibid., 308.
595 Ibid., 309, 311.
596 Giglio, *Presidency*, 141.
597 Ibid.
598 Ibid., 237–238.
599 Knott, *Coming to Terms*, 224, n.8.
600 Knott, *Coming to Terms*, 37–38.
601 Beschloss, *Presidential Courage*, 238.
602 Ibid., 239.
603 Dallek, *Unfinished Life*, 291–292.
604 Updegrove, *Incomparable Grace*, 81l; Knott, *Coming to Terms*, 42.
605 Ibid., 20–21.
606 Beschloss, *Presidential Courage*, 242; Knott, *Coming to Terms*, 34–36.
607 Dallek, *Unfinished Life*, 292, 580.
608 Sheldon Goldman, *Picking Federal Judges: Lower Court Selection from Roosevelt through Reagan* (Yale University Press 1997); Dallek, *Unfinished Life*, 494.
609 Beschloss, *Presidential Courage*, 245.
610 Dallek, *Unfinished Life*, 388.
611 Updegrove, *Incomparable Grace*, 163–167; Beschloss, *Presidential Courage*, 250–255.
612 Giglio, *Presidency*, 176–178.
613 Dallek, *Unfinished Life*, 380.
614 Updegrove, *Incomparable Grace*, 214.
615 Beschloss, *Presidential Courage*, 262.
616 Updegrove, *Incomparable Grace*, 221.
617 Knott, *Coming to Terms*, 57, 63–66.
618 Kennedy's televised address to the nation on Civil Rights, June 11, 1963.
619 Boston, *Cross-Examining History*, Stern interview, 277.
620 Ibid.

621 Kennedy's "Special Message to Congress on Civil Rights," June 19, 1963.
622 Beschloss, *Presidential Courage*, 276.
623 Knott, *Coming to Terms*, 71.
624 Sherwin, *Gambling with Armageddon*, 466.
625 Boston, *Cross-Examining History*, Stern interview, 282.
626 Dallek, *Unfinished Life*, 573.
627 Boston, *Cross-Examining History*, Stern interview, 284–289.
628 Sherwin, *Gambling with Armageddon*, 9.
629 Boston, *Cross-Examining History*, Stern interview, 284–285.
630 Ibid.; Knott, *Coming to Terms*, 84–86.
631 Sheldon M. Stern, *Averting 'The Final Failure': John F. Kennedy and the Secret Cuban Missile Crisis Meetings* (Stanford Nuclear Age Series) (Stanford University Press 2003), 368; Sherwin, *Gambling with Armageddon*, 445.
632 Boston, *Cross-Examining History*, Stern interview, 289–290.
633 Ibid.
634 Ibid.
635 Ibid., 285.
636 Ibid.
637 Knott, *Coming to Terms*, 86.
638 Dallek, *Unfinished Life*, 470, 576.
639 Sidey, *Kennedy*, 204, 278.
640 James MacGregor Burns, *John Kennedy: A Political Profile* (Harcourt, Brace & World 1959), 263.
641 Knott, *Coming to Terms*, 151.
642 Giglio, *Presidency*, 207.
643 Giglio, *Presidency*, 209; Dallek, *Unfinished Life*, 547.
644 Ibid.
645 Updegrove, *Incomparable Grace*, 187.
646 Giglio, *Presidency*, 213.
647 Sherwin, *Gambling with Armageddon*, 223.
648 Ibid., 358.
649 Sidey, *Kennedy*, 274–275.
650 Sherwin, *Gambling with Armageddon*, 286.
651 Ibid., 209–210.
652 Sidey, *Kennedy*, 273, 278.
653 Walter Pincus, "Transcript Confirms Kennedy Linked Removal of Missiles in Cuba, Turkey," *Washington Post*, October 22, 1987.

654 Sherwin, *Gambling with Armageddon*, 326, 331.
655 Ibid., 403–404.
656 Ibid., 242.
657 Boston, *Cross-Examining History*, Stern interview, 284–285.
658 Ibid., 287.
659 Ibid., 288–289.
660 Giglio, *Presidency*, 224.
661 Sherwin, *Gambling with Armageddon*, 450.
662 Ibid., 431, 449.
663 Brinkley, *John F. Kennedy*, 125–126.
664 Updegrove, *Incomparable Grace*, 197.
665 Updegrove, *Incomparable Grace*, 226.
666 Knott, *Coming to Terms*, 216–218.
667 Updegrove, *Incomparable Grace*, 199.
668 Dallek, *Unfinished Life*, 335–336.
669 Executive Order 10924: Establishment of the Peace Corps, March 1, 1961.
670 Ibid.
671 Dallek, *Unfinished Life*, 340.
672 Kennedy's Address to Joint Session of Congress, May 25, 1961.
673 Charles Fishman, *One Giant Leap: The Impossible Mission That Flew Us to the Moon* (Simon & Schuster 2019), 6, 17.
674 Knott, *Coming to Terms*, 210–211.
675 Updegrove, *Incomparable Grace*, 149.
676 Kennedy's Address at Rice Stadium, September 12, 1962.
677 Updegrove, *Incomparable Grace*, 245.

CHAPTER EIGHT: RONALD REAGAN

678 H. W. Brands, *Reagan: The Life* (Doubleday 2015), 733.
679 Richard Reeves, *President Reagan: The Triumph of Imagination* (Simon & Schuster 2005).
680 Henry Olson, "How the Right Gets Reagan Wrong," *Politico Magazine*, June 26, 2017.
681 Steven F. Hayward, *The Age of Reagan: The Fall of the Old Liberal Order 1964–1980* (Forum 2001), xi.
682 Brands, *Reagan*, 458; Lou Cannon, *President Reagan: The Role of a Lifetime* (Public Affairs 1991), 434.
683 Ibid., 177.

684 William Inboden, *The Peacemaker: Ronald Reagan, the Cold War, and the World on the Brink* (Dutton 2022), 17–18.
685 Jacob Weisberg, *Ronald Reagan* (Times Books 2016), 4.
686 Scott Borchert, "'Unlikely Heroes' Review: FDR's Key Quartet," *Wall Street Journal*, February 24, 2023.
687 Cannon, *Role of a Lifetime*, 435.
688 Ibid., 147.
689 Inboden, *Peacemaker*, 13; Cannon, *Role of a Lifetime*, 194; William F. Buckley Jr., *The Reagan I Knew* (Basic Books 2008), xii.
690 Arthur Schlesinger Jr., "The Man of the Century," *American Heritage* 45, no. 3 (May/June 1994).
691 Cannon, *Role of a Lifetime*, 19.
692 Weisberg, *Reagan*, 5.
693 Boston, *Cross-Examining History*, Brands interview, 362.
694 Inboden, *Peacemaker*, 475, 479.
695 Cannon, *Role of a Lifetime*, 764.
696 Cannon, *Role of a Lifetime*, 147.
697 Garry Wills, *Reagan's America: Innocents at Home* (Penguin Books 1987), 9.
698 Ibid., 31, 67.
699 Ibid., 18–19.
700 Cannon, *Role of a Lifetime*, 181.
701 Weisberg, *Reagan*, 6.
702 Edmund Morris, *Dutch: A Memoir of Ronald Reagan* (Random House 1999), 3.
703 Cannon, *Role of a Lifetime*, 147.
704 Ibid.
705 Ibid., 17.
706 Cannon, *Role of a Lifetime*, 121, 198.
707 Ibid.
708 Ibid., 752; Wills, *Reagan's America*, x.
709 Weisberg, *Reagan*, 52.
710 Cannon, *Role of a Lifetime*, 178.
711 Weisberg, *Reagan*, 52.
712 Inboden, *Peacemaker*, 22; Beschloss, *Presidential Courage*, 283; Reeves, *President Reagan*, 6.
713 Hayward, *Age of Reagan 1964–1980*, xxiii.

714 Ken Adelman, *Reagan at Reykjavik: Forty-Eight Hours That Ended the Cold War* (Broadside Books 2014), 325.
715 Hayward, *Age of Reagan 1964–1980*, 142.
716 Brands, *Reagan*, 737.
717 Adelman, *Reykjavik*, 339.
718 Steven F. Hayward, *The Age of Reagan: The Conservative Counterrevolution 1980–1989* (Crown Forum 2009), 142.
719 Morris, *Dutch*, 435.
720 Reagan's "Time for Choosing Speech," October 1, 1964.
721 Stuart Spencer Oral History Transcript, University of Virginia Miller Center, November 15–16, 2001.
722 "California's Governorship Race," *TIME* magazine, October 7, 1966.
723 Inboden, *Peacemaker*, 22; Hayward, *Age of Reagan 1964–1980*, 481; Morris, *Dutch*, 404.
724 Wills, *Reagan's America*, 456.
725 Reagan's debate against Jimmy Carter, October 28, 1980.
726 Morris, *Dutch*, 424.
727 Cannon, *Role of a Lifetime*, 442.
728 Boston, *Cross-Examining History*, Brands interview, 347.
729 Lee Edwards, "'Dutch': Less Than Meets the Eye," The Heritage Foundation, October 12, 1999.
730 Fred I. Greenstein, "Reckoning with Reagan: A Review Essay on Edmund Morris's *Dutch*," *Political Science Quarterly* 115 (November 1, 2000).
731 Brands, *Reagan*, 311.
732 Julia Simon and Kenny Malone, "Looking Back on When President Reagan Fired the Air Traffic Controllers," NPR Network, August 5, 2021.
733 Ibid.
734 Reagan's remarks at Reagan Presidential Library, November 11, 1991.
735 Kissinger's Keynote Speech Commemorating President Ronald Reagan's 112th Birthday, Ronald Reagan Presidential Foundation & Institute, February 6, 2023.
736 Cannon, *Role of a Lifetime*, 108–109.
737 Ibid., 109.
738 Hayward, *Age of Reagan 1964–1980*, xx.
739 Morris, *Dutch*, 415.
740 Boston, *Cross-Examining History*, Baker interview, 438.

741 James A. Baker, III, *"Work Hard, Study...and Keep Out of Politics!"* (Northwestern University Press 2006), 125.
742 Boston, *Cross-Examining History*, Brands interview, 358.
743 Beschloss, *Presidential Courage*, 324.
744 Inboden, *Peacemaker*, 4–5.
745 Adelman, *Reykjavik*, 322.
746 Kissinger's speech at Reagan Library, February 6, 2023.
747 Buckley, *Reagan I Knew*, xix.
748 Morris, *Dutch*, 414.
749 Cannon, *Role of a Lifetime*, 241.
750 Hayward, *Age of Reagan 1980–1989*, 3.
751 Reagan's announcement for his presidential candidacy, January 13, 1979.
752 Cannon, *Role of a Lifetime*, 241.
753 Reagan's speech accepting nomination at Republican National Convention, July 17, 1980.
754 Inboden, *Peacemaker*, 42, 67.
755 Adelman, *Reykjavik*, 318.
756 Philip Taubman, *In the Nation's Service: The Life and Times of George P. Shultz* (Stanford University Press 2023), 317–318.
757 Inboden, *Peacemaker*, 372.
758 Brian Domitrovic, "George H.W. Bush's Voodoo Rhetoric," *Forbes*, December 2, 2018.
759 John Kenneth Galbraith, "Recession Economics," *New York Review of Books* 29, no. 1 (February 4, 1982).
760 Beschloss, *Presidential Courage*, 281.
761 Ibid., 299.
762 Inboden, *Peacemaker*, 20–21.
763 Ibid., 20, 408, 433–434, 459.
764 Reeves, *President Reagan*, 109.
765 Hayward, *Age of Reagan 1980–1989*, 1.
766 James Mann, *The Rebellion of Ronald Reagan: A History of the End of the Cold War*, xvii.
767 Beschloss, *Presidential Courage*, 323.
768 Mann, *Rebellion*, 343–345.
769 "DeSantis's First Big Mistake," *Wall Street Journal*, March 16, 2023.
770 Inboden, *Peacemaker*, 10.
771 Taubman, *Nation's Service*, 355.

772 Ibid., 361.
773 Reagan's speech at Moscow State University, May 31, 1988.
774 Taubman, *Nation's Service*, 364.
775 Reagan's remarks at Moscow's Vnukovo II Airport, June 2, 1988.
776 Reagan's Farewell Address, January 11, 1989.
777 Kissinger's speech at Reagan Library, February 6, 2023.
778 Inboden, *Peacemaker*, 7.
779 Cannon, *Role of a Lifetime*, 59.
780 Reeves, *President Reagan*, 14.
781 Morris, *Dutch*, 499.
782 Inboden, *Peacemaker*, 421.
783 Cannon, *Role of a Lifetime*, 36, 64, 107.
784 Ibid., 133.
785 Weisberg, *Reagan*, 77–79.
786 Boston, *Cross-Examining History*, Brands interview, 347.

INDEX